Pittsburgh Series in Social and Labor History

PITTSBURGH SERIES IN SOCIAL AND LABOR HISTORY
Maurine Weiner Greenwald, Editor

And the Wolf Finally Came: The Decline of the American Steel Industry
John P. Hoerr

The Correspondence of Mother Jones
Edward M. Steel, Editor

Don't Call Me Boss: David L. Lawrence, Pittsburgh's Renaissance Mayor
Michael P. Weber

The Speeches and Writings of Mother Jones
Edward M. Steel, Editor

Trade Unions and the New Industrialisation of the Third World
Roger Southall, editor

What's a Coal Miner to Do? The Mechanization of Coal Mining
Keith Dix

Women and the Trades
Elizabeth Beardsley Butler

OTHER TITLES IN THE SERIES

The Emergence of a UAW Local, 1936–1939: A Study in Class and Culture
Peter Friedlander

Homestead: The Households of a Mill Town
Margaret F. Byington

The Homestead Strike of 1892
Arthur G. Burgoyne

Immigration and Industrialization: Ethnicity in an American Mill Town, 1870–1940
John Bodnar

Out of This Furnace
Thomas Bell

Steelmasters and Labor Reform, 1886–1923
Gerald G. Eggert

Steve Nelson, American Radical
Steve Nelson, James R. Barrett, & Rob Ruck

Working-Class Life: The "American Standard" in Comparative Perspective, 1899–1913
Peter R. Shergold

What's a Coal Miner to Do?

The Mechanization of Coal Mining

KEITH DIX

University of Pittsburgh Press

Published by the University of Pittsburgh Press, Pittsburgh, Pa., 15260

Library of Congress Cataloging-in-Publication Data

Dix, Keith.
  What's a coal miner to do?

  (Pitt series in social and labor history)
  Includes index.
  1. Coal-mining machinery—Social aspects—United States—History—
20th Century.   2. United Mine Workers of America—History—20th Century.
I. Title   II. Series.
HD6331.18.M615D59   1988   331.25   88–1337
ISBN 0–8229–3585–6

CONTENTS

Preface   vii

Acknowledgments   xi

1.   The Hand Loading of Coal   1

2.   Evolution of Underground Machinery   28

3.   The Joy Loading Machine   61

4.   Transformation of the Miner's Job   77

5.   Miners' Response to Technological Change   107

6.   The Union and Mechanization   126

7.   Evolution of the UMWA's Mechanization Policy   149

8.   Union and Industry During the Great Depression   168

9.   Government Intervention in the Industry   185

10. Miners' "Freedom" Under Increased Mechanization   199

11. Opportunities Lost   211

Appendix   217

Notes   221

Index   246

PREFACE

It is often said that modern society has chosen efficiency in production rather than richness in the working life; that it has chosen the possibility of fuller and more varied living outside working hours rather than the possibility of a creative life on the job itself. . . . Society makes no choices as such, and the countless individual decisions out of which come mass production as efficient as that at Ford's and jobs as dull as those at Ford's have most of them been made without the slightest reference to the quality of working life that would result.

—Carter Goodrich, *The Miners' Freedom*, 1925

THIS STUDY joins many in recent years that have focused on what historian Jeremy Brecker calls "the hidden history of the American workplace." From shoemaking to shipbuilding, a new generation of scholars has shown that traditional histories of union organization and union leadership have failed to deal with fundamental historical forces shaping the nature of work and the quality of working life. Inspired by the new history, this volume examines underground bituminous coal mining and the technological changes that transformed the labor process in that industry during the 1920s and 1930s.

My interest in the impact of technology at the workplace evolved from my earlier study of work relations in the coal mines during the hand-loading period. It also grew out of the current concern in the industrial relations field over the important link between technology and quality of work. Throughout the book, I will be using the word *technology* in a very narrow sense of the term: a mechanical process, simple in design and function, which was developed for the purpose of eliminating the hand loading of coal. While this mechanical coal loader may not have pushed forward the frontiers of the engineering profession, it had a complicated and fascinating history, which raises many questions concerning the development and diffusion of an invention not only in the coal industry, but throughout our economy.

The path from initial inventive concept to widespread adoption of the coal-loading machine was a rocky one indeed. Economic, social, and political forces sometimes retarded its development, while at other times conditions moved the mechanization process forward with great speed. It is the mix of these forces—involving business, government and the union—that makes it so clear that technology is not just a question of engineering feasibility, but rather a social process affected by personalities, institutions, and traditions.

Certainly it is important to explain the mechanical features of the loading machine, to show how it evolved from the drawing board to working model to actual use. In doing this, I have pursued answers to questions such as, What motivated the inventors? Who did the experimental work on the inventors' ideas? How was experimental and development work financed? Who built the new machines once perfected? And how were their sales promoted?

All of this led me to an investigation of the capital goods industry in mining machinery, an essential ingredient in the technological process. But having a new machine available is only part of the story; business incentives to invest are influenced by an array of factors such as national economic trends, government policies, and the responses of workers and their unions.

While having very little direct involvement in the decision-making process relating to technology, workers have an obvious personal stake in change, because new methods affect the number of jobs available and alter the nature of the jobs that remain. These concerns were reflected in a folk song George Korson recorded in 1940 in southern West Virginia:

> Tell me, what will a coal miner do?
> Tell me, what will a coal miner do?
> When he goes down in the mine,
> Joy loader he will find.
> Tell me, what will a coal miner do?

Recognizing that mechanization would mean a loss of jobs, the first stanza of the song laments

> Miners' poor pocketbooks are growing lean,
> Miners' poor pocketbooks are growing lean,
> They can't make a dollar at all,
> Here is where we place the fault,
> Place it all on that coal-loading machine.[1]

Rather than focus on the employment impact of technological change, a disaster about which others have written, I have been concerned primarily with the effect new technology had on the social relations of production and on the quality of working life. Further, I have been particularly interested in how miners reacted to the new machinery and what, if any, effect their response had on the diffusion of technology in the industry. To do this it was necessary to review the evolution of collective bargaining in the industry, and this in turn involved a rather detailed look at some aspects of the miners' union history, its leadership, its internal structure, and the formation of the union's goals and objectives. In this effort I repeatedly found myself trying to understand the relation between the local unions of miners and their national union.

At the outset I need to make the disclaimer that there is not an antitechnology, Luddite, assumption underlying this study. It is true, however, that in searching for some answers to the questions about the sources and uses of technology in this industry I have tried to do what David Noble urges us all to do, that is "to transcend the myth of the machine, the fetish for technological transcendence."[2] Implicit in these pages, therefore, is the view that industrial technology is, in part, a control mechanism to promote the accumulation of private wealth. By rejecting the conventional wisdom, which equates technology with social progress, I feel that I have been better equipped to search for the many private and social costs associated with the introduction of a new industrial process and to weigh those costs against claimed benefits. This view has been especially important in the chapter on the impact of the loading machine on the health and safety of coal miners.

When production was organized under a system of hand loading, workers largely controlled the production process.[3] The primary responsibilities of the coal operator were to raise the capital necessary for the mine to function and to sell the coal. The highly competitive nature of coal markets, coupled with depressed coal demand in the 1920s and 1930s, forced a transformation in this relation between workers and owners. Increasingly, coal operators were forced to find ways to lower costs and rationalize production. It was not just a matter of buying a new machine to increase productivity; what was needed was a fundamental reorganization of the workplace, with a machine at its center. When the reorganization took place, management could more effectively direct the work force in much the same way that workers were disciplined in the modern factory. And with the expansion of management's control, there was a corresponding loss of workers' control—or what Carter Goodrich called "the miner's freedom." In focusing my research on the qualitative changes workers experienced from the new technology, I am not trying to romanticize some earlier period when working conditions were ideal, for no such period ever existed. The point I hope to emphasize is simply that the impact of technological change is so far-reaching that we need to find ways for all of those affected by it to share in making the decisions that bring it about.

ACKNOWLEDGMENTS

I WOULD LIKE to express my appreciation to all those West Virginia coal miners who, over the past eight to ten years, have been so generous with their time in telling me about their underground work experiences. District union officials, local union officers, and rank-and-file miners have contributed to my understanding of the process by which coal was mined in an earlier day, and while they may not agree with my assessment of things—especially my views on John L. Lewis—I hope these pages will help them, in turn, understand their own past a little better and help them appreciate the fact that they, too, helped shape history.

I also want to express a special thanks to several people who made substantive comments and helpful criticisms of early drafts of this book, notably Jeremy Brecher, Peter Gottlieb, Betty Justice, and Rick Simon. Sarah Etherton provided invaluable editing assistance, Deloris Ratliff spent many hours on the word processor, and Sharon Mayfield helped with secretarial work. Through it all, Richard Humphreys, director of the Institute for Labor Studies at West Virginia University, where this project was undertaken, gave continual support and encouragement.

WHAT'S A COAL MINER TO DO?

CHAPTER 1

The Hand Loading of Coal

FOR MORE than a hundred years, from before the Civil War to well into the 1930s, the production of coal depended on the simple act of taking shovel in hand, scooping up a pile of the material, and throwing it into an empty mine car. During the period that bituminous coal provided energy for the nation's industrial revolution, each year human muscle lifted nearly half a billion tons of coal an average of three feet from ground to mine car. It is ironic that the advance in technology and management, which gave modern industry its momentum, bypassed the one industry on which most others depended. While a few mine owners experimented in the 1920s with ways to substitute mechanical for muscle power for loading coal, as late as 1948 a third of the nation's underground coal was still loaded by hand.

This chapter describes the work practices and social relations of production associated with traditional hand loading.[1] The chapter also presents a case study of a typical coal mine that employed hand loaders in the 1930s.

Over the years, tradition has classified underground bituminous mining by the approach used to gain entry to the seam of coal. When coal reserves are found at some depth from the surface, the method was to sink a shaft and erect a hoist for transporting workers, supplies, and coal. If the coal lay beneath the surface but not at a great depth, access to the seam might dictate a sloping entry, permitting movement of workers, supplies, and coal by rail. Drift mining, the third method of gaining entry to a coal seam, was a simple, direct approach to a seam of coal conveniently exposed on the side of the hill. In the drift mining of an earlier day, workers frequently walked to and from their workplaces, while supplies

1

and mined coal moved by mule haulage on an underground railway system.

Selection of one approach over another was largely a matter of geography and geology. That is, it was a question of whether the coal seam outcropped on a hillside or lay buried some distance below ground level. The mine entry decision was not, however, neutral in its impact on overall economic conditions in the industry or on work relations inside the mines. Sinking shafts and the initial development of a coal seam that lay several hundred feet below the surface required a much larger capital investment than that necessary for a coal seam exposed along the contour of a hill. Ease of entry in a literal sense—as in drift mining—has meant ease of entry in an economic sense, with the resultant problems of overexpansion during prosperous times and excess capacity and unemployment during depressed times.

Once the coal seam has been penetrated by shaft or drift entry, there are two basic systems for removing the coal: the room-and-pillar system and the long-wall system. Historically, the room-and-pillar system has been the most widely used, although long-wall mining was well understood and in use as early as the turn of the century. In recent years, with the development of new methods of roof support and coal shearing machines long-wall mining has been replacing the room-and-pillar system. Each system must be described to establish the physical context within which the miner did his job.

The Room-and-Pillar Method

In the hand-loading days of the 1920s, room-and-pillar mining involved the opening of tunnels, called main entries, that were driven forward horizontally into the coal seam from the bottom of the shaft or from the drift opening. Along a main entry, at intervals of approximately 400 feet, side entries 1,200 to 1,500 feet long were driven, blocking out a rectangular panel of the coal seam (figure 1). From the side entries and at right angles to them, "rooms" were opened up. And it was in these rooms that the principal mining activity took place.

Depending on special conditions in each mine, rooms ranged in width from twelve to forty feet, with a twenty-foot width being close to an average. When completed, these rooms traversed the distance from one side entry to another, say 400 feet. As the room was being worked, the end wall was referred to as the coal face, the place where the miner and

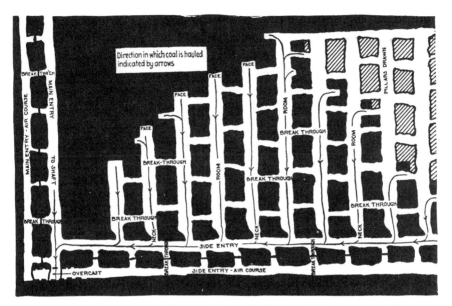

FIGURE 1. *A portion of a working panel shows the location of the main entry, side entry, working rooms, and the face. Shaded area indicates that pillar removal is in progress, while the arrows show the direction in which the coal is being hauled.*

his helper performed their jobs. The dimensions of the working face were determined, therefore, by the mine owner's decision on how wide the rooms should be and by the thickness of the coal seam.[2] For example, if the coal seam was six feet thick, a miner's workplace might be twenty feet wide, six feet high and any length, depending on how near to completion his room was. The rooms were connected to one another by "breakthroughs" cut through the walls separating the rooms. That part of the coal seam bounded by the walls of the rooms and the breakthroughs was called a pillar of coal, hence the name, room and pillar.

A panel, as delineated by the side entries, might contain fourteen or more rooms, enough places for fourteen or twenty-eight miners, depending on whether the rooms were considered single or double size. The size of the mining property and customer demand determined the number of panels in operation at any one time. By design, work in the different rooms of a panel did not move ahead simultaneously, but rather proceeded at different rates so that a diagonal advancement took place.

When all the rooms in a panel had been completed, the task of removing the pillars between the rooms began. This process, called pillar drawing, was accomplished by retreating from the end of the finished room back toward the room entrance and had to be performed simultaneously and quickly since, in removing the pillars, no support remained to hold up the roof. Proper pillar removal could greatly reduce the amount of coal left in the mine—and therefore lost to production. But the process required both the careful management of advancing workplaces and the use of very skilled workers to "pull" the pillars.

The Long-Wall Method

Unlike the room-and-pillar system, long-wall mining involved the removal of the entire seam of coal, or very large sections of it. The working face of coal might be a hundred feet or more, depending on the type of equipment used, and the roof of the mine was supported only close to the face. The mined-out area was filled by allowing the overburden to fall down behind the miners as they moved forward into the seam. The cutting and removal of the coal could begin at the shaft bottom and move toward the outer limits of the property, called advancing. Alternatively, coal removal could be postponed until entries for ventilation and haulage had been driven to the property limits. Mining by moving backward toward the point of origin was referred to as retreating. Regardless of the direction of removal, long-wall mining had several advantages over room-and-pillar mining, not the least of which was that the rate of recovery of coal was much greater.

By 1900, long-wall mining was used extensively in Europe, having been in place in some countries as early as the eighteenth century.[3] In this country, the system had staunch supporters. They claimed that the many economic advantages of long-wall mining might offset the higher capital costs generally associated with it. One mining official in 1911 claimed that the system concentrated the men and thus minimized the cost for day laborers, such as track men, drivers, and mechanics, which in some traditional mines, were substantial. He also observed that it would make supervision easier and in every way tend to lessen the work of the mine superintendent, which also would reduce the cost per ton of coal.[4]

Successful long-wall mining depended on uninterrupted production schedules, a condition difficult to achieve in the early days of mining. The failure to maintain regularity in the removal of coal often caused the roof to shear at the face, possibly resulting in a loss of equipment and inevitably incurring a considerable cost to reestablish the working face.

Since the availability of steady customers and the regular delivery of empty railroad cars affected production schedules, mine owners were reluctant to commit their mines to the long-wall system. Work stoppages, which were frequent in some coalfields, interrupted production and tended, thereby, to discourage the adoption of this system. The mining official cited above noted that "even a short stoppage of operation may result in serious damage to the working area through the caving of the roof. In the pillar method this is less important." Thus, while long-wall mining made supervision of the work force possible, it also gave workers a strategic bargaining advantage not available to them in room-and-pillar mining.

The economic feasibility of long-wall mining depended, therefore, on a risk-free market and on the availability of a peaceful and disciplined work force. Neither condition prevailed during the hand-loading period in this country. Furthermore, the long-wall retreating system did not lend itself to a rapid return on an owner's investment because of the long delay between initial commitment of capital and first production of coal. Because there was little room for patience in the competitive push to exploit the nation's coal resources, long-wall mining was little utilized during the hand-loading period.

The Labor Process

Mining coal by hand methods in the room-and-pillar system involved four basic tasks: undercutting the coal face with a miner's pick, drilling the face with a hand auger (sometimes called a breast auger), blasting of the coal, and finally, shoveling the broken coal into empty mine cars (figure 2). Other elements of the job at the face included setting timbers to support the roof and laying new track to the face after the room had been cleaned up.

While timbers and track were supplied by the company, the pick miner owned his own tools and, out of his own pocket, paid the company blacksmith to keep them sharp and in repair. The miner also bought his own blasting powder, lamp oil, and other supplies. Working mostly without much supervision, the early miner was an independent craftsman who was paid for the number of tons of coal he mined. The job required a high level of knowledge, experience, and dexterity, which were acquired, as with most skilled jobs, by serving an apprenticeship of variable

FIGURE 2.   *After blasting the coal from the face, the coal miner loaded it by hand into the mine car.*

length, depending on law and custom. In some states, such as Illinois and Indiana, two years' experience were required before a miner could obtain a certificate enabling him to work alone at the face.

Undercutting the coal face with a pick was the first task to be mechanized. As early as the 1880s, undercutting machines were introduced to coal mining, and by the turn of the century a quarter of all bituminous coal was mechanically cut.[5] Even with this development, the labor process remained essentially as it had earlier. Shot holes were still drilled by hand, blasting powder was still used to break down the coal face, and loading coal remained a hand-and-back operation. Coal loading was, however, no simple matter. It was strenuous work, done with the knowledge that the daily wage depended on how fast one shoveled. While loading coal, the miner had to remove pieces of rock and slate to avoid having his pay docked for loading "dirty" coal. Once loaded, the coal car had to be pushed from the room by the miner and his helper. (In some mines, the loaded cars were "gathered" by mule or small locomotive.) Interviews with retired coal miners who remember the hand-loading days explain the human side of this process.

Room-and-Pillar Mining in Northern West Virginia

Howard Raber, born in 1909, started working in the mines of northern West Virginia in 1924.[6] Moving about from one mine to the next in his early years because, in his words, "the grass was greener on the other side of the fence," Raber settled down for a short time in 1928 when he began loading coal at a large captive mine near Wheeling (that is, the mine was owned by a steel company). This mine employed 750 hand loaders and 150 day men, all of whom worked a seam of coal considered to be low coal, three to five feet thick. Raber recalled that tonnage rates for the miners were higher than at other mines because the company wanted to keep the union out. "The company hated the union like God hates sin." The mining process at this particular mine was similar to that used elsewhere. The coal face was twenty-four feet wide and was undercut by machines on the midnight shift so that the drilling-blasting-loading cycle could begin as soon as the miners arrived at their rooms.

After the company undercut the coal face, would it also drill and blast it?
RABER: No, not there. Some places they did, but not there. You drilled your holes with a breast auger. I don't know why they called it a breast auger, 'cause you placed it on your knees in that low coal.

How many holes would you drill?
RABER: About four holes. It was up to you, because you paid for the powder. You paid for your powder and your detonator caps.

Did the company prefer that you mine mostly large "lump" coal?
RABER: No, at this mine they didn't care. But you were supposed to pick out the binder [impurities]. Of course, we had a sledge hammer, and sometimes we'd bust it up and load it, too. If you could get by with it, that saved time cleaning it. You could do that; but if you got caught they would dock you for that car. They'd take the whole car and you didn't get paid anything. Of course, you would pick that binder out if the boss was around.

How often did the boss come around?

RABER: You'd only see him once a day. A section boss would have four or five sections, generally about sixty men. By the way, my uncle was a section boss. That's one reason I got a job. You also had a fire boss, and you'd see him once a day. He carried a safety light, and he checked for gas; and then he inspected the haulage and the rooms, and if you needed a post he'd tell you.

So you drilled, blasted, loaded, and cleaned the coal.

RABER: And did the timbering.

How many timbers did you generally set?

RABER: Fourteen per cut. When I tell you fourteen per cut, that depended on whether you were holding the rock up or taking the rock down. When you hold your rock up it took more posts. If you took the rock down you had to pry it down and then gob it. We called "gobbing it" putting it back some place. At times you had to shoot [blast] your rock to get it down.

Was this considered "dead" work?

RABER: Oh yeah. You didn't get paid. If the rock was over a foot thick you got paid so much per inch per cut.

How large were the coal cars?

RABER: Two tons. I'll say at that time they didn't steal any weight off of you. I'll say that much.

How much coal could you load in a shift?

RABER: I have loaded twenty-six tons. Of course I was young and I didn't have much for brains. That was pretty good money.

How many hours would it take to clean up your room?

RABER: It depended on how long you wanted to stay in there. We didn't have what they call the clean-up system. But when you did clean up, the cutting machine operator was there to give you a fresh cut. Unless he went home at noon and you cleaned up late in the afternoon. We didn't clean up every day. They didn't require you to come out when they run a man trip. If there was something you wanted to do you just stayed in there and walked out . . . about seven miles.

After loading coal for about three years, Raber got a job as a cutting machine helper. He and the machine runner, like the hand loaders, were paid on a tonnage basis—eight cents a ton—which they split evenly. He said that a room when cut "would throw twenty-five to thirty tons," so that the two machine men each made roughly a dollar each per room. A machine man "could cut a place in fifteen or twenty minutes if he had good power." The machine men cut for thirty or thirty-five hand loaders but apparently not on any fixed schedule. They would go in the mine at midnight and start cutting in those rooms that had been cleaned up the day before. When the loaders came to work, some would finish loading the coal in their rooms before others, and the machine men would come in to cut their coal.

While the hand loaders depended on the men who operated the cutting machines, it seems that the principal duty of the machine runners was to provide a service for the men who broke down the coal and loaded it. Raber confirmed this by pointing out that the machine operators were generally there when you needed them, and "you never lost any time on account of his not being there." In the same way that motormen provided empty cars and supplies to the loaders and that the fire boss checked for gas, the machine operator's job was to improve the efficiency and productivity of the miners at the face. It is clear from Raber's description in the coalfields of northern West Virginia that machine technology did not give management control over the pace of production while coal was loaded by hand.

Room-and-Pillar Mining in Southern West Virginia

Another retired coal miner from a different coalfield confirmed many of the impressions of underground work that Howard Raber gave. Wylie Erwin began working in a southern West Virginia mine in 1938, when the coal was still being loaded entirely by hand.[7] The mine employed approximately 1,200 workers and, using the room-and-pillar system, was divided into sections with twelve or fourteen working places each. The company's hiring policy was quite informal, according to Erwin: "The young men they hired were kids of the men who were already working. It was just one big happy family." His first job in the mines was as a trackman's helper. He and the trackman laid the track for the loaders, keeping the track moved right up to the face for a whole section.

Track-mounted cutting machines undercut the coal face for the loaders, who in turn drilled the face, blasted it, and loaded the coal. Loaders also had to clean the coal. According to Erwin, "If you had slate or what we called 'gray band,' they would clean that out, throw it back on the rib, and you would have to load it out later. But it wasn't worth what it took. If you loaded up a car or two cars, they might give you a dollar." While not rigidly enforced, the loaders worked by a clean-up rule that dictated they could not leave their workplaces until the coal was loaded and the room readied for the cutting machine. All the cutting was done on the hoot owl, or midnight, shift. If a loader didn't clean up, "when he went in the next day all the coal he would have would be what was left" from the day before. "Nobody worked in your room," Erwin pointed out. He also noted that "the tools belonged to the coal loader. See, he bought his own shovel and everything and, of course, the coal loaders had to pay for the powder, too."

Erwin later became a brakeman (called a spragger in some locations) on what was called a pull-n-place gathering locomotive. The job of the motorman, who drove the motor, and his brakeman was to provide empty cars for the loaders and to remove the cars as soon as the loaders had filled them. As a brakeman, Erwin would go into the mine with the motorman around 6 A.M. and they "stayed on the section until all the coal loaders had cleaned up." There were no restrictions on how long he stayed at work, but if he left early "that would mess up the loaders. Everybody was a family . . . so you wouldn't run off and leave that poor coal loader [without enough empties to clean up] knowing that the next day that man wasn't going to have a fresh cut of coal." He said that "the biggest majority of your hand loaders would start walking out of the mine around 2 P.M." but usually he, as a brakeman, had to stay until early evening, around 7 or 8 P.M.

A general mine foreman walked the mine each day, and each working section of the mine also had a boss. When asked what the section boss's responsibilities were, Erwin said, "he really didn't have much to do, just made sure the hand loaders had cars and, of course, if the motor crews had any wrecks from bad track he'd tell the [trackmen] to go fix it. He was also in charge of 'turning the rooms,' that is, the opening of new rooms. You see, in the hand-loading days you would turn your places on a 45 [degree angle]." The section boss would "order the size posts his loaders needed for the working places," and they would be delivered on the hoot owl shift. All activity was directed toward providing a service to the loaders so they could do their jobs.

An Alabama Miner in West Virginia

William H. Veasly began in an Alabama coal mine at age fourteen.[8] After working there with his father and three brothers until 1923, Veasly moved to the Fairmont field in northern West Virginia, where he found work at the Grant Town mine. A year later, the mine shut down when the operators in northern West Virginia and Pennsylvania decided to abrogate their union contracts and operate their mines without a union representing their workers. Veasly returned to Alabama for two years but then came back to Grant Town in 1926. He joined the many miners who reluctantly returned to work on a nonunion basis during the late 1920s. The miners refer to this period—from 1924 to 1933 when the union was reorganized—as the scab period.

Veasly became active in the union after it was recognized in 1933 and served on the mine committee for five years. He studied for and passed the state examination for mine foreman but was refused advancement by the company because, he believes, of his race. When loading machines were introduced in the mine in the early 1940s, Veasly was laid off. He drifted south and found work in the Kanawha field, where he worked until 1952, still loading coal by hand. After 1952 he worked for the West Virginia Department of Mines, until his retirement. Veasly's mining career covers the period being studied and his experiences were typical, especially of black miners.

When you first went into the mines did you work with your father?

VEASLY: Yes, that's the only way you could go in the mines. Now you've got a different thing, they have official training for the mines; but the only way you could get in the mines in those days was if your daddy carried you in or your uncle or somebody carried you in.

How long did it take you to become an experienced miner?

VEASLY: He'd keep you with him about a year or maybe two years if he didn't have another boy to bring in. Say you got a boy here who's sixteen or seventeen and you carry him in, but you got one behind him who's fifteen. After he trains you, you can go to a place by yourself and he can carry the other boy in and right on through, see?

Why did you move to West Virginia?

VEASLY: You could make better money than you could in Alabama. What really happened, understand, there was a man in Alabama called Bowlegged Jones, and he was an agent for the coal operators in West Virginia, Kentucky, and all around. The coal operator would take a Negro preacher and give him $400 to $500 and send him to Alabama and tell him to bring back so many people. He'd have a ticket for you and give you $25 or $30, what they called "transportation." Bowlegged Jones said he was gonna ship them till his legs get straight.

Were these experienced black miners?

VEASLY: Yes. That's why they came there. You couldn't go get a miner and bring him to West Virginia if he didn't know how to mine.

What did your job involve, from the time you started work each day until the time you left?

VEASLY: You'd go in the mine and catch a man trip at 6:30 A.M. and you'd be at your place about 7:00. You laid your track, set safety posts, drilled your own coal, shot your coal, and loaded it. Your place, understand, is a room twenty to twenty-five feet wide and six feet high. The machine came in and cut the coal. When I first went to Grant Town in 1924 they'd drill your holes. They had air drills and would drill your holes, but after they broke the union, why, they quit drilling your holes.

How did they determine who got which place?

VEASLY: There would be favoritism when the boss would find a fellow he liked better than another fellow. When it came down to the scab job [during the 1924–33 period], the company told the foreman to do this kind of thing—give the men that traded with the company store the best breaks. Some were nasty enough to let a man come home with another man and go with his wife to get a good place.

The Miner's Freedom

The very fact that the knowledge of the mining process belonged to the body of miners at work in their respective rooms and that this knowledge was passed on through an informal apprenticeship system gave miners a considerable amount of control over their job. Carter Goodrich, in his 1925 book *The Miner's Freedom,* pointed out that "the miner does in practice pick up his trade almost entirely from his buddy or his neighbors and hardly at all from his boss."[9] In addition, the miner developed a proprietary interest in his room and rarely was transferred until it had been worked out. Even if a miner was absent from work for a considerable time, his room was ordinarily held for him. Further, the handloading coal miner worked without supervision, being almost an independent contractor.

One of the most powerful features of the miner's control of the production process was his freedom to leave the workplace whenever he decided to do so. According to the 1922 U.S. Coal Commission, the reasons generally given for leaving the mine before its official closing time were that the miner got "cleaned up" or that he had earned enough for the day. A miner also might leave his work if empty cars were unavailable for loading, if his shots misfired, if his tools broke, or if other factors left him without sufficient coal to load. The point is, he was free to do so. Even where the eight-hour day was established under a union contract, the tonnage men still retained the right—by virtue of management's inability to change it—to leave the mine when they pleased. One Ohio mining official reported to the Coal Commission that "in actual practice 60 percent to 70 percent [of the loaders] do not observe the eight-hour rule." And "for these employees even the six-hour day is the exception and not the rule."[10]

When the industry was faced with an economic crisis in the 1920s, this lack of industrial discipline became increasingly incompatible with management's need to plan, to coordinate, and to control the labor process for maximum productivity. L. E. Young, vice president of the Pittsburgh Coal Company, reported on an industry survey made in 1929, confirming the contradiction between the miner's freedom to leave his workplace and a rational labor process: "The one point which is stressed most by the [owners] is the difficulty of operating a coal mine economically when the daily output is contingent upon the whims of the coal loader who works when, as long, and as hard as he pleases."[11] It is not surprising that the establishment of a standard workday became an integral part of the movement for increased productivity that brought about an end to the hand-loading era.

One of the most important characteristics of work relations in the early period of coal mining was the lack of direct and continuous supervision of the work force. Unlike the factory, where workers are concentrated and foreman/worker ratios are high, the widespread dispersion of workplaces under the room-and-pillar mining system and the industry practice of hiring only one inside foreman for each mine made close supervision of mine workers practically impossible. The long distances between workplaces meant that a single mine foreman had only minimal daily contact with the miners. Although by 1915 some state safety laws required that mine foremen visit each workplace at least once a day, it is doubtful that such laws were routinely followed. Instead, management continued to depend on the skill and individual initiative of the miner, a fact that gave the miner a freedom and an independence found in only a few other industrial settings.

Alternatives to Direct Supervision

Given this lack of supervision in the early days, payment by the ton evolved as the only reward system that could assure that mine workers would put forth a reasonable effort to load coal. Tonnage rates were determined by competitive market forces or, where the mines were organized, by collective bargaining. However, the history of the industry is replete with evidence that mine owners, while relying on piece-rate payments, continually tried to increase their profit levels by various manipulations and abuses of the system. For example, the practice of short weighing became so common in the industry that one of the first demands of miners when they formed unions was for a checkweighman to assure them an honest weight for the coal they sent to the surface. Dockage, an arbitrary reduction in payment because of impurities loaded with the coal, was another abuse of the piece-rate system that provided management with a partial control of the miner's efforts. Howard B. Lee, former West Virginia attorney general, reported that operators admitted it was their policy "to dock considerable [sic] more than the waste in their cars . . . to punish the miner and make him more careful in the future."[12]

A modification of the piece-rate system came with the practice, common in some nonunion mines in West Virginia, of making payment by the car rather than by the ton. Increases in the size of cars and nonpayment for improperly loaded cars were frequent complaints of miners under this system. The introduction of screens, which allowed only lump coal to pass onto the scales, was yet another management effort to get greater production and profits out of the tonnage system.

Mine owners also tried to maintain their profitability by the use of an elaborate system of off-the-job control mechanisms. Because of the isolated nature of most mining operations, miners were usually dependent on the company to provide housing, stores, and recreation. This provided an opportunity for direct economic exploitation, which frequently was seized. There is evidence, as the Greenbrier story in the next section shows, that some companies made greater profits from their company-run stores than they did from their mining operations.[13] Intimidation and physical violence from company-hired armed guards and spies were other forms of control common in many coalfields, especially during the nonunion era.[14]

The labor situation in West Virginia illustrates the conflict that existed in unorganized coalfields from Colorado to Alabama to central Pennsylvania. West Virginia miners lived in company-owned houses and in company-controlled communities; paid high prices at company-owned stores; received annual wages that were generally insufficient for an adequate family diet; and worked under constant threat of eviction, discharge, and blacklisting. When economic reprisals failed to keep miners from trying to organize a workers' union, the coal operators maintained their sovereignty by political oppression and force of arms. During the 1920s and early 1930s, detectives were hired as spies to infiltrate the union, armed guards patrolled the coal camps, county sheriffs were put on company payrolls, state legislators were bribed, and the judicial system was dominated by the companies. Lee has described these conditions:

> To keep the miners' union out of the fields, and thus maintain their feudal proprietorship, the operators employed six principal methods of defense and attack: (a) injunctions; (b) martial law; (c) suzerainty over county government; (d) elaborate espionage and spy system; (e) coercion and intimidation of workers by the use of mine guards; and (f) blacklisting all miners who favored the union.
>
> Injunctions, martial law, and espionage violated no existing laws, but were greatly subversive of the public welfare. But the use of company-paid deputy sheriffs (mine guards) was in violation of law, and frequently resulted in such wholesale killings as to be unbelievable in a supposedly civilized and law-abiding State.[15]

Looking back on the early hand-loading period, it seems that these forms of exploitation and control of miners off the job were substitutes for management's lack of control over miners on the job. But this contrast is too sharp. Management did exercise control over certain aspects of the job and working conditions. For example, the power of the mine foreman to hire whomever he pleased was more or less an unchallenged right that gave management the opportunity to show favoritism or to honor blacklists of union supporters. More importantly, the mine foreman's authority to discharge workers and evict them from company-owned houses gave significant disciplinary power to mine management. During periods of recession in coal markets when jobs were scarce, such discipline was quite effective. The power of the foreman in nonunion mines to assign workplaces, to determine the distribution of empty mine cars, and to establish rates of pay for so-called dead work gave him influence over the miners' earnings.

Mine workers were not, however, without their own defenses against these practices. From the very early years in the industry, when mine management attempted to alter the terms and conditions of employment or to impose arbitrary disciplinary actions, miners frequently resisted such interference—even before union organization came to the coalfields—by a concerted refusal to work. There are numerous reports of local strikes resulting from management's attempt to increase productivity and to effect greater profits at the miners' expense.[16] These local job actions were a corollary to, if not dependent upon, the control that workers in the mines exercised at the point of production. Before the coal industry could take its place among the technologically advanced industries of the twentieth century, this control, rooted as it was in the hand-loading system, had to be broken or at least severely limited.

Other factors also slowed the transition of this industry to more modern methods of production. Even after new technologies had been developed and proven profitable, many coal firms still found it advantageous to continue using the traditional labor intensive system. A close look at a mine in southern West Virginia helps explain why some owners resisted the sales pitches of the mine machinery manufacturers and continued using traditional hand-mining methods long after new technology became available.

The Greenbrier Story

The Greenbrier Coal Company operated a medium-sized mine in McDowell County, West Virginia, throughout most of the hand-loading period.[17] This mine, which began operating in 1893, was favorably situated as a drift operation in the six-foot Pocahontas seam of high-quality, "smokeless" coal. Shipping its output over the Norfolk and Western Railroad, the annual production of the Greenbrier mine averaged 150,000 tons between 1896 and 1932. Production closely paralleled both the long-run trends and the cyclical swings in national coal output. When national output reached a post–World War I peak in 1926, the mine experienced its best year, producing 264,000 tons, and as national output dropped precipitously with the Depression years, Greenbrier production fell to 128,000 tons in 1932. Annual fluctuations in output were accompanied by changes in the number of miners hired and, more importantly, by variations in the average number of days the mine was in operation. During the whole period, irregularity of employment was as characteristic of this particular mine as it was of the industry in general.

The work force at this southern West Virginia mine averaged 150 employees up through the years of high demand for coal during World War I. Thereafter, a gradual reduction in the work force by the end of the 1920s left approximately 110 employees on the payroll. Part of the cutback came when the company closed down its small coke-producing facility in 1919, and the rest of the work force reduction followed increases in productivity with the introduction of two undercutting machines in 1924. Traditional production relations existed at the Greenbrier mine, with all of the coal being loaded by hand. Unlike the payment-by-the-ton system common at most mines, coal loaders at Greenbrier were paid by the number of three-ton cars they loaded each day.

Using the room-and-pillar mining system, rooms were driven sixty feet from center to center and were twenty-one feet wide.[18] Haulage was accomplished by a combination of electric locomotives and animal power; mules were used extensively as late as 1932. Mine management consisted of two persons, a general manager and a mine foreman, until 1932, when the company added an assistant mine foreman to help direct the underground work force. For the most part, miners worked alone in their rooms with only infrequent visits from management.

A company-owned store supplied food, clothing, and other merchandise to employees in exchange for company scrip, the medium of exchange in the coal camp. Miners and their families, without any choice in the matter, lived in company-owned houses, and their rent payments were deducted by the company from their biweekly paychecks. New employees were recruited from among recent immigrants by labor agents in New York City or brought in "on transportation" from rural areas of the South. In the isolated mining community, management was able to keep the mine workers from organizing a union by threat of discharge and eviction. The mine was run nonunion for forty years, from its opening day to the mid-1930s.

In almost all respects, then, the Greenbrier mine was typical of the thousands of medium-sized mines in operation throughout the coalfields during the hand-loading period, from the Civil War to the 1930s and later. Since company records have been preserved and are available, it is possible to take a closer look at how the mine owners controlled the miners and how they made their cost and output decisions in a way not possible when data is limited to government or other secondary sources. Of particular interest is the question of why this firm did not mechanize its underground coal loading when the equipment became available.

Incorporated in West Virginia in 1892, the Greenbrier Coal Company in 1932 listed sixty individuals, banks, and other corporations as owners of its 2,000 shares of outstanding common stock. While ownership may have appeared to be widely held, controlling interest lay in the hands of Justus Collins, who owned several mines in the nearby Winding Gulf coal district. Collins and his family held 747 of the 2,000 shares, making him the largest single shareholder.[19] In the late 1890s Collins's brother Jairus assumed the duties of general manager of the Greenbrier mine, a position he held until his death in 1932. Justus Collins remained an executive officer of the firm until his death in 1934. Isaac Mann, who held the second largest number of shares, was appointed president of the Greenbrier Company and held the position for many years. Mann also was president of the Bank of Bramwell in Mercer County, West Virginia, and owned extensive coal-bearing land in the Pocahontas field. In fact, Mann, along with Elbert H. Gary and William Edenborn, had organized the syndicate that sold 300,000 acres of coal land to the Norfolk and Western Railroad in 1901. The Greenbrier Coal Company, in turn, leased its coal land from the Norfolk and Western for a ten-cent-a-ton royalty and shipped all its coal over the Norfolk and Western rails.[20]

From outward appearances, the Greenbrier was an independent coal company. However, the firm in fact was well integrated—through joint stock ownership and family ties—into the Winding Gulf Collieries, a much larger coal-producing network under Justus Collins's control. Further, the sales agency through which all the Greenbrier coal was sold provided a linkage with Collins's other operations in southern West Virginia. In 1932, Collins and his family held 90 percent of the common stock of this sales agency, which they called the Smokeless Fuel Company. Ownership of the sales agency provided Collins profitable commissions even when, during depressed coal markets, mining operations were showing losses. The sales agency was an important creditor of the operating companies held by Collins, providing operating and investment capital when needed.

Detailed financial reports of the Greenbrier Company are available for 1932,[21] and with them it is possible to probe into some of the problems facing local mine management and to understand some of the management policies that emerged during the hand-loading period. It is also possible with this data to determine ways in which economic decisions of the firm affected workers on and off the job, as well as the various ways workers' decisions on the job affected management and stockholders. This discussion is divided into two parts. First is an analysis of the demand side of the price equation, at least insofar as this coal company is concerned. The second part considers questions relating to the costs of production, which determine the quantity produced and sold by the company.

The price for a ton of Pocahontas no. 3 coal, or rather the prices for the various sizes of this coal, were negotiated prices incorporated in short-term contracts (three to six months) between the sales agency and any one of dozens of customers. The Smokeless Fuel Company, in competition with other agencies and producers who sold directly, made commitments for delivery of specific quantities of coal in specified sizes. Coal prices were quoted f.o.b. (free on board) the mine, and deliveries under the contracts were generally subject to "car supply, strikes, labor agitations or disturbances and causes beyond the control of the coal operator."[22]

The price of coal was largely outside the control of the local coal operator; competition dictated that a single seller could have little effect on market price. It is true that by advertising and aggressive salesmanship the Greenbrier Company, through the Smokeless Fuel Company, might have had some slight effect on the demand for Pocahontas no. 3 coal. But for the most part the f.o.b. price of Greenbrier coal was a fixed consideration. By the same set of circumstances that made it difficult for the operating company to affect price, the firm had little difficulty in selling all the coal it produced at the going price. The availability of empty railroad cars set an upper limit to local mine production, but within that limit management made output and employment decisions based on production relations and production costs, and not on market price. In the terminology of the economist, the firm's demand curve was elastic.

The coal operator during the hand-loading period actually was faced with an array of prices for different sizes of coal. The smaller sizes were less desirable at that time and sold for much lower prices than the "lump" and "egg" sizes. Complicating managerial decisions was the additional fact that the relative prices of the various sizes—produced under conditions of joint costs—changed monthly. Each size had its own conditions of demand and supply, and as those conditions changed there were adjustments in the relation among the various prices.[23] Table 1 shows how relative prices fluctuated from one period to the next.

Total revenue for any period not only derived from the number of tons of coal mined but also depended quite heavily on the mix of sizes in each coal car sent to the surface. In 1932, the Greenbrier records show that the various sizes were produced in the following proportions: lump, 12.5 percent; egg, 18.6 percent; stove, 6.1 percent; nut, 7.2 percent; slack, 51.9 percent; and other, 3.7 percent. These averages obscure wide variations in the monthly size composition of the mine's output. For example, the percentage of slack, the lowest priced size, varied from a high of 62.0 percent in July to 37.9 percent in December. Given the relative prices of the different sizes, mine revenues would have been substantially lower in months when the slack ratio was high. From these figures, it is easy to understand why management during the hand-loading period continually pressured the miners to load as much lump coal as possible.

The size mix was, indeed, a matter largely determined by the individual miner. It depended both on his skill in making the undercut (when it

TABLE 1

Coal Prices, Greenbrier Coal Company, 1932
($ per ton)

Size	July	October	December
Lump	1.91	2.59	1.71
Egg	1.86	2.75	1.78
Stove	1.60	2.40	1.90
Nut	1.04	1.18	1.40
Slack	0.28	0.22	0.31

was done by hand) and on how he placed his shot and how much powder he used to bring down the face. An excessive amount of powder would shatter the coal and reduce the proportion of larger sizes. The size mix of any coal mine also depended simply on the decisions of miners as to how much of the smaller sizes would be loaded into each mine car and how much would be gobbed along the sides—called ribs—of their rooms. Management efforts to the contrary, the slack ratio was controlled by the mine workers while coal was being loaded by hand. (Machines for loading coal, of course, gathered everything, from lump to slack.)

The Greenbrier figures on mine output by size of coal suggest a reason for loading more slack in some months than in others. When faced with the prospects of shorter workweeks or even layoffs during summer months, Greenbrier miners might well have wanted to load as many cars as possible each day they were allowed in the mine. Even though it required greater effort to load a single car with more slack than usual, the miners wanted to load as many cars as possible with all the coal loosened with each shot. Rather than gob the slack and ultrafine "bug dust," they loaded it along with the larger sizes. Since this mine paid by the number of cars loaded, this practice was a matter of self-protection, an "income-maintenance" plan during summer months. For management, on the other hand, receiving so much slack at the tipple was a costly propositon.

Two monthly financial statements from the available 1932 data for the Greenbrier mine have been selected for closer scrutiny. These two months, July and October, represent contrasting situations because of the substantial difference in mine output. Detailed profit and loss statements for the mine permit an examination of trends in costs of production as output was expanded from 7,612 tons in July to 13,880 tons in October, an increase of 82.3 percent. While it is true that 1932 was a Depression year both in coal mining and for the nation as a whole, there is no reason to believe that short-run cost trends would have behaved any differently had there been full employment and good markets for coal.

In the Pocahontas field, prices for all sizes of coal increased with the seasonal increase in demand during August and September. For the Greenbrier mine, the price increase meant greater output and greater profits, as shown in table 2.

The familiar boom-or-bust phenomenon long associated with the coal mining industry is highlighted by this particular experience at the Greenbrier mine. In this case, the increase in market demand and price stimulated a substantial expansion in output, employment opportunities, and total personal income. It is not likely that the mine owner hired new employees for this short-run expansion but rather that he increased the workweek from a two- or three-day schedule to a full-time schedule.[24] In the four-month period from July to October, the company's profit picture made a complete turnaround, going from a net loss of $524 in July to a net profit on coal sales of $5,058 in October. (At the same time, company records show that total payroll for all nonsalaried employees at the mine rose from $3,533 to $6,277, for a 77.7 percent increase.)

Unfortunately, the data are not available to determine per capita income, nor to determine the general level of economic welfare of miners and their families during this period in the Greenbrier mine community. The available data do show, however, that there were dramatic fluctuations in income within fairly short periods of time, and it follows that miners and their families found ways to survive during the periods of few or no work opportunities. Of course, this suggests dependency on the company store and company-owned homes, a question discussed below.

The monthly profit-and-loss statements for the Greenbrier mine show in detail the various costs of production, such as the cost for mining and loading the coal by hand, the timbering and track work, the haulage and preparation of coal, the supplies, taxes, salaries of bosses, and so forth. For the sake of discussion, these costs can be divided into two categories: those that are variable and those that are fixed. The fixed costs of production include salaries and other traditional overhead items, which are incurred regardless of the level of output. Variable costs depend on the level of output and fluctuate with it. When computed on an average or per-ton basis, fixed costs decline as output expands, while the variable costs may go up or down or, as in the case of the wage payment by the carload or a tonnage royalty payment, remain the same.

From the data, it is quite clear that the single most important cost

TABLE 2

Coal Production and Profit, Greenbrier Coal Company, 1932

	July	October
Average price per ton	$0.99	$1.19
Tons of coal mined	7,612	13,880
Total revenue from coal sales[a]	$7,550	$16,547
Total cost of coal mined	$8,074	$11,488
Net profit (+) or loss (−)	−$524	+$5,058

a. Total revenue depended not only on total output but on the mix of the various sizes of coal and on the prices for these sizes.

item was the labor cost of mining and loading coal (table 3). At the Greenbrier mine, traditional hand-loading practices were used, and the miners were paid seventy cents for loading a three-ton car, that is,

TABLE 3

Cost of Production, Greenbrier Coal Company, 1932
($ per ton)

	July	October
Variable costs		
LABOR		
Mining	0.2341	0.2395
Timbering	0.0149	0.0057
Dead work	0.0347	0.0446
Track	0.0202	0.0292
Drainage/ventilation	0.0227	0.0213
Haulage	0.0529	0.0356
Preparation	0.0763	0.0669
Smithing	0.0083	0.0095
Worker's compensation	0.0125	0.0104
Total	0.4856	0.4627
SUPPLIES		
Timbering	0.0119	0.0378
Drainage/ventilation	0.0017	0.0023
Haulage/stables	0.0849	0.0083
Preparation	0.0172	0.0240
Smithing	0.0009	0.0004
Total	0.1166	0.0728
OTHER		
Electric power[a]	0.1224	0.0760
Depletion	0.0405	0.0327
Gross sales tax	0.0037	0.0048
Operators assistance	0.0163	0.0089
Royalty	0.1000	0.1000
Other[b]	0.0048	0.0029
Total	0.2879	0.2253
TOTAL VARIABLE COSTS	0.8901	0.7608
Fixed Costs		
Superintendent	0.0368	0.0202
Foreman	0.0184	0.0100
Section boss	0.0147	0.0081
Engineer	0.0049	0.0036
Insurance	0.0299	0.0152
Expenses[c]	0.0582	0.0207
TOTAL FIXED COSTS	0.1629	0.0777
Grand Total	1.0530	0.8385

a. Electric power is not entirely a variable cost. Even when the mine is closed down, electric fans and pumps are kept in operation.
b. Includes "supplies" for the superintendent and foreman.
c. An unexplained item, $443.17 in July and $286.75 in October.

roughly twenty-three cents per ton. The small increase in the labor cost per ton between July and October resulted from a reduction in the amount of coal the miners loaded, on the average, into each car. Loaded cars averaged 2.9 tons in October, while the carload average in July was 3.0 tons. This may have been a random occurrence or it may have resulted from the miner's decision to exert a little less effort on the job as the workweek approached full time and their incomes increased.[25] Payment by the car rather than by the ton gave miners some control over the pace of production, but over the long run was a dubious advantage since management controlled the size of the cars. The company sometimes effected a speed up by increasing the size of the cars.[26]

When the labor cost of mining and loading the coal is added to all other variable labor costs, the total is forty-nine cents per ton in July, or 46.1 percent of average total cost per ton. In October the labor cost was forty-six cents per ton, or 55.7 percent of average total cost. The costs of supplies per ton declined as output expanded, and the costs of all the other variable items, taken together, also declined. The decline in average variable costs suggests that production could have been increased even further without increases in the cost per ton. This means that mine output had not reached capacity levels. The nature of coal mining during the hand-loading era was such that rather dramatic output expansion could be achieved with constant or, in this case, declining costs per ton.

All of the fixed costs per ton declined, of course, as output expanded. The combined effect of a decline in average variable cost and average fixed cost was a drop in the per-unit cost of mining coal over this range of output: with the 82.3 percent increase in output, the average cost per ton of coal decreased by 20.0 percent, from $1.05 to $0.84. Losses were quickly turned into profits when the mine moved to full-time operation. Even if coal prices had not gone up, operating profits would have resulted from the cost cuts. The boom in the financial picture for the Greenbrier owners occurred in part because the company had unused capacity that could be brought into production rapidly.

Good business sense probably would have kept the operator from closing the mine as long as revenue per ton was equal to or greater than average variable cost. When revenue from the sale of coal was greater than variable cost, some of the fixed costs that continued in the short run were covered, and economic logic dictated that production continue. However, there was in the mining industry at that time, and particularly in the Greenbrier operation, an equally compelling reason for the mine to remain open and operating at a reduced workweek and with losses on its mining operations as it did in July: the system of company-owned subsistence.

The miners and their families at the Greenbrier mine lived in company-owned houses and bought their food and other necessities from the company-owned store; it was a typical mining community. For the company, the work force was a captive one on which it could depend regardless of the condition of coal sales. Even in the low-production year of 1932 and in the slow summer month of July, store sales and rent payments amounted to $3,266.06, a sum which absorbed 79.6 percent of the total income of all employees including the bosses (table 4). When output and incomes increased in October, store sales increased, but not as much as incomes. The ratio of sales and rents to income fell to 67.0 percent that month. If prices in the company store were not raised in October, the longer workweek and higher monthly incomes meant that the standard of living had gone up and it might also have been possible for the average family to save a little. At least it would have been possible to pay for postponed medical care, to retire some debts, and to make preparation for the next downturn in the coal market.

The company store profits and rental income are particularly significant because their combined value for July turned what would have been a net loss on mining operations into a net profit for the company as a whole. It is no surprise to anyone familiar with the economic history of the coalfields that the company store was an important adjunct to the mining process for many coal operators, but these records show the extent to which overall profits were linked to the successful operation of these

TABLE 4

**Company Store Profits and Rental Income on
Company-Owned Houses, Greenbrier Coal Company, 1932**
($)

	July	October
Company Store		
Sales	2,773.08	3,888.74
Operating expenses	2,239.96	3,053.70
Profits	533.12	835.04
Rent on company houses	492.98	709.01[a]
Total, store profits plus rent	1,026.10	1,544.05

a. Actual rent collections were $501.01 in October. An entry marked Sundry was included in this total for that month.

ancillary activities. The store manager in the company town must have surely been as important an official as the mine superintendent, especially during periods of slack demand for coal.

The opportunity to continue operating in the black while incurring actual production losses affected both long-run and short-run decisions, such as the appropriate level of output, the level of wages, the use of machinery, and the type of mining system to employ. Coal mining was more than the extraction of a mineral from the earth; it was a technical process combined with a mercantile process, with considerations for the former affected by the latter. Within this economic context, a partial answer to the question concerning mechanization in the coalfields might be found.

On the one hand, as long as short-run company profits could be maintained at the company store, the incentive to mechanize the mines was weak. Pressures that might have been exerted by higher labor costs and low productivity due to hand-loading methods were partially ameliorated by the knowledge that part of what was lost by mining would be made up through the sales of flour and potatoes. On the other hand, company store profits depended on maintaining a large work force. If mechanical loading machines were introduced, they would necessarily replace labor. With fewer workers, company store sales would drop and company houses would be vacated.

Mercantile profits and rental income were not the only factors that kept coal operators in business during the long period of recession in the industry, but for many companies these sources of income were inseparable in the corporate profit picture and logically had an impact on policy decisions relating to mine mechanization. The company store and the company house were more than symbols of exploitation of workers. If the Greenbrier experience is typical, they were as much a part of "mining" as drilling, blasting, and loading coal.

At the end of 1932 the Greenbrier financial statement showed that production had hit the lowest level in the company's history and coal prices were at their lowest Depression levels. The company mined 128,368 tons of coal at a cost of $145,492, while the sale of this tonnage brought in only $133,331 in revenues. The difference between production costs and sales ($12,161) represented a substantial loss on the company's mining operations. Indeed it was as bad a year for the company as it was for the whole industry.

The annual profit and loss statement for all of the Greenbrier operations—store, houses, mine, and even insurance sales to employees —shows a somewhat different picture, however. Partially offsetting the losses on coal sales were the rather substantial profits of the company store, amounting to $8,037 (an 18 percent return on sales). Company-owned rental units, powder sales, and commissions on insurance sold to employees yielded additional revenues, which brought the total profit on nonmining operations to $11,785. These profits nearly offset the losses on the production and sale of coal. At the end of the year, the company reported a loss of only $366 on its total activities, rather than the $12,161 it would have lost had it been engaged in coal mining alone.[27]

The conclusions to be drawn from the analysis of the July and October profit and loss statements are further confirmed by figures for the whole year. The Greenbrier accountant reported that revenues from coal sales were not sufficient to cover all of the company's variable costs of production, not to mention any of its fixed costs. Economic reasoning would have dictated that the mine be closed down rather than be operated with such heavy losses. Of course, this did not happen at Greenbrier because the company store and company houses provided an economic cushion, which made the mining operations viable. This coal company earned a substantial return on its nonmining operations, and while not being sufficient to offset mining losses totally, profits were high enough to keep the mine operating. In an industry that had experienced many such periods of low or negative profits on actual production of coal, it made good sense to view these ancillary operations as indispensible to economic survival.

One final thought follows from this analysis of a typical mine during the hand-loading period. The important role of the company store and the boom-and-bust experience of the industry help explain why coal operators might have been hesitant to move toward full mechanization of their mines. Even if they understood that mechanization would lower their labor costs and increase their profit potential, the mechanical loaders would displace a large number of workers. And as noted, a smaller work force would mean sales at the company store would go down and company houses would go unrented. It follows that insurance against catastrophic losses during periods of declining prices depended on continuing to use hand methods, at least under the economic conditions that existed well into the 1930s.

CHAPTER 2

Evolution of Underground Machinery

MINE MECHANIZATION involved more than just the use of machinery for undercutting the coal face and loading the load. Haulage underground was converted to mechanical power as the mine mules were retired; drilling of shot holes was soon done by air or electrically driven drills; ventilation of the mine was more scientifically undertaken; and screening and cleaning of coal in the preparation plants was mechanized. But it was the machinery developed for cutting the coal and the mobile loading machine more than any other development that altered the work of the traditional pick miner and set the stage for the transformation of the social relations of production in the nation's coal mines. A brief history of these two machines is presented as a basis for understanding the additional factors that made the modernization of coal mining such a slow process. Principal focus will be on the more important of the two, the loading machine.

Nineteenth Century Undercutting Machinery

British inventors developed the earliest machines for cutting the coal face, giving serious attention to the use of mechanical power more than a decade before their American counterparts. After a Glasgow mine owner showed in 1850 that compressed air could be used to power underground machinery, there was a flurry of engineering interest in designing equipment to replace the time-consuming and often hazardous task of undercutting coal by hand. A practical design for a machine incorporating a cutting chain was developed in 1853, and eleven years later another chain machine known as the Gartsherrie was patented and installed in a mine in Scotland. The Gartsherrie is now regarded as the precursor of modern coal cutters, although many similar machines were tested in the same period. In 1856, for example, a cutting machine utilizing a bar with cutting bits was built and tested in several mines, and in 1861 a machine with a cutting disc was patented and gained favor in some British mines using the long-wall mining system. Also in 1861, a machine that tried to replicate the miner's hand pick was patented and put to work with some success. [1]

American inventions often incorporated ideas from the British experience, the most notable case being the chain-type machine. In 1876, according to British mining professor G. Hibberd, one of the Gartsherrie chain machines was sent to the Philadelphia Exhibition, and "there is little doubt that it was from this exhibit that American engineers obtained their first knowledge of the principles of the chain machine as, during the exhibition, numerous photographs were taken and drawings made of the exhibit."[2] After the 1870s, American inventive effort began to overshadow that of the British, and the flow of ideas and machinery began to move in the opposite direction across the Atlantic.

American interest in cutting machines began in earnest in the late 1870s and took three forms: a cutter-bar machine, a pick or punching machine, and a chain machine. Francis M. Lechner of Columbus, Ohio, is credited with inventing the first practical coal cutter in this country. In June 1876, Lechner received a patent for a machine that used a revolving steel bar on which were mounted small, sharply pointed bits, or picks. The cutter bar, an idea probably taken from a similar British invention, was rotated by chains from a power shaft driven by compressed air. Mounted on a frame that could be moved forward and backward, the cutter bar was pushed into the coal face, or "breast," at ground level. When the machine had cut to its full depth of five or six feet, the cutter bar would be pulled out from the face and moved into position to make the next cut. In this manner the machine cut across the whole coal face.

Development work on the Lechner cutter-bar device was carried out in an Ohio coal mine with the financial backing of several Columbus bankers, the most notable of whom was Joseph A. Jeffrey. In 1878, when Lechner sold his patent to Jeffrey, the Lechner invention became the foundation for the first mining equipment manufacturer in this country, the Jeffrey Manufacturing Company.[3] Several years of experimentation were required to bring this undercutting machine to market, but the technical difficulties were overcome during the 1880s. When electricity became a workable alternative to compressed air, the Jeffrey Company began manufacturing a cutter bar machine driven by an electric motor. Even though this approach to undercutting proved its worth, in 1894 the company discontinued production of the machine when the new chain machine proved to be technically superior.

Although the basic technology of chain-type machines originated in Britain, machines incorporating cutting discs or cutting bars were preferred because they were better able to withstand the rigors of British long-wall mining. But in 1913 the Sullivan Machinery Company, an American firm, built a chain machine especially designed for long-wall work. When it was exhibited in England, coal mine owners were duly impressed. In the following years, many Sullivan cutting machines, which operated much like a modern chain saw, were exported for use in British mines where they "gave a high standard of service."[4]

The British failed to maintain their early initiative in development work on mining machinery, because no firms were established that specialized in manufacture of coal face machinery. Without such firms, the building of a new machine to a particular specification was entrusted to "one or another firm of engineers, whose concern obviously began and ended with the construction." According to historian Hibberd, these engineering firms "had no knowledge of, or even interest in the actual operation of the machine, that being left to the designer, who when difficulties revealed themselves, endeavoured to overcome them by modifications in the design of the machine, which frequently resulted in the creation of a mechanical monstrosity."[5] In this country, by contrast, manufacturing firms specializing in building and testing mining equipment were organized in the 1870s and 1880s. By the turn of the century, a viable capital goods industry in this field had become well established, with seven U.S. firms manufacturing coal mining machinery.[6]

Next in order of importance in the history of undercutting machinery was the punch, or pick, machine patented in 1877 by J. W. Harrison (figure 3). This machine incorporated a compressed-air-driven piston to which was attached a steel bit about two inches in diameter. This bit undercut the coal in much the same manner as the miner traditionally had done with a hand-held pick. It was claimed that this puncher could do the work of six to fifteen skilled miners working with hand picks.[7] The small size, integral strength, and simplicity of design made the Harrison machine easy and inexpensive to repair, a characteristic frequently lacking in most other forms of early coal mining technology. The serious disadvantage of the punch machine was that the use of compressed air

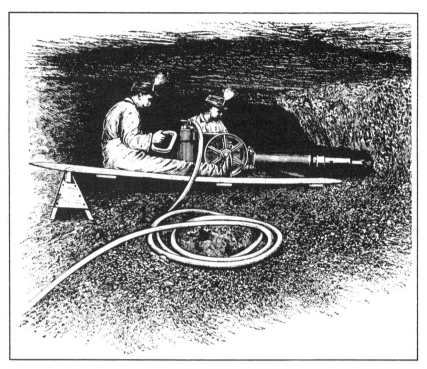

FIGURE 3. *The punch, or pick, undercutting machine was driven by compressed air.*

required a rather expensive installation of pipes and hoses from compressor to mine face. Friction within these pipes severely reduced air pressure as the distance between compressor and machine increased, adding to the expense of supplying punching machines with adequate air pressure.[8] But even with that handicap, the air-driven machines remained popular, and by the turn of the century there were three companies—the Whitcomb Company, the Sullivan Company, and Ingersoll-Sargeant Company—engaged in manufacturing essentially similar punchers.[9]

Reliability and low operating costs were not sufficient, however, to meet the needs of a rapidly expanding coal industry at the turn of the century. Mine owners were looking for greater cutting speed so that a larger number of coal loaders could be accommodated on each shift of work. The chain machine passed the test, with claims that it was at least twice as fast as the puncher (figure 4). Although the chain machine did not make its appearance on the market until 1893, within a decade it

FIGURE 4. *The chain cutting machine was faster than other designs and became the industry standard after the turn of the century. (Ohio Historical Society)*

surpassed its competitor and soon thereafter dominated the market for coal-cutting machinery. (The history of this popular piece of equipment will be pursued further in the discussion of the Jeffrey Company and the Goodman Company below.)

1920s Coal-Loading Machinery

Much of the early inventive effort in mechanical loading originated at the mine site, where experienced mining men tried one idea after another in a search for a machine that would meet the needs of their particular mining conditions. Some of the machines never left the drawing boards, but many were built locally and tried out in the inventor's own mine. Some of these machines were good enough to be manufactured and sold commercially. This process led to the emergence of several small firms, each initially focused on the development, manufacture, and sale of a single loading machine. The Coloder Company of Columbus, Ohio; the Joy Manufacturing Company of Franklin, Pennsylvania; the McKinley Mining and Loading Machine Company of Fairmont, West Virginia; the Myers-Whaley Company of Knoxville, Tennessee; and the Oldroyd Machine Company of Cincinnati, Ohio, are examples of firms starting out in the loading machine business.[10] Other firms already established in mining machinery got into the race in the 1920s and 1930s to develop a mobile loading machine for underground mining. These were the Jeffrey Manufacturing Company of Columbus, Ohio, the Goodman Manufacturing Company of Chicago, the Ingersoll-Rand Company of Chicago, and the Sullivan Machine Company of Chicago.

There were some who believed that the push in this country for a device to load coal was a result of the control that mine workers exercised over the pace of production. For example, in 1918 E. N. Zern, editor at the Keystone Publishing Company, presented a paper to the Coal Mining Institute of America in which he summarized the state of the art in loading machine technology. Referring to war labor shortages and the wave of postwar strikes, Zern argued that the push for mechanization of coal loading was a direct result of the industry's labor problems. He was not certain, he said, whether the problem was "due to the scarcity of labor, its indifference, its inefficiency, or its antagonism," but "the fact that it exists is sufficient." We can, he then asserted, "ascribe the development of the mechanical loader to the persistent endeavors of the industry to solve the problem of labor."[11]

The social forces that contributed to the development of machinery to eliminate the hand loading of coal were more complex than Zern's analysis implies, and his own description of the various machines then available attests to the fact that inventive effort had long preceded wartime labor shortages. While many of the machines he pictured were in developmental stages, the number alone is impressive evidence of the sizable effort invested in developing machines for coal loading. Names such as Ingersoll-Rand, Hamilton, Jeffrey, and Myers-Whaley were prominent among the manufacturers who had put machines on the market by 1918. Even though some of these did not survive the competition in the formative years of this capital goods industry, newcomers took their places so that by the mid-1920s there were numerous loading machines from which a mine operator could select to mechanize his mine.

In 1924, the journal *Coal Mine Management* surveyed the industry and reported that at least thirty-six mechnical loading devices had been developed. While nine were still in the process of design and building, twenty-seven had been operated underground "with varying degrees of success."[12] Through advertisements in the trade journals and through articles in these journals extolling the virtues of particular machines, the mining industry was becoming increasingly aware of the wide range of possibilities for mechanical loading. In 1924, at the American Mining Congress's first convention, a full range of coal loaders was exhibited to the public. Industry awareness was further raised in 1925, when the Carnegie Institute of Technology published the results of a nationwide study on the use of various types of coal loaders.[13] Not all of the machines on the market in the mid-1920s could be used under all mining conditions, of course, but for each operation there were several machines to choose from. If there were any doubt in a mine owner's mind about the efficiency of mechanical loading, it was allayed by the publication of the 1922 Presidential Coal Commission's report. Two types of loading machines were studied intensively, and the recommendation was made that the whole industry should move rapidly to mechanize.

Early loading machines varied in both function and design; some were supposed to mine and load the coal, others loaded the coal after it had been broken from the face; and still others were simply conveyors that had to be fed by hand. There was little similarity in basic design, except that practically all of the early machines, except the power shovels and scrapers, incorporated some sort of chain conveyor in their mechanism. These conveyors were generally powered by electric motors. Some sense of this variability can be conveyed by dividing the machines on the market in 1925 into four categories defined by function and, then, by discussing some of the more important machines in each category.

> *Mining and loading machines:* McKinlay entry driver, Jeffrey-Morgan entry driver, and O'Toole mining and loading machine.

> *Digging and loading machines:* Hamilton pit car loader, Jones Coloder, Jeffrey Shortwaloader, Myers-Whaley coal loading shovel, and Joy loading machine.

> *Room conveyors:* self-loading conveyors and pit car loaders.

> *Scraper loaders:* Goodman scrapers.

Mining and Loading Machines

The McKinlay entry driver and the Jeffrey-Morgan entry driver were combination machines that not only sheared or broke the coal from the face but also loaded it, anticipating the modern continuous mining machines. The O'Toole invention was based on principles similar to modern long-wall mining. In a generic sense, these machines were loading machines, but their applicability was severely limited. The McKinlay and the Jeffrey-Morgan machines were so large and cumbersome that they were used only in entry driving, where they did not have to be moved from one location to another. The O'Toole system had some success in mechanizing hand operations, but its success depended on special mining conditions like those in the McDowell County, West Virginia, coalfield, where it was first used. While these machines may in some ways be considered predecessors of modern mine technology, they did not figure importantly in the development of the mobile loaders, which dramatically altered room-and-pillar mining.

The McKinlay entry driver was patterned after the early Stanley header, a British import from the late 1880s.[14] It was essentially a boring machine that simultaneously cut two large overlapping circles in the face of the coal (figure 5). The two circular cuts left a triangular section at the

FIGURE 5. *The McKinlay entry driver sheared coal from the face and loaded it into coal cars* (Mining Congress Journal 11 [1925]:213)

top and bottom, which was cut by a cutter chain working on the same principle as the undercutting machine. As the machine moved forward, boring and cutting its way into the face, the coal fell down onto an internal conveyor, which moved it to the rear of the machine and dumped it on a second conveyor. The second conveyor delivered the coal to a waiting mine car. The cycle of operation could be a continuous one if empty cars were made available at appropriate intervals.

Manufactured by the Marietta Manufacturing Company of Point Pleasant, West Virginia, the McKinlay machine was well adapted to entry driving. Even in mines with poor roof conditions, the natural arch left by this piece of equipment meant very little timbering was necessary. In 1926, two of the machines were installed in the New Orient mine in Illinois, where they proved quite successful. According to E. M. Warner, a mining machinery company executive, these two machines, with improvements, remained in this mine for twenty-five years and drove approximately a hundred miles of entry.[15] Experience gained at the Illinois mine and at other mines, notably in West Virginia and eastern Kentucky in the 1920s and 1930s, provided the basis for successful development of the Marietta machine and all other boring-type, continuous, mining machines put on the market after World War II.

The Jeffrey-Morgan entry driver (figure 6) was akin to the McKinlay

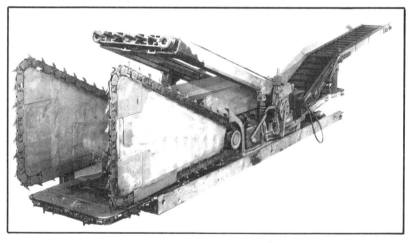

FIGURE 6. *The Jeffrey-Morgan Entry driver, like the McKinlay, broke coal from the face and loaded it into cars. (Ohio Historical Society)*

machine in that its primary purpose was to speed up the opening of new entries in a coal mine. Based on patents purchased from inventor E. C. Morgan, the Jeffrey Company devoted considerable resources to the building and testing of this invention between 1910 and 1926.[16] Although there is no lineal descent from this machine to modern coal mining equipment, it was, in fact, a continuous mining machine. It cut the coal, broke it down, and loaded it while moving forward at a slow pace. The prinicpal elements in its design were an undercutting chain about five feet wide, two vertical shearing chains, and a heavy reciprocating frame carrying a number of picks that punched down the coal after it had been cut on the bottom and on both sides by the chains. The broken coal fell onto a conveyor in the middle of the machine and was transferred back to an empty car.

During experimental work, the Jeffrey machine, later named simply the 34A and 34B, loaded an average of twenty-one tons an hour, with a cost saving of thirty-two cents per ton over traditional hand methods. But even with these advertised advantages, the Jeffrey miner had some serious drawbacks that prevented its general acceptance in the industry. Reportedly, a major disadvantage lay in the large number of working parts, because "in spite of the care taken in design, failures due to breakage of vital parts are sure to occur." Another problem was that it was "necessarily cumbersome" and moved "with difficulty from place to place, even though such movement is not often required."[17] Manufacture of the Jeffrey entry driver was discontinued in 1926, being to some extent superceded by the company's Shortwaloader (see below).

Colonel Edward O'Toole claimed that he had developed and built the first "real" cutting and loading machine in the country. Working for the H. C. Frick Company, which later became part of the United States Steel Company, O'Toole installed a mining system incorporating his ideas at two mines in western Pennsylvania between 1896 and 1898. The experimental work was transferred to southern West Virginia when O'Toole was put in charge of all captive mines of U.S. Steel.

In recounting the history of his work, O'Toole told an industry gathering in 1925 that, after his initial efforts in the 1890s, development work at U.S. Steel on new machinery lagged because of the "excessively low labor rates prevailing at that time."[18] Just prior to and during World War I, however, "immigration from foreign countries practically ceased and a great scarcity of coal mine labor developed." This meant "labor costs of coal production became excessively high; which in turn directed the minds of inventors to coal-loading machines." O'Toole's experimental work during the war and postwar years resulted in the installation of a novel mining and loading machine in a company mine near Gary, West Virginia. Design work and model building were carried out by O'Toole in company shops in McDowell County,[19] but the Jeffrey Company actually manufactured his machine and marketed it for a short while in the 1920s.

The system devised by O'Toole involved a cutting chain mounted on a very long cutter bar—on one machine it was forty-two feet long—which was used to cut and load simultaneously along the coal face.[20] In back of and parallel to this cutter bar was a drag-type flight conveyor extending the full length of the machine and elevated at one end so the coal could be loaded into a mine car. The novel feature of this setup was that it did not require drilling and blasting to bring the coal down after it was cut. Instead, the weight of the rock strata, which was 600 feet thick in the area of O'Toole's experimentation, was sufficient to crush the coal as rapidly as it was cut. The broken coal fell onto the conveyor as the cutter bar made the kerf, making the operation practically a continuous one.

Instead of the traditional room-and-pillar mine layout, the O'Toole machine required a long-wall, retreating system. Long-wall "rooms" were worked out to a distance of 600 feet, with forty-eight-foot pillars of coal left between each room. Roof support for the coal face and track was provided by a network of hydraulic jacks and collapsible timber cribs. Cribs are simply stacks of squared mine timbers piled in log-cabin fashion from floor to roof. The coal face and the miners were protected by a double row of 150-ton hydraulic jacks set in staggered fashion, with the first row placed immediately behind the machine. Water was used as the hydraulic fluid for the jacks, which were hand pumped. In addition to supporting the roof, the jacks anchored a screw-threaded propulsion bar, which pushed the whole machine forward into the face. As mining progressed, the cribs set behind the jacks were removed and the roof was allowed to cave in. The contribution O'Toole made to mining technology is obvious to those familiar with modern long-wall mining, but in the 1920s the industry was firmly committed to room-and-pillar mining, so his system attracted little attention at the time.

Digging and Loading Machines

Digging and loading machines were generally referred to as mobile loaders, and they became the keystone for mechanization in the bituminous industry. One of the earliest, if not the first, mobile loading machine on the market in the United States was the Hamilton pit car loader manufactured in Columbus, Ohio, by the Hamilton Manufacturing Company (figure 7). After several years of experimental work in the late 1890s, W. E. Hamilton of Zanesville, Ohio, obtained a patent on his loading machine in 1900.[21] His invention was built in two parts. The first was simply a gathering conveyor made of a continuous chain to which flights were attached to scoop up the coal. This part constituted the loading mechanism and would sweep across the room gathering coal and sending it up the trough on the other side. The coal thus loaded was deposited on the second element of the machine, which incorporated a second conveyor running horizontally. This flat conveyor was to be used as a picking table, from which the mine workers could remove slate and other impurities before the coal was loaded into mine cars.

Numerous advantages over hand loading were claimed for the Hamilton loading machine. For example, skill requirements for the mine work force were greatly reduced. The recommended machine crew consisted of

FIGURE 7. *The Hamilton pit car loader was one of the earliest mobile loading machines on the market. (Ohio Historical Society)*

three men, two unskilled mine laborers and a machine runner, and the latter could be "any man of ordinary intelligence," for he could "learn to operate a loader within one week's time."[22] Also, track and timbering costs would be lower because, with greater speed in loading, the same amount of coal could be mined in less territory. "Rooms can be quickly worked out and the rails and timber used over again. Maintenance of the mine will be proportionately less." Further, the early promoters of the Hamilton machine understood the indirect advantages accruing to management from a reorganization of the workplace. "Superintendance will be rendered more effective at a lessened cost, as there will be fewer men in the mine; and these will be concentrated in fewer working places."

Offsetting these claimed advantages were several problems associated with the use of this and all other mechanical loaders in these early years. For example, mines were surveyed and laid out for hand loading and could not accommodate machinery and a faster pace of production. Haulage systems became a veritable bottleneck, and even the most vocal proponents of mechanization warned of the folly of putting a loading machine in a mine without first modernizing the facilities for moving the coal from the face. It was pointed out that "the loading machine will not load coal any faster than the cars are delivered to the room." If mine cars are delivered on the hand-loading schedule or "turn," the mine owner will get hand-loading results from the machine and "the machine will be idle four-fifths of the time."[23]

When put into commercial operation, the Hamilton loader met with resistance from both mine workers and local mine management. Soon after obtaining a patent, the manufacturer sold a machine to a southern Illinois mine where, on an experimental basis, it was able to load 150 tons of coal on each shift. When an owner of a nearby mine, impressed with this performance, ordered ten of the Hamilton loaders, miners realized that mechanical loading was no longer an experimental undertaking. Believing that they should share with the owners the profits realized from mechanization, the miners went out on strike for nearly a year to force management's hand on this issue. Although they gave up the struggle without winning any concessions from the company, miners returned to work still quite hostile to the new machines. When a fire of unexplained origin destroyed one of the loaders, the operator decided to discontinue their use and to return to hand loading.[24]

E. N. Zern told of a visit to a West Virginia mine in 1906 with the aim of observing a Hamilton machine in operation. He related that the mine superintendent was typical of the old school of management who "regarded a strong arm and stronger language as the handmaidens of authority." Zern described his tour in the mine in the following manner:

> With the expectancy of the small boy about to behold his first aeroplane, we explained that the object of the visit was to see the Hamilton coal loading machine at work. The effect was instantaneous. The words "coal loading machine" pricked the bubble and let loose a volley of expletives that would have done credit to the profanest driver that ever started a mule. It was plainly evident he had gone through some unpleasant, perhaps, painful, experiences. After deleting the torrid portion of his tirade, the substance was that the Hamilton machine was not a coal loader, but rather an infernal machine, devised to send mine superintendents to an untimely end, and that so far as my seeing it, this was impossible for the reason that they had quit its use and abandoned it in some working place, he didn't care a hang where.[25]

Several years later, Zern returned to the same mine on an inspection tour and, in an old section of the mine, he "chanced to observe, barely protruding from beneath a fall of slate, the diplodocus-like tail of the Hamilton machine. Its fate was but the common fate of the pioneer. Like the flying machine of Langley, it came into existence too early and failed."

It is not certain when the Hamilton Company closed its doors and went out of business, nor is the full history known of why it ceased its development work on what was apparently a good idea. One observer, summarizing the Hamilton experience, suggested that "in spite of its good features [the machine] did not prove to be a success, largely because existing conditions in coal mines rendered it impossible to keep the machine in continuous operation."[26] It is true, however, that the ideas Hamilton put into his loading machines were important in the overall development of this technology. The Jeffrey Company purchased the patents to the Hamilton loader in 1909 and manufactured the machine for a year or two. Later, we find the flight chain idea that Hamilton used incorporated into the Jeffrey L400 loading machine put on the market in 1936.

James Elwood Jones, at the time general manager of the Pocahontas Fuel Company in McDowell County, West Virginia, received the first U.S. patent for an underground loading machine in 1893.[27] While this design did not result in a commercially successful loader, Jones, a college-trained engineer, continued development work on loading machines of various design for more than thirty years. Most of the experimental work was carried out in his own machine shops at the Pocahontas mines, but on at least one occasion, he approached the Jeffrey Company to design and build one of his loaders. In 1902, the inventor received a patent on a machine, which he later called the Jones Coloder, a machine quite similar in design and function to the Hamilton machine.

In 1918, in partnership with Norton Newdick, a draftsman formerly employed by Jeffrey, Jones established his own manufacturing company in Columbus, Ohio, and started taking orders for his Coloder. The loader enjoyed a brief period of success in the early 1920s, and was one of two loaders selected by the 1923 U.S. Coal Commission to be studied for its report on mine mechanization. By 1924, Jones had twenty-three of his machines at work in his own mines; the combined total of mechanically loaded coal at Pocahontas that year was 1.5 million tons, or 40 percent of the company's total annual output. In the late 1920s, the Coloder Company responded to the need for a machine that could load coal in lower seams by building a smaller loader. And in 1928, the company announced the availability of a loader with a newly designed gathering mechanism that reduced the weight of the overall machine. Unfortunately, almost as soon as this new machine was advertised, the company began to suffer a loss of sales, as coal markets collapsed and operators cut back on capital investments. When both Jones and Newdick died in 1930, their loading machine business was permanently closed.

The Jeffrey Manufacturing Company did not enter the race for the mechanical loading machine market until 1924, when the company introduced its 43A Shortwaloader. Unlike most of the other loaders then available, the Jeffrey machine was not intended as a mobile loader that would be moved from room to room in the mining cycle. The company's engineers based their design on the notion—an incorrect one as it turned out—that mining men would prefer to keep their equipment in a single workplace until that place was worked out. The Shortwaloader had very limited success, and it was not until the mid-1930s that Jeffrey was successful in selling a mobile loading machine. The company's history explains why Jeffrey lost the opportunity to be a front-runner in the new technology of coal loading.[28]

The Myers-Whaley shoveling machine was based on a workable design, which gave it fairly widespread use in the coalfields (figure 8). In

Special No. 3, Myers-Whaley Shovel

Approved permissible Myers-Whaley Shovel

FIGURE 8.   *The Myers-Whaley coal loading shovel featured a powered scoop, or shovel, to lift the coal.* (American Mining Congress, 1928 Year Book on Coal Mine Mechanization)

an effort to duplicate the motions of the hand shoveler, the Myers-Whaley machine was one of several on the market that utilized a power scoop or bucket to lift the coal from the mine floor and deposit it in a mine car.[29] First manufactured in 1907 in Knoxville, Tennessee, the Myers-Whaley shovel went through a three-year experimental period in Tennessee mines. When modifications to the original design were made and a machine was sent to a mine at Holden, West Virginia, it performed better than predicted by the manufacturer. A concerted effort was made at the time the machine was installed to supply it with an adequate number of empty cars and, as a result, the shovel was able to load 128 tons per day. Based on this successful showing, the Myers-Whaley Company went into full production, and by the 1920s its machines could be found in mines in Utah, Illinois, Pennsylvania, and West Virginia.[30]

Retired miner U. G. Jordan, was working in a West Virginia mine in 1925 when the company decided to instal a Myers-Whaley loader.[31] He remembered that the machine had "a shovel up front which worked off a drive like the wheels on a locomotive. It was just a bucket which scooped up the coal and threw it back on a conveyor which carried it back in to a car." Operating with a reasonable degree of efficiency, this loader continued to be used in the mine where Jordan worked until the 1930s, when it was replaced by a mobile loader, a pattern that repeated itself in many mines. The Myers-Whaley Company continued to market its shoveling device well into the 1930s, but its popularity suffered from the competition of other designs, notably that of the Joy machine.

The digging and loading machine by which others were eventually judged was the one designed and patented by Joseph Joy. This mobile loader met the needs of the mining industry: it could be built for various thickness of coal seams, it was fast and efficient, and it was reasonably inexpensive. Its important role in the mechanization of the nation's coal mines is discussed in the next chapter.

Room Conveyors

Coal operators had experimented with room conveyors in one form or another for many years before the development of the various machines discussed above.[32] By the 1920s, there were numerous room conveyors of various configurations on the market; some were used in long-wall mining and others were used in narrow rooms and loaded by hand. In 1926 the engineers at the Union Pacific Company mines developed a self-loading shaker conveyor, which they called the Duckbill. When one central Pennsylvania coal operator experimented with a room conveyor system, he found a substantial increase in labor productivity. In thirty-five-foot rooms, he placed short conveyors parallel to the face, with longer, sectional conveyors positioned at right angles along one rib the full length of the room. The second conveyor moved the coal from the room and dumped it into mine cars on the main haulage track. Timbers and supplies could be sent to the face by reversing the motor on this sectional conveyor. Each of five men in a crew—cutting, drilling, shooting, and loading the coal by hand on the face conveyor—produced an average of sixteen tons per shift, in contrast to seven tons each when the coal was loaded by hand into mine cars.[33] However, mainline haulage by conveyor, a common practice in modern mines, was infrequently employed in the coal mines of the 1920s.

One of the most popular forms that conveyors took in this early period was the electrically driven elevating conveyor, which came to be known as the pit car loader. The basic idea of this mechanism was simply to "reduce the height a man raised the coal to one foot in place of four feet," explained a Jeffrey Company engineer.[34] The Jeffrey pit car loader was mounted on a self-propelled truck, which moved on mine rails (figure 9). Others were mounted on wheels and pushed into place by hand. Operation of the pit car loader involved positioning the lower end of the

FIGURE 9. *The Jeffrey pit car loader was mounted on a self-propelled truck.* (Coal Age, January 23, 1919, p. 177)

conveyor close to the coal after it had been drilled and shot down. The higher end was positioned directly above an empty mine car. The miner shoveled the coal onto the lower end or, in the case of wide rooms, onto an auxiliary conveyor placed parallel to the face. The availability of horizontal capstans on each side of the pit car loader also allowed the coal to be dragged from some distance by rope and scoop. The pit car loader was quite popular in the late 1920s and early 1930s, especially in Illinois and Indiana.

Scraper Loaders

Finally, coal was loaded in some mines by a mechanical arrangement called a scraper, which was simply a scoop pulled along the mine floor by a motor-driven hoist. Because their use required a certain freedom of motion, scrapers could not be used effectively in narrow rooms with close timbering, so they were used primarily on long-wall faces with fairly good roof conditions. The expense of moving and setting up the equipment also limited scrapers to fairly long working faces. The most popular scraper was probably the Goodman type A scraper, although the simplicity of design made local fabrication possible.

Major Manufacturers of Coal-Loading Machinery

As the inventory above shows, a variety of equipment was available for any mine owner who wanted to convert his mine to mechanical loading. The conversion process for the industry did not, however, parallel this growing availability of equipment. In fact, it was not for another decade that the mine mechanization movement began to pick up momentum. And when the industry did turn to mechanization, it favored the mobile loading machine over all other forms of mechanical loading.

In the decade from the mid-1920s to the mid-1930s, the capital goods industry went through some major changes. Most of the small loader manufacturers closed down. In some cases, their patents had been purchased by the larger, established mining machine firms, and in others their machines simply had not met the needs of the industry. Only one of these small firms, the Joy Company, produced a loading machine that caught the fancy of the mine operators across the country and grew to challenge the better established equipment manufacturers. By the mid-1930s, there were three principal firms engaged in manufacturing the popular mobile loading machines: the Goodman Manufacturing Company, the Jeffrey Manufacturing Company, and the Joy Manufacturing Company. Each of these is examined in detail for the role it played in the introduction of new mining technology in general and the mobile loader in particular.

Goodman Manufacturing Company

The Goodman Company made its entry into the loading machine market with the introduction of the Goodman electric-hydraulic power shovel, a large power-driven scoop that worked on the same principle as the miner's shovel.[35] The Goodman Company had a long history in the mining machinery business in the manufacturing of cutting machines, locomotives, power-generating apparatus, and other electrically operated equipment. In fact, during the first two decades of this century the Goodman Company and with its two competitors, the Jeffrey Company and the Morgan-Gardner Company, dominated the market for undercutting machinery. And for several years, the Goodman Company ranked with General Electric and Westinghouse as the main suppliers of electrically driven locomotives and haulage equipment for the nation's coal mines.

Elmer A. Sperry, who did pioneer work in the field of electricity and its practical applications in industry, was the owner of the company that later became the Goodman Manufacturing Company. In the late 1880s, Sperry designed an electrically driven coal-punching machine at the request of Albert L. Sweet, president of the Chicago, Wilmington, and Vermillion Coal Company, the second largest coal company in Illinois. A company was formed to manufacture the machine which, its inventor and sponsor hoped, would challenge the then-popular air-driven puncher. With Sperry providing the inventive genius and Sweet providing the capital, a prototype was built and tried out in one of Sweet's mines at Seatonville, Illinois. The first machine failed in its test because its parts could not withstand the impact from blows as the pick hit the coal face. Both poor workmanship and poor design contributed to its failure. When modifications were made, it was decided that the machine warranted commercial production. The Sperry Electrical Mining Machine Company was organized in 1889 to sell the machine throughout the industry. Sweet became president of the new company, Sperry was titled "electrician," and Sperry's brother-in-law, Herbert E. Goodman, became the secretary-treasurer.

Even before the company could claim success with any of the early models, it began a promotional campaign in trade journals and newspapers. To demonstrate his confidence in the machine, Sweet ordered ten of the machines for his own mines and also signed a territorial agreement that gave him exclusive use of the Sperry machine within a 120-mile radius of his mines. In addition to promoting the sales of the electrical puncher and hoping to improve the efficiency of his mines, Sweet had another reason for installing a mechanical mining machine. His workers had been on strike for several months in 1889 against a wage cut, and he wanted to break the strike by reducing the bargaining power of the skilled miner. The second order for the Sperry machines came from the Watson, Little, and Company mine in Brazill, Indiana, which was also experiencing labor difficulties. In this case, local miners refused to run the machines, and machine operators had to be imported.

Unfortunately, the optimism of the inventor and his associates was unfounded. Within a few weeks of its first installation, it became clear that the Sperry machine was a failure. The machine was not sturdy enough to cut coal. With downtime for repairs being greater than operating time and without a system for supplying replacement parts, Sweet withdrew his financial support and resigned from the Sperry Company. Despite the early failures and Sweet's dropout, Goodman and Sperry convinced William D. Ewart, founder and president of the Link-Belt Company, to help capitalize continued manufacture and sales of the electrically powered punching machine. It soon became evident, however, that their punching machine was not going to be accepted by the industry, so they ceased production. Undaunted by this failure, Sperry and Goodman continued in the mining machinery business, with factory space rented from the Link-Belt Company. In 1891, Sperry designed and built for sale his first electric mining locomotive and at the same time began to experiment with a new design for a coal-cutting machine.

This new Sperry coal cutter incorporated an old idea that had originated in Great Britain—the cutting chain—in an electrically driven design for long-wall undercutting. Manufacture of the long-wall cutter lasted only a short while, but the experience gained with it gave Sperry and Goodman further proof that there was money to be made in undercutting machinery if the right design could be developed. They found that machine, not on Sperry's drawing board, but in a small machine shop in Columbus, Ohio, where Frank N. Slade was trying to manufacture a chain breast machine using a cutting chain based on several patents he purchased from Francis Lechner. Sperry and Goodman bought the Lechner patents from Slade and, still operating from the Link-Belt factory, began the manufacture of the Lechner-Slade machine in 1893.

From the very beginning, the Lechner-Slade machine was a success, so much so that it called forth unexpected competition from two well-established manufacturing firms—the Jeffrey Company of Columbus, Ohio, and the Morgan-Gardner Electric Company of Chicago. Almost simultaneously in 1894, three electrically driven, chain breast machines were put on the market, launching a rivalry that lasted for several decades. Convinced that their patent should protect them from imitation by competitors, Sperry and Goodman turned to the courts, where, after a lengthy and costly battle, they failed to sustain their claim to prior ownership of the chain breast design. During the rest of the decade, the competition heated up, and price wars, misleading advertising, and high-pressure salesmanship substituted for competition based on improved products or quality service. The competition became so intense that by the late 1890s the three firms held secret meetings to determine whether a joint selling company with a patent pool could be established. Although the three companies thought it was a good idea to eliminate the cutthroat competition, they could not agree on the details for a monopoly for this mine machinery.

Sperry left the mining machinery business, and in 1900 Goodman raised money from friends and from the sale of stock to coal operators to purchase the Link-Belt interest in the mining machine business. He formed a new company, the Goodman Manufacturing Company, and launched an aggressive sales and promotion campaign to challenge Jeffrey and Gardner on the economic battlefield. The Goodman Company also was involved in manufacturing power-generating equipment for underground mines and electrically driven locomotives for underground haulage. As the lineal descendant of the inventor Elmer Sperry, the Goodman Company claimed a full package of mine mechanization during the first two decades of this century.

Although successful in many of its product lines, the Goodman Company was not a leader in the development of loading machine technology. It manufactured its shovel-type loader in the 1920s and 1930s and then in the early 1930s tested a track-mounted machine that was later marketed as the Goodman 260 loader (figure 10). The gathering head of this loader continued to be the novel feature in subsequent modifications of the 260 and in the tread-mounted Goodman 660, which

FIGURE 10.   *The track-mounted Goodman 260 loader was the predecessor of the tread-mounted Goodman 660 loader. (American Mining Congress,* 1937 Year Book on Coal Mine Mechanization)

was not put on the market until 1947.[36] These loaders completed the Goodman line of equipment from "face to tipple," as their ads claimed, but at no time did the Goodman loaders challenge the superiority of their chief rival, the Joy loading machine.

Jeffrey Manufacturing Company

The oldest mining machinery company in the United States, the Jeffrey Manufacturing Company, traces its history to the late 1870s when two Columbus, Ohio, bankers, Joseph A. Jeffrey and Francis C. Sessions, decided to financially support an undercutting machine invented by Francis M. Lechner.[37] The three men organized the Lechner Mining Machine Company in 1878 to develop a workable air-powered cutting machine based on Lechner's patent. The idea was to imbed cutting bits in a rotating bar that would be mechanically forced into the coal face. By withdrawing the cutter bar, moving the machine, and repeating the action, the length of the face could be undercut in a manner similar to that performed by the miner with his pick. After many initial setbacks, the Lechner machine was finally developed to a point that commercial production was possible.

The company's name was changed to the Jeffrey Manufacturing Company when Jeffrey bought out Lechner's interest. It continued its development work on undercutting machines and also began the manufacture of an electric mine haulage system. In 1888, it sold the first mine locomotive made in the United States (figure 11) and branched out into the manufacture of chain conveyors, ventilating systems, preparation equipment, and other mining machinery. By the turn of the century, the Jeffrey Company was the leading producer of capital goods for coal mining.

The evolution of the mining machinery industry is replete with case histories of individuals with inventions who could not afford the great cost involved in building their machines and testing them under actual mining conditions. But the Jeffrey Company from its early days had sufficient venture capital to undertake the lengthy development work necessary to bring a machine or piece of equipment to market. The company also had an advantage in that it had well-established connections with some of the nation's largest coal firms, which allowed Jeffrey engineers to test equipment in their mines. In some cases, the ties between mine owners and manufacturer were close ones and worked to everybody's advantage. Mine owners with ideas for new machines but without the facilities to build them often had prototypes built in the Jeffrey shops. And at other times, the Jeffrey Company loaned its en-

FIGURE 11. *The Jeffrey Company manufactured the first electric mine locomotive in the United States. (Ohio Historical Society)*

gineers to mine owners for the purpose of designing and building equipment the owner had conceived at the mine site. The Pittsburgh Coal Company, the U.S. Coal and Coke Company, the Pocahontas Fuel Company, and the Hanna Coal Company were a few of the producers who, during the early years, had reciprocal dealings with Jeffrey that strengthened the company's position in the mining machinery industry.

Advertising was important to the company's early growth (figure 12). The company also took advantage of the pages of the trade journals to extol the virtues of its equipment and to explain company policy.[38] As the company grew, it came to dominate the mine machinery market, not only in this country but worldwide. While it shared the market for undercutting machinery with others, many of the Jeffrey product lines had very little competition. Yet with all the advantages that its size bestowed, the Jeffrey Company was not in the forefront in the development of loading machine technology. It was inflexible in some ways and misdirected in others, so that in the mid-1930s, when mechanical loading began to revolutionize underground coal mining, the Jeffrey Company found itself taking a backseat to a relative newcomer to the field.

Jeffrey's first attempt to produce a loading machine came in 1909, when it purchased the patents of W. E. Hamilton and built one of the

FIGURE 12. *Jeffrey Company advertisement in the* Coal Trade Bulletin.

Hamilton machines in 1911. This machine, the Jeffrey 33A coal loader, was sent along with a demonstrator and mechanic to the Monongah mine of the Consolidation Coal Company. The results obtained from these tests were "just fair," according to company records. Apparently, the track-mounted machine was slow in its handling, and its single-jointed conveyor was not well suited to the existing narrow rooms and room necks. Modifications were made, but the second trial proved no more encouraging, so the company decided to discontinue work on this model. Rather than move ahead with more development effort on a machine incorporating the novel Hamilton loading mechanism, the company began work on machines of entirely different design.

Jeffrey made a major commitment to the development of a combination cutting and loading machine after it purchased certain patents from E. C. Morgan in 1910. The Morgan machine was designed primarily for entry work. Before it was put on the market, the machine was tested in several mines in West Virginia and Pennsylvania. The company scientifically selected mines for development work on its machinery, seeking variations in roof and bottom coal seam conditions and different mine layouts to permit a comprehensive analysis of the machine's capabilities.

While the physical characteristics at the mine site were important, the Jeffrey demonstrators also learned that successful testing of a machine depended on local management attitudes and, more importantly, on the labor situation. For example, Bert Norris, a Jeffrey engineer, was sent in 1913 with the entry driver to the Cannelton Coal Company mine at Smithers, West Virginia, and found that, for successful use of the machinery, worker resistance had to be overcome:

> Cannelton was a union mine and on Saturday and Sunday the opposition became very pronounced. In fact the miners did not want the machine unloaded. Rumor had it that this machine was one of a dozen ordered by the coal company. The best argument that we could make was this was an experimental machine and our company desired to test it out in a variety of coals and conditions. . . . We were given permission to go ahead and we hired one of their men as a helper.
>
> The coal company was willing to run the risk of the miners interfering with their regular output if our company would assume the risk of damage to our machine. Consent was authorized by our company, but to minimize our risks, our shop management sent a watchmen from Columbus armed with a pistol that could be easily hidden in the palm of one hand.[39]

Under armed guard, the Morgan-Jeffrey entry driver proved its worth in this Kanawha field mine and was sent to the Pocahontas field, where it also encountered resistance by miners who saw it as a threat to their jobs. Again the miners were mollified by the promise that the use of the machine was only experimental. Next, the machine was sent back to Columbus to the Jeffrey shops for modifications and then sent to Illinois for a test at the Old Ben mine near West Frankfort under the supervision of a young demonstrator named Joseph Joy. At this mine, the superintendent decided that, to avoid labor troubles, the best policy would be to operate the machine at much slower speeds than its rated capacity. According to Norris, "the reason the Old Ben Company was not primarily interested in quick development was due to the uncertainty of the labor situation. This class of work was new so slow progress might alleviate antagonism from labor. Illinois labor was as independent as a hog on ice."[40] The strategy of designating the machine as experimental and running it at slow speeds so its full job-threatening potential would not be so apparent worked to avoid labor troubles in Illinois. And the entry driver got a good workout under physical conditions quite different from those in West Virginia mines.

From Illinois, the machine was sent in February 1916 to the Pittsburgh Coal Company's Somers no. 2 mine, where several loading machines from Jeffrey competitors also were being tested. This nonunion mine, operated by the nation's largest coal company, had been set aside as an experimental mine and provided an opportunity for inventors to try out their ideas under realistic mining conditions. The Pittsburgh Coal Company, by this important subsidy of technological development, hoped to be the first in the industry to find a suitable loading machine. In tests of the Jeffrey entry driver, the Pittsburgh people were impressed enough to order five of the machines and put them to work in the company's mines. Over the next few years, the entry driver was sold to commercial mines throughout the country, but its career was short-lived. In 1926, fifteen years after E. C. Morgan had first brought the idea to Jeffrey, sales faltered and manufacture of the machine was permanently discontinued. Competition from lighter weight, less expensive loading machines may have killed the industry's interest in the Jeffrey entry driver; what is more likely is that sales dropped off with the collapse of coal markets in the mid-1920s.

The Jeffrey Company at an early date decided not to pursue the idea of a mobile loading machine. It believed, apparently, that the industry would not accept the changes in mining methods that mobile loaders required. So on several occasions before World War I, the company turned down the opportunity to purchase patents to build a mobile loader designed by Joseph Joy. Until the 1930s, the loading machines that it did build were not based on the concept of room-to-room mobility. Jeffrey's chief engineer, N. D. Levin, shed some light on the company's crucial policy toward loading machines when he asserted in 1920 that the idea of moving a machine from one room to the next was not feasible. "A machine that picks up coal from the bottom and delivers it into mine cars is necessarily heavy and expensive," he wrote, and "it appears that such a device must remain in the same place for an appreciable length of time if it is to be financially successful."[41] Levin was convinced that mining men would not purchase a machine that required a crew of ten to twenty workers to run effectively.

Therefore, the Jeffrey Company's perception of what the industry needed—and it was simply a matter of personal judgement, since others in the industry acted on opposing views—led the company to manufacture and promote the use of pit car loaders. Such simple conveyors "can be used to advantage in room-and-pillar work, as this device is light and convenient to move from one place to another," Levin wrote.[42] The policy continued well into the 1920s, when the company brought out its cutting and loading machine, the 43A. This was not a mobile loader but a machine designed "to remain in one room until it was worked out."[43] This crucial failure to appreciate the potential of mobile loaders must surely have been a costly one for this largest manufacturer in the mining machinery industry.

Inspired by the growing competition in the loading machine business, the Jeffrey Manufacturing Company did put its engineers to work in 1923 to design a combination machine that would both cut and load coal in room work. Taking advantage of their years of experience in building cutting machines and conveyors, they developed a machine called the 43A Shortwaloader (figure 13) and shipped it to the New River Company in West Virginia in 1924. The 43A consisted of three sections. The first was an undercutting chain plus two auxiliary chains that could be swung into position for loading. The second section was an inclined drag flight conveyor very similar in design to the Hamilton loader. Finally, it included a discharge pivoting conveyor, which could be kept in position as the loader moved across the coal face. The 43A was designed to stay in one place, rather than move from room to room, and the company's

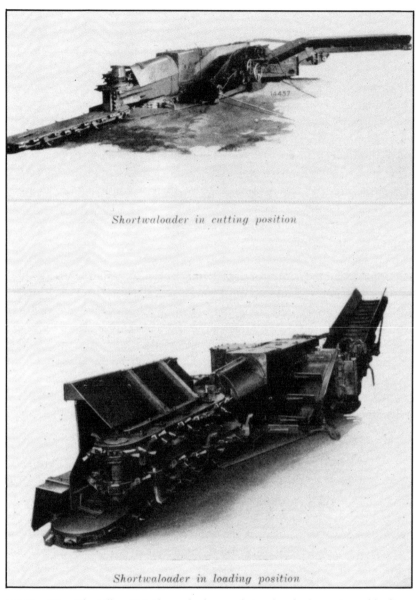

Shortwaloader in cutting position

Shortwaloader in loading position

FIGURE 13.   *The Jeffrey 43A Shortwaloader was designed to do the cutting and loading in room-and-pillar mining. (American Mining Congress, 1928 Year Book on Coal Mine Mechanization)*

promotional literature suggested that it could work to the best advantage with a stationary conveyor system. N. D. Levin, chief engineer at Jeffrey, claimed that one of the chief advantages of the 43A was that it "works more continuously than those that are moved from place to place. In fact, it operates all the time except while coal is being shot, unless there is slate to handle."[44]

The early response to the Jeffrey loading machine encouraged its designers. Reflecting on this period in the company's history, a Jeffrey official wrote: "It is agreeably surprising the eagerness with which the mine people took hold of the 43A Shortwaloader. A hurried check recently showed that during 1925 and 1926 forty of these machines were sold."[45] After the initial enthusiasm, however, mine operators found that under continuous use the 43A experienced frequent breakdowns. Armature shafts were a frequent source of trouble, as were "bearings, gears and pinions, clutch jaws, chains and sprockets, worms and wheels."[46] After 1926, sales of the Shortwaloader dropped off as quickly as they had increased. The company soon dropped its production and shifted its facilities to the manufacture of the popular pit car loader, which it had first marketed in 1916. The pit car loader was a simple elevating conveyor that reduced the effort involved in the hand loading of coal. It became an important item in the company's line of mining equipment, especially from 1927 to 1932.

Even during the late 1920s, when the coal industry was in the doldrums and operators seemed reluctant to make large investments in mining equipment, interest at the trade shows in a self-loading mobile machine continued to grow. Finally impressed with this trend, the Jeffrey Company in 1929 began work on its own mobile loading machine. What came off the drawing boards was a track-mounted loader incorporating the familiar Hamilton gathering mechanism. This loader—the 44A —was at first well received in some areas. It was flexible in use and relatively low priced, which influenced mine owners to try it. The company reported that thirty-three were shipped to mines in Illinois and Indiana in 1930. Within two years, however, it became apparent from a sharp drop in sales that the company had again failed to produce a product with industrywide acceptability. Company historian Bert Norris lamented, "The strange part of the whole matter was we furnished the mining industry a light machine, easily handled, suitable for various conditions, and capable of producing coal at a reasonable cost, and immediately they demanded a more powerful machine to increase the output one third and we were compelled to double our power output."[47] After five years of experience with the 44A and several modified versions of it, the company gave it up in favor of a new design, the L400 (figures 14 and 15).

A December 1935 memo between the Jeffrey research and development department headed by R. K. Jeffrey, son of the founder, and the engineering department indicates the lagging state of the company's technology and its determination to catch up: "The design of a satisfactory loading machine is the most important item that the research and development department has to consider and I trust that through mutual cooperation we will be able to conceive a loading machine that will outload anything on the market."[48] A major effort was put forth at the Columbus, Ohio, shop to design and build a mobile loading machine in time for the annual exhibition of mining equipment at the May 1936 meetings of the American Mining Congress. The Jeffrey L400 mobile loader was a track-mounted machine powered by a fifty-horsepower electric motor and equipped with a gathering mechanism of two opposing flight chain conveyors. Although being somewhat limited by being track mounted, the L400 was the Jeffrey Company's entry in the race to mechanize underground coal mining with mobile loaders in the period 1935–48.[49]

FIGURE 14.   *The Jeffrey 44A mobile loader incorporated the Hamilton gathering mechanism from a turn-of-the-century design.* (American Mining Congress, 1934 Year Book on Coal Mine Mechanization)

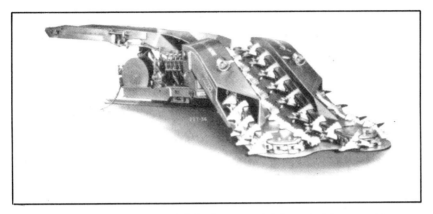

FIGURE 15.   *The Jeffrey L400 mobile loader superceded the 44A.* (*American Mining Congress,* 1936 Year Book on Coal Mine Mechanization)

Advertisements promoting the L400 loader said that the machine, equipped with hydraulic controls, "takes difficult drifting in stride. . . . Its long flat-nosed head undermines a standing shot with minimum crowding." Ruggedness, low maintenance costs, and long operating life were also claimed by the manufacturer.[50] Mike Murphy, a West Virginia miner with personal experience with the early edition of the L400, was not particularly impressed, however. The machine "sounded like five threshing machines running over cobblestones. [It was] the most poorly designed piece of machinery I have ever seen. You have to develop the mine, the curves and everything, for it. It wouldn't go around a sharp curve."[51] Yet company records show that the L400 must have lived up to most of its advertised claims. Within five years of its first installation in the summer of 1936, 150 of the L400 leaders were sold. This number represented a respectable percentage of the 700 or more mobile loaders installed in U.S. coal mines during the same period.[52]

A modified version, called the L600, was particularly popular in the 1940s in the higher coal seams in the Pittsburgh field, where many mines continued to use room track systems. The closest competitor that Jeffrey had in these particular mines was the Goodman Company with its 460 loader. Between twenty and thirty-five of the L600 machines were sold each year from 1941 to 1949. At that time, the industry began its shift to a new technology, the continuous miner, and sales of mobile loaders dropped rapidly.

Joy Manufacturing Company

During the period of rapid expansion of mechanical loading of coal after 1935, the industry's favorite machine was one that could be easily moved from room to room and was quite adaptable to various coal seams and different mining conditions. This coal loader was developed by a man named Joseph Joy, who had at one time been a Jeffrey employee and had approached the company with his invention. Jeffrey officials rejected his ideas and thereby missed the opportunity to be in the vanguard of new technological developments. Joy's contribution to mine mechanization is so important that the next chapter is devoted to his history. For some miners, the name Joy was synonymous with the loading machine.

CHAPTER 3

The Joy Loading Machine

JOSEPH JOY went to work in the coal mines when he was twelve years old. Some say that it was the hard work involved in loading coal by hand that prompted him to search for some mechanical device that would do the job better. While this truly may have been an important motivation for him, it is more likely that Joy was caught up in the turn-of-the-century rush to develop labor-saving machinery for the rapidly expanding coal mining industry.[1] With coal output doubling every decade and labor shortages anticipated, it was not unreasonable to expect that fortunes would be made by those who could first develop and market technology to replace the centuries-old hand methods of mining.

Whatever the motivation, Joseph Joy over his lifetime contributed more than any other individual to mine mechanization. Lechner, McKinley, Hamilton, Morgan, O'Toole, and Jones made important contributions to coal technology, but Joy heads the list of inventors in this field. For several generations of coal miners, Joseph Joy was known as the inventor of the best mobile loading machine ever put in the mines; his name is still carried by the major mining equipment company he founded in 1919. Between 1904, the time of his first invention, and 1944, the U.S. Patent Office awarded him 106 patents on various types of mining equipment, including cutting machines, loading machines, drills, and conveyors. In the thirty years between 1914 and 1944, more than $100 million worth of mining products were manufactured and marketed under these patents. The most important of Joy's inventions was his coal loader, a machine that dominated the market for coal-loading equipment for decades. In 1954, for example, when the Joy Manufacturing Company put together a brief history, it claimed that Joy loaders accounted for 72 percent of all coal loaded mechanically.[2]

Joseph Francis Joy was born in 1883 on a farm in Somerset County, Pennsylvania. Few details of his childhood are known, but it is quite likely that he attended public school while also working hard on the family farm. If the configuration and operation of some of his early mine machinery is any indication, Joy acquired his general mechanical skills from his work as a young boy on the family's farm. For example, in the early 1920s he developed a coal-loading and -transporting machine, a prototype of the modern shuttle car, incorporating a chain conveyor almost identical to the conveyor system found on all manure spreaders. With his schooling interrupted at age twelve, Joy's subsequent education was limited to only one correspondence course in mechanical engineering from LaSalle University, which he completed at age fifteen.

By the time he was nineteen, Joy had submitted drawings and an application to the U.S. Patent Office for a machine designed to undercut the face of the coal in preparation for drilling and blasting.[3] The patent was awarded, but there is no history of the machine's being developed or even a model made. The technology for mechanical undercutting had been around for thirty years or more, and Joy's idea was not a particularly significant improvement to that technology. But in that same year, 1903, Joy made some sketches for a mining and loading machine incorporating an idea that was to revolutionize the underground loading of coal (figure 16). However, it took twenty years from the date of conception to the marketing of a successful machine. Most of the development work was concentrated in the last six years of this period, as Joy devoted his full energies to building a machine that the market would accept.

Historians of technology usually identify the period between an invention—the "Eureka, I found it" event—and the point of innovation —the production of a machine or product for the market—as the development phase of technological change. It has been characterized as a "persistent, sweaty, sometimes grim, comparatively monotonous" experience,[4] which involves taking the idea off the drawing board and converting it into a working model that must be tested, modified, retested, and then manufactured. If development work is carried on outside the shops and labs of established corporations, it is likely to include financial hardship and lawsuits over patent claims, not to mention adverse affects on personal and family life. The development of technology is a social process, and the career of Joseph Joy during the development phase of his coal-loading machine demonstrates some of the forces that shaped the history of technology in that important industry.

From 1895 to 1913, Joy worked in several coal mines in Maryland and western Pennsylvania. He moved up from mine laborer to miner to master mechanic and then, in 1910, he continued to make drawings and

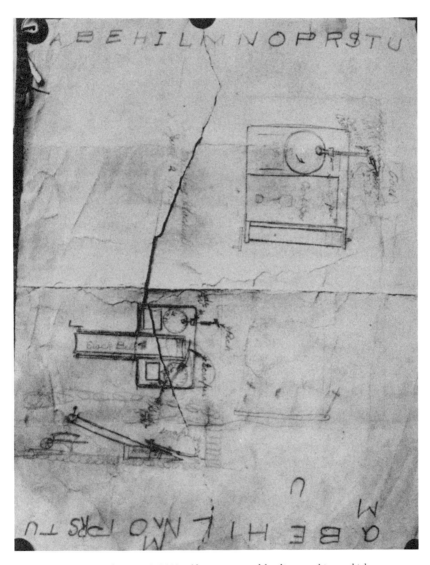

FIGURE 16. *Joy's drawing (1903) of his mining and loading machine, which was to revolutionize the loading of coal. (Ohio Historical Society)*

to discuss his ideas with practical mining men whenever the opportunity presented itself. About 1906, he made his first scale model and continued to make drawing board improvements. These must have been particularly frustrating times for the young inventor, since he lacked the resources to build a prototype of his loader. According to later testimony before the U.S. commissioner of patents, "he was compelled to labor that he might support his wife and indigent father. Consequently he could give but little time to the machine. But if he could spare the time, he was without the necessary money to procure material and facilities for the construction of the device."[5] On two separate occasions, he secured employment in mines where he had heard that mine management was favorably disposed to the development of mechanical mining, but in neither mine was he able to obtain the necessary support. In 1912, he accepted a position as mine superintendent, thinking that he finally would be in a position to devote some time to building his dream. Unfortunately, he was disappointed again for "the company which owned it . . . was not financially strong and it was imperative that he should give every moment of his time to its affairs."[6]

In September 1913, Joy made an important career decision when he resigned his job as a mine superintendent and went to work for the Jeffrey Manufacturing Company. Not only did the job change involve a cut in pay from $140 a month to $100 a month, but it also meant that he would have to travel and spend long periods of time away from home. The primary advantage to him apparently outweighed these drawbacks. For the first time, he would be in a position to persuade a machine manufacturing firm to build his coal loader. His first assignment with Jeffrey was to work with Bert Norris, a company engineer, at a mine near Pocahontas, Virginia. The men were testing the company's new 34A entry driver, an early form of a continuous miner. Following that assignment, Joy was sent to the Old Ben Mining Company in Illinois to continue testing the same machine under different mining conditions.

The practical experience he gained while demonstrating and testing the new Jeffrey equipment aided Joy in redesigning his own loading machine, and when he finally showed his plans to the company's engineers they were at first well received. However, when the engineers referred him to the company executives, they refused to support him and "endeavored to discourage him from further prosecution of his thought."[7] According to his own recollection of the event, their attitude "was due to the fact that they believe [the Joy] machine would conflict with one their company was working on."[8] During 1915, Joy used his spare time to build a small working model of his loading machine and tried once again to interest the Jeffrey executives in building it. Again, he was turned down. "Their general disposition toward it was still discouraging," he recalled later.[9] Their decision was not based on technical consideration, because company engineers had recommended it, but rather on factors relating to their prior investment in other equipment and to their own projections of the market for loading equipment.

From Illinois, Joy was sent to the mines of the Pittsburgh Coal Company to test the Jeffrey machine at the Somers no. 2 mine. As it turned out, this was a fortunate assignment for the frustrated inventor, because the Pittsburgh Coal Company was experimenting with several types of loaders and was actively seeking ways to mechanize its mining operations. As the nation's largest coal producer, principally owned by the Mellon family, it could easily afford to underwrite the expenses of experimentation with mining equipment. When Joy took the Jeffrey entry driver to the coal company, the Somers no. 2 mine had been set aside for the exclusive use of equipment manufacturers for testing their new mining devices. Armed with a letter of introduction from a Jeffrey engineer who liked his idea, Joy went to the headquarters of the Pittsburgh Coal Company to confer with the company vice president, John A. Donaldson. Joy took his model with him (figure 17). As Bert Norris, Joy's associate at Jeffrey, remembers it, "He appeared at the office with a small, hand-operated model of a loading machine. The distinguishing feature was two gathering arms at the front end of the conveyor. One area on each side would reach out and sweep the material in small chunks inward and then backward onto the conveyor where it would be carried to the rear into a hopper. With the use of mixed nuts it gave a very good demonstration of gathering coal."[10] The coal company officials were so impressed with the model that they immediately contacted Jeffrey to request that a machine be built to Joy's specifications. Unable to refuse such a request from the nation's largest coal producer, the Jeffrey Company finally built the first Joy loader. It took ten months and $22,000 worth of parts and labor to complete the job, and when it was finished, Joy proudly had his picture taken with his machine (figure 18).

In the fall of 1916, Joy resigned from his Jeffrey job when the Pittsburgh Coal Company offered to hire him as a consulting engineer. At that time, he applied for a patent on his mobile loader with its unique loading arms. Unfortunately, the examiners at the U.S. Patent Office

FIGURE 17.   *Joseph Joy holds a hand-operated model of his loading machine. (Joy Manufacturing Company)*

were not sufficiently impressed with his claims of originality and refused to award him a patent. It took two years for Joy to convince the Patent Office that his loading machine was sufficiently different from the prior inventions of Hamilton (1903), Doss (1907), Howley (1908), and others to warrant a patent. During this time, he also had difficulties with the

Jeffrey company, which claimed that he had developed his invention while in its employ. Finally, the patent was awarded in November 1918. However, it was not until 1924 that a U.S. Court of Appeals decision settled the legal issue in his favor and supported his claim to conception prior to his employment with Jeffrey.[11] The sketches Joy had drawn as early as 1903 helped him win his case.

During the next two years, the Pittsburgh Coal Company built four Joy loading machines in its own shops, using Joy as an engineer to supervise their construction and testing. Experimentation continued in the Somers no. 2 mine, where the new machines were put to rigid production tests under the scrutiny of time-study experts. Preliminary results appeared to be quite favorable, with average production of 111 tons of coal loaded per day and only 8.6 percent of lost time resulting from machine failure. The tests were run in a mine where the miners had to handle from 40 to 60 tons of draw slate for every 100 tons of coal, so "if the machine had been operating in a bed free from troublesome draw slate the production would have been nearly if not quite doubled."[12]

FIGURE 18. *Joseph Joy stands with first Joy loader in the Jeffrey company yard. (Ohio Historical Society)*

Two conveyors were incorporated into the mechanism on these machines. The first ran from the gathering arms to a storage hopper, while the second discharged the coal from the hopper into a mine car. Both conveyors were flexibly mounted and could be swung to nearly any angle, permitting entry into rooms through narrow entrances. The gathering mechanism was the novel feature of the loader, and Joy was credited at the time with having made an important contribution to mining technology. The editor of *Coal Age* wrote that "the principles involved in the construction of the machine are departures from any other attempts that have been made along this line. . . . The gathering mechanisms with its horizontal, penetrating, undermining action is effectual in winning coal from a semi-undisturbed state."[13]

Joy claimed that design of the gathering arms allowed for a fairly conservative use of explosives, an obvious advantage to miner and mine owner alike. The storage hopper was another new feature, which in theory was to solve the transportation problem at the face by enabling continuous loading of coal during the switching of mine cars. Joy put a lot of faith in the hopper idea, having noted in one of his patent applications that "coal production may be increased from 30 percent to 50 percent if a means is provided for the storage of coal" while a loaded car is being replaced by an empty.[14] But the use of a storage hopper added substantially to the overall weight of the machine. The track-mounted machines built in 1917 and 1918 weighed nearly nine tons and were difficult to maneuver and slow to move from room to room in the mining system used in the Pittsburgh seam.

Records are not available to explain why, but the Pittsburgh Coal Company decided to discontinue the experimental work with the Joy loader. Wage rates were high and labor was scarce during World War I, and from outward appearances it would have been an opportune time to pursue mine mechanization.[15] But at some point, probably near the end of 1918, corporate executives decided that no more funds would be expended in this effort and that Joseph Joy's employment would be terminated. Circumstantial evidence indicates that there was labor resistance to the new technology. The Pittsburgh field was part of the Central Competitive Field organized by the United Mine Workers of America; and coal operators had often met with objections, usually from local unions, to the introduction of new machinery.[16] The Pittsburgh Coal Company simply may have been unwilling to risk a strike or other job actions at that particular time by moving ahead with installation of labor-saving equipment.

Joy found himself without a job, a misfortune that worked to his long-run advantage because, at this point, he decided to organize his own company and to raise money for manufacturing and marketing his machines. The practical experience he had gained while working with the coal company must have given him the confidence he needed to make this move. The Joy Machine Company was organized early in 1919 as a patent-holding company without the right to manufacture. John Donaldson, production vice-president of the Pittsburgh Coal Company, who had encouraged Joy to form his own company, subscribed to $5,000 in company stock and served as a member of the board of directors.[17] But Joy had not yet received a patent on his new loading machine, although he had applied for and received patents on various other types of mining equipment.

It was not until five months after he formed his company that he was awarded the patent for the loader with the unique gathering arms. U.S. Patent 1,306,064 was the basic patent on which the now famous Joy loader was built. This patent, with various modifications, protected the Joy Company in the manufacture of these loading machines until 1941.[18] In the patent application, Joy summarized the primary purpose of his machine:

> In the mining of coal it is the common practice to break the coal from its natural bed by blasting fragments from the face of the vein. By this method the broken coal is left in heaps adjacent to the working face from which it must be loaded into the car, entailing labor of the most arduous character. I am aware that machines have been proposed having inclined conveyors adapted to gather the coal from the floor of the mine and transfer it to conveniently placed cars but great difficulty has been experienced in the operation of such machines owing to the irregular size and shape of the fragments into which the coal is broken by the blast, to the irregular surface of the floor and to the restricted space, especially vertically, in which the machine must operate.
>
> It is the special object of the present invention to provide in a machine of the class described, improved devices by which the coal is gathered from the floor of the mine onto the conveyor by which it is deposited in the pit cars.

He claimed that he had designed a machine with "a gathering mechanism including substantially horizontally arranged fingers and means to move said fingers longitudinally to penetrate a pile of material and then laterally and rearwardly to engage said material and move it onto the conveyor."[19]

Lacking the capital to manufacture any of the machines, Joy approached the Thayer Engineering Company of Allentown, Pennsylvania, to build several of the loaders. According to T. J. McNabe, who worked for Thayer at the time, the company built four machines; two were truck mounted and two were put on caterpillar treads.[20] The first Joy loader was shipped to Logan County, West Virginia, and installed in a mine owned by Harry S. Gay. According to Robert Spence, historian of Logan County, Gay was an innovative mine operator and worked closely with Joy in redesigning the loader after it had been used in the Gay mine.[21] Joy sold the second loader to the Consolidated Coal Company,[22] which also operated a mine in Logan County. These two mines may have been Joy's first customers because they were located in the staunchly nonunion territory of southern West Virginia.[23] That union resistance to the new machine was a problem for the inventor-turned-entrepreneur is further suggested by the fact that the third machine was sent to a mine in Illinois where the miners were out on strike. The fourth machine was sent on trial to a nonunion mine in Saskatchewan, Canada.

In 1921, Joy was in a position to move ahead with the manufacture of his loading machine on a production basis, and again he had financial backing from John Donaldson. He organized the Joy Manufacturing Company as a wholly owned subsidiary of the Joy Machine Company and contracted with the Charleroi Iron Works in Charleroi, Pennsylvania, to build the loader for marketing throughout the coal fields. Joy then moved to Evansville, Indiana, where he set up a shop for assembling and servicing the loaders made by Charleroi and other subcontractors.

Why Joy chose to move his company to Evansville in 1921 remains unclear. The official company history states that "it was believed that the Indiana and Illinois progressive and productive coal fields would yield a market."[24] If "progressive" meant that there might be less opposition from local unions in these fields, then an explanation of the move can be offered. In most organized coalfields, the leaders of the national union paid lip to mine mechanization, but local unions usually refused to negotiate wage rates for operators of machinery that coal companies wanted to instal.[25] This, of course, had the effect of retarding the development of mechanization by virtue of the fact that union miners would not work in a mine where no wage scale had been established for a job.

Indiana was part of the long-organized Central Competitive Field, but the first negotiated local union agreement to establish a wage scale for a loading machine operator and helper was signed there in January 1921 by the Pike County Coal Company, which operated a mine just a few miles from Evansville.[26] Joy's relocation of his company to the same county, in the same month, must surely have been more than mere coincidence. Within a short period of time, other operators in this southern Indiana field successfully negotiated local wage agreements comparable to the one at the Pike County Company mine. In 1922, the Ingle Coal Company in the same county was credited with being the first fully mechanized mine in the country.[27] Joy surely thought then that his move was a wise one and that it was only a matter of time before his machines would be accepted throughout the coalfields.

Winning union approval in other districts did not come very easily, however. In fact, for the most part, it did not come in the organized fields until later in the decade.[28] In 1924, *Coal Age* lamented that "the strong effort to introduce underground mechanical loading . . . is handicapped by labor in such solidly unionized districts as the states of Illinois and Indiana."[29] In a survey of the extent of mechanization in 1924, the trade journal reported that "although the unionized Middle West [operators are] keen to use them, only twenty-five have ever penetrated Indiana and a bare fourteen in Illinois, whereas there are nearly 100 in West Virginia . . . and only a little less than fifty in Pennsylvania, most of these in the non-union mines of that state."

Experimental work continued in Evansville, and by 1922, after three different series of loaders had been built, tested, and then rejected, the first signs of success came with the production of model 4A. At that time, Joy decided to replace the track wheels with caterpillar treads. He called this more mobile machine the 4B loader. Company records show that the first of the 4B machines was sold in September 1922 to the D. J. Kennedy Center, a Pittsburgh building supply firm that used the machine as an above-ground yard loader. The next sale was to the Lang Coal Company, which used the machine underground, so Joy designated it the 4BU (figure 19). The classification BU continued to be used by the Joy Company to specify underground loading equipment.

In 1922 and 1923, the new company sold 184 of its 4BUs to coal

FIGURE 19. *Joy 4BU loader at work in Ingle Coal Company mine in southern Indiana* (*Joy Manufacturing Company*)

companies, both large and small, in the major coalfields. The Chicago, Wilmington and Franklin Coal Company, a large coal operator in Illinois, bought seven of the loaders, but most of the coal operators moved slowly to purchase the new loader and placed orders for only a single machine. It was a common practice for management to purchase one machine and place it in the mine to clean up a roof fall or to do other nonproduction work. In this way, mine management could test the new equipment under its own particular mining conditions before making a full-scale commitment to mechanization. This gradual approach had the added advantage of giving management an opportunity to determine workers' reactions to the loaders before making a substantial financial investment in minewide mechanization.[30] Interestingly, the Pittsburgh Coal Company bought only one 4BU Joy Loader prior to 1927, when it moved ahead with mechanization and placed an order for fourteen machines.[31]

It was Joy's next model, the 5BU, that is considered to be the real granddaddy of the modern coal loader. According to a company history, the first steel casings were used on this model, and the tail conveyor assembly was powered horizontally so that it could swing ninety degrees in each direction. "This, coupled with the vertical movement offered in earlier models, gave complete articulation to the rear assembly of the loader."[32]

Loading coal was only one of the problems of underground mining to which Joy directed his inventiveness in the 1920s. Another problem that substantially reduced the productivity of any type of loader was the production delay caused by the switching of filled mine cars for empty ones. The storage hopper on his earlier models had been one solution to the problem, but these machines were not mobile enough for fast-paced production. In 1921, Joy patented a modified version of his loader, which offered a different solution to the coal face transportation problem (figure 20). Designed for thin seams, this loader consisted of a flat bed with a conveyor on it, four feet eight inches wide and twelve feet long, that would hold one-and-a-half tons of coal. Joy called this machine a "self-loading shuttle car . . . especially designed for use in thin veins, either flat or pitching, for gathering coal from the floor at the face, transporting it out of chamber to gangway and loading it into mine cars."[33] This was

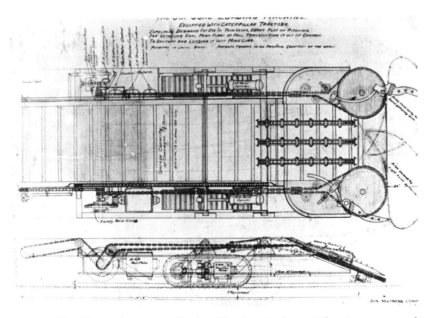

FIGURE 20. *Engineer's drawing of Joy's self-loading shuttle car. (Photo in possession of Herman Van Houten)*

the manure spreader from his childhood days on the farm, and while it was never manufactured on a commercial basis, Joy's idea of a shuttle car between loader and rail haulage was a decade or more ahead of its time. The Joy 4BU, 5BU, and subsequent loaders did not contain any form of storage facility, so the problem of switching or "gathering" continued to limit the potential of his loading machine. Otherwise, Joy had a good machine. It was capable of rapid and efficient loading, it was lightweight and quite mobile, and it could be built for low-coal seams.

After three years in Evansville, Joy began to run into financial difficulties resulting from an inability to obtain quality parts from his subcontractors and increasing machine failures in the field. For example, steel castings were difficult to obtain, so gray-iron castings were used. Even operators who found Joy's machine the most efficient on the market publicly complained of machine breakdowns and troubles with repair. After experimenting with Joy loaders for two years, a Pennsylvania coal operator abandoned the effort. "In justice to the Joy machine it must be admitted that the plan of construction was very clever but an idea no matter how clever will not load coal alone; such must be incorporated in a sturdy, practical machine which can be operated and repaired by the ordinary run of labor found around the coal mines."[34] Joy's financial position became so precarious that he was forced to refinance his company. As an inventor he may have been without equal in the industry, but as a businessman he seemed unable to keep his company solvent.

Joseph Joy approached the Colburn Machine Tool Company of Cleveland for financial aid, and a deal was made whereby the Colburn Company agreed to refinance the loading machine in return for common stock and a small amount of cash. The transaction also included turning over the Colburn-owned plant in Franklin, Pennsylvania, to the Joy Machine Company. The new plant offered complete manufacturing facilities to Joy and proved to be an advantageous move, since it was near steel foundries and other sources of raw materials. In March 1924, Joy occupied the Franklin plant and began manufacturing the 4BU and 5BU loaders. (The Joy Company, today a worldwide corporation, continues to maintain its headquarters in Franklin.)

Within a year of the move to Franklin, Joy was again in financial trouble, this time more serious. The inventor was forced to resign as president and the company was taken over by a committee of its creditors, chaired by John Donaldson. This committee directed the company's operations for a year until it was reorganized with Donaldson serving as president and sales manager. During this time, the Joy Machine Company continued to market the 5BU and its successor models. In 1928, the Joy Machine Company, the parent company, was dissolved and renamed the Joy Manufacturing Company. Conveyors, locomotive specialties, the shuttle car, and various other types of mining equipment were added to its manufacturing line in the 1930s as the company continued to expand its role in the mining capital goods industry.

With Joy's departure from Franklin in 1925, his role in the development of the coal-loading machine came to an end (more or less), but his career as a designer of mining machinery did not end. Following his disappointments in business, Joy went to work for Allen and Garcia, a Chicago consulting firm that had a contract with the USSR to assist in the mechanization of coal mines in the Ukraine. Joy moved to Kharkoff, Russia, in 1925 and stayed there for nearly four years assisting the Soviet government in its efforts to modernize the mines in the Donnetz Basin. When he returned to the United States, he went to work for the Marion Shovel Company, where, according to Herman Van Houten, he designed two important improvements for the company's strip-mining equipment. He engineered the counterweights on the back of big stripping shovels and suggested the system of hydraulic leveling, using stabilizing jacks, for the big shovels so they could move over irregular terrain.

In 1930, Joy organized a new mining equipment company, the Joy Brothers, Incorporated. Three of his brothers joined the organization, and under Joseph's leadership as president the new firm began manufacturing "saws," a type of chain-cutting machine that literally sawed blocks of coal from the face. Since lump coal was marketable but the market for slack and small sizes was negligible or nonexistent during the Depression years, the coal saws were well received by the industry. In 1934, he sold this company to the Sullivan Machinery Company, a Claremount, New Hampshire, firm that had been in the mining machinery business for many years. Joy was then employed by Sullivan from 1934 to 1938, where he designed improved coal cutters and began working on the design for a continuous mining machine that would eliminate the separate operations of undercutting, drilling, blasting, and loading. Development work on this machine was dropped, however, and others were later credited with the invention of the continuous mining machine. From 1940 to 1944, Joy worked for the U.S. Army, designing various types of military equipment.

Joy had not been associated with the Joy Manufacturing Company for twenty years, but when this company purchased the Sullivan Machinery Company in 1945, it offered Joy a lifetime contract to serve as an engineering consultant. The company set up a small, well-equipped shop for him to build working models from his new ideas. When he wanted to move to Florida, the company moved his shop and tools to Fort Pierce where he lived in semiretirement until his death in 1957. He completed several models for new mining machines in the last few years of his life,[35] but none were accepted by the younger engineers in the Joy Manufacturing Company's research center. They just weren't interested in Joseph Joy's ideas any longer.[36]

Joseph Joy's contributions to the mechanization of the mines, notably the loading of coal by machine, far exceed those of any other inventor. In 1942, when he was applying for an appointment as a commissioned officer in the Army's Ordnance Engineering Division, he asked several coal operators to write letters of recommendation. These letters indicate the importance of his contribution to the industry. The president of the Old Ben Coal Corporation, a large mining firm in Illinois, said "I have known Mr. J. F. Joy for more than 20 years. He is an engineer of exceptional ability and probably is more responsible for the complete mechanization of coal mines than any other engineer in the United States." Eugene McAuliffe, well known as president of the Union Pacific Coal Company, wrote, "My relations with Mr. Joy over some nineteen years have been most satisfactory, and I look upon him as the man most responsible for the development of our modern coal loading machinery." And E. R. Coombes, of the magazine *Mechanization,* praised Joy as "a noted authority upon the coal loading machine."[37] By 1942, when mining people thought of the coal-loading machine, they thought of the Joy loader. The fact that, by 1954, 72 percent of all coal loaded underground was loaded by Joy loaders confirms the importance of the inventive efforts of Joseph Joy.

CHAPTER 4

Transformation of the Miner's Job

THE SET of work relations that characterized the hand-loading period became increasingly inefficient from the standpoint of management's interest in increasing productivity—an interest that became acute during the depressed times of the 1920s. Workdays of variable length, a tradition of single shifts, individual proprietorship of working places, the lack of meaningful supervision, quality control that depended on the miner's skill, worker ownership of tools, and a generally undisciplined work force all stood in the way of rational (i.e., efficient) production. Two things were needed: mechanization of traditional hand methods to increase the physical output of mine workers and a reorganization of the labor process to make it more factorylike.

The conversion of underground coal mining to a more efficient process took almost twenty-five years, and its path during that period was not a smooth one. Many miners, if not most, objected to the new technology because it involved a loss of jobs and an adverse impact on the quality of working life for those who remained on the job. This chapter focuses on the impact of the mechanization and reorganization movement on the miners' working conditions.

The End of Hand Loading

The principal motivation of the early inventors of mine machinery was to develop an individual machine for each of the separate tasks embodied in the age-old miners' craft. As early as the 1890s, some inventors were working on ideas that would incorporate all the tasks into one machine, but these precursors of the modern-day continuous mining machines were not commercially successful until the late 1940s. Therefore, the technology that evolved prior to successful continuous mining systems included separate machines for undercutting, drilling, and loading, all linked to the surface by various forms of mechanized transportation.[1]

During the days prior to mechanization, the miner daily confronted the unbroken coal at the end of the room by lying on his side to undercut the face across its width so that several tons of coal could be easily dislodged with blasting powder. Because this first task in the mining cycle was quite arduous and time consuming, it became the focus of the first efforts to increase labor productivity with machinery. In chapter 2 it was pointed out that the first cutting machines were patented in the 1870s and that by the turn of the century mine owners could choose among several models. By 1920, 61 percent of all underground coal was mined with an undercutting machine.[2] Some coal was "shot from the solid," that is, it was blasted without being undercut. But this practice generally was deplored by those concerned for the miner's safety because it involved using an excessive amount of powder to break the coal.

The second task for the skilled miner of an earlier day was to drill one or more shot holes for the blasting powder. Long, hand-held breast augers, resembling in design the carpenter's brace and bit, were used for this purpose until air-powered, and later electrically driven, drills were developed. Installation of compressed-air-powered drills for use in bituminous mines began as early as 1890, and in 1911 electrically propelled augers, including types that were mountable on cutting machines, were placed on the market. Mine owners' interest in power drilling did not advance very fast, however, even after one-man portable machines were developed. Hand augers were most common in the industry until mechanical loading made it economically feasible to mechanize the whole mining cycle. As late as 1936 only 27.2 percent of all underground coal was produced from working places in which the shot holes were drilled by mechanical drills.[3]

Paralleling the improvements available for drilling were improvements in explosives and methods of blasting. The U.S. Bureau of Mines, established in 1910, very early began testing various types of explosives and made known to the industry its approval of certain "permissible" explosives, which were safer and more efficient than the traditional black powder. In the 1920s, some mines began switching from chemical explosives to methods using mechanical force, such as hydraulic pressure, compressed air, and the heaving action of carbon dioxide, the latter being called the Cardox system.[4]

Along with, and in many cases preceding, the changes taking place at the face were major changes in coal haulage from the face to the surface. Mules, horses, and ponies had been the traditional source of transportation until the electric motor proved to be much more efficient. The original wooden rails were replaced with steel rails, while larger cars and more powerful locomotives made it possible to speed mine cars filled with coal to the surface and return them quickly to the loading machines. Conveyor systems were also being installed during the 1920s and 1930s, and in 1938 one manufacturer marketed a truck mounted on rubber tires powered by a small electric storage battery that delivered coal from the loading machine to the main haulage system. This shuttle car proved to be an important link in the search for an integrated transportation system, which would help the mine owner realize the full potential of mechanical loading.

Each new technological development increased productivity, but the labor process itself remained largely unchanged until the advent of the loading machine. After the introduction of the cutting machine, for example, miners still worked alone or with a partner in separated and rather isolated rooms. They still set their own pace of production (with an upper limit set by the amount of coal cut by the cutting machine), and they continued to be paid according to the amount of coal they loaded. The tonnage payment system was so accepted in the industry that the cutting machine operator and his helper were also paid in this manner. Electric drills, better blasting powder, improved ventilation, and more efficient mine haulage all worked to increase output per man-hour, but taken together they had little impact on the organization of work underground.

Scientific Management in the Mines

It was apparent to those who knew the industry well that substantial productivity gains would not come until the miners' control over production at the face could be broken. By combining the new loading machine technology with new management practices, industry experts saw a way to take away that control and make production more efficient. In a forthright, and perhaps exaggerated, statement of what was needed to put "the industry on a sound basis," mine superintendent Thomas A. Stroup in 1923 thought it would be necessary "to abolish the contract system, to mechanicalize [sic] the mines thoroughly," and "to standardize every operation down to the minutest detail so that no responsibility of any kind will fall on the worker."[5] Stroup had some ideas on the probable effect that such a reorganization of the labor process would have on workers: "Silly sentimentalist alone will decry this conversion of the coal miner into a routine worker whose tasks and duties are minutely set and closely supervised, while the full responsibility for results is assumed by the management. Engineers and others responsible for the introduction of the 'mass production system' and 'efficiency methods' into industry have long known that the workers thereunder are more contented, happier and less susceptible to the corrupting influences of unionism, than are the highly skilled workmen upon whom responsibility devolves."

After a detailed study of underground mine management, the 1922 U.S. Coal Commission recommended a program of both mechanization and reorganization, which, it argued, would make mining a more rational and profitable endeavor. Sanford E. Thompson, a protégé of Frederick W. Taylor and the first time-study expert of the Taylor movement, was hired by the commission to prepare a study on underground mine management. In his report to the commission, Thompson suggested four areas for improvement: (1) development of machinery "to replace the irksome and solitary operation of hand loading"; (2) improved control of underground operations; (3) improvement in the work of the individual; and (4) standardization of equipment.[6]

Also in 1923 *Coal Age* editor R. Dawson Hall picked up this theme and chided the industry for remaining a "cottage industry" that used outdated management techniques.[7] "In manufacturing fields," he noted, "the intrinsic value of proper organization was realized long ago. . . . Most large manufacturing concerns have spent much energy and money in installing, or attempting to install, a system. Many such firms have engaged efficiency engineers whose business it is to search out the rough spots in the working of their industrial plants. Unfortunately, the managements of a large majority of the coal companies have not even approximated a system."

Throughout the 1920s, the industry itself, through its trade journals and professional associations, called for improvement of management techniques. For example, in a 1924 *Coal Age* editorial titled "How Many Sub-bosses Have You," the industry's attention was focused on the problem of inadequate underground supervision. "As men rarely exert their best efforts," the editor noted, "still more do they need to be under supervision."[8] It was argued that in the long run money spent on supervision "is money well invested. Many mines fail to get out cheap coal because all the supervision is left to one mine foreman." At another point, the journal warned that "supervision must be more intent. . . . Companies can no longer countenance superficial observance of processes by foremen."[9]

Consulting firms sprang up and made their industrial engineering services available to the industry in the 1920s. One such firm reported intensive studies it conducted at one of the large mines owned by a steel company. Part of this study focused on company-owned housing: "An interesting study was made of the houses, and in analyzing the returns from these the gauge used was the labor obtained from each house as measured in gross returns. This indicated that some of the houses were occupied by men whose productive ability was below the standard and gave an indication of those men who were occupying better quarters than was their worth to the company in comparison with others."[10]

An industrial engineer for one of the nation's largest independent coal companies reported to the West Virginia Coal Mining Institute that in the mid-1920s his firm had embarked on a program of management improvement based on two elements: "First: The use of machines to replace man power. Second: The breaking up of any activity into component parts, arranging these parts so each can be performed with a minimum of lost time and motion, by hand or by machine, and reassembling these into an efficient composite."[11] This firm had initiated daily production quotas for each of its mines, "with a quota of labor on each of the [job] classifications." And "consistent low productivity of any classification is a signal for investigation and study."

To study and investigate inefficiencies and to call for the introduction of scientific management techniques such as "driving methods easily applied in factory organization" was one thing; to implement these reforms throughout the industry was quite another, however. The problem was in the labor process itself. As long as coal was loaded by hand by workers who labored in isolated rooms, they would be the ones to establish the pace of production and to determine how the coal would be mined. It became increasingly clear that scientific management techniques did not lend themselves to mining, at least not until the installation of machinery to load the coal.

Once loading machines were introduced, the door was wide open for management to make fundamental changes in the way coal was mined. The Coal Commission understood this relation when it detailed the impact that the use of a mechanical loading device would have: "With the use of a machine loader many duties which now fall to the hand loader pass over to company men. Such work as timbering, laying track in rooms, clearing up after the loader, and removing rock or slate, is necessarily done entirely by men who can be specially trained for it. Furthermore, these men work in a small area and under constant supervision of the foreman, which is impracticable where individuals are scattered in work places widely apart. Consequently they can be more effectively employed and at correspondingly lower unit costs."[12]

Following the commission's 1923 report on mechanical loading, two mining engineers at the Carnegie Institute of Technology conducted a comprehensive study of loading machines in sixty-five bituminous mines.[13] A wide variety of machines working under diverse conditions were reviewed with "a view of ascertaining the conditions under which such machines may be employed to economic advantage." This study was much more than an engineering feasibility study; it was also a management study, because the authors found that many early failures had resulted from poor organization and bad attitudes. "It is not fair to expect a machine to make a good showing if the car supply is faulty, the coal improperly shot, the voltage too low, or the management or the men 'bucking' the machine." The authors concluded that, once "mechanical and psychological" obstacles were overcome, mechanical loading was superior to hand loading. In addition to direct cost reductions through increased productivity, the authors found four advantages of machine loading, yielding indirect cost savings to the operator. These indirect factors were continuity of output, increased safety, concentration of mining operations, and closer supervision.

Machine loading not only changed the pace of production but it also made output more dependable. The freedom of hand loaders to leave the workplace caused delays and uncertainties in production that were beyond the mine owners' power to regulate, whereas machine loading made production levels almost predictable. "From a certain number of working places in a closely defined area the mine foreman can then expect a certain number of cars of coal per shift, a situation rarely reached with hand loading," the Carnegie engineers reported.[14] In contrasting the two systems, they pointed out that under a hand-loading system, "if a man is sick he lays off and his place is idle. If he doesn't feel like working he may clean up part of a cut and go home, with a consequent loss of coal in the section and at least slight disruption of the cycle of duties of the night cutting crew. If there is a major delay in the haulage or the hoist the miners will start home, and once started it is difficult to get them to return. The result is a greater loss in tonnage than is warranted by the delay. These factors do not influence the operation of loading machines."

Noting that one of the greatest problems in connection with machine loaders was that "of leaving a large area of unsupported roof to give space for the machines to work in," the authors claimed that during their study they heard of only two serious accidents to machine operators, "both of which were caused by carelessness." Their favorable conclusion regarding the safety value of machine production was based on the notion that "with most machines the dangerous part of the room or entry is occupied by the machine. A roof fall will do little damage to the machine when it might easily kill a man." In pillar removal, they thought the machine had even greater safety value because "the retreat is so rapid that the coal is out and the machine is gone before the working of the roof has time to dislodge the slate." But these conclusions regarding safety were not supported with empirical evidence, thus weakening their validity.[15]

The authors were on firmer ground when they concluded that machine loading concentrated operations and made closer supervision possible. Based on their field survey, they reported that "it is now possible for a loading machine to replace fifteen or twenty hand loaders and produce the same tonnage from an area one quarter as large." This meant that gathering locomotives worked in a more restricted area and could handle more cars in a shift. This fact alone could reduce the operating costs, as well as the initial investment in the haulage system. The concentration of working places with machine loading also made it possible to impose closer supervision of the work force. In contrast with hand loading, where the foreman's brief visit each shift was "the only contact the hand loader has with any authority during the day," the advent of loading machines "has made possible a closer contact between the boss and the job."[16] Concentration of mining operations means that "most of the boss's time does not then have to be spent in traveling from one place to another."

This study and others like it during the 1920s pointed to the advantages of mechanical mining, although the perspective was almost entirely a management one. Coal miners were not consulted, nor their interests considered, when the decision was made to instal machinery. Yet when it happened, they were the ones most adversely affected. Many lost their jobs at a time when there were no unemployment compensation or severance benefits. Those who remained on the job found that they would be working under drastically altered conditions.

The Arrival of the Loading Machine

Wylie Erwin started working at age sixteen in a large southern West Virginia mine in 1938, just one year before the mine installed its first mechanical loading machine.[17] Erwin recalled that the first machine used at his mine was called a Clarkson loader. "We knew it was coming," he said, "but we didn't know it was going to be as quick as it was." Although rumors were flying, the company gave no advance notice to the hand loaders that their jobs were being eliminated. "The day they put the loading machine on our section, the coal loaders went in to work but the boss was already there and he said that the men not on his list could pick up their tools and leave. And the men walked out of the mines," Erwin recalled. Fortunately, for these miners, there was an upswing in the coal trade, so others jobs were available. "The biggest majority of the men fired just laughed it off 'cause at that time you could—if you really wanted to work—you could go anywhere and get a job. There was a lot of work."

Of the men left on the job to run the new machinery, few liked loading coal mechanically. For one thing, it was hazardous work. Erwin said that "when you had hand loading, your faces stayed clean. You didn't have accumulation of dust because the coal loader was responsible. You could eat off the bottom, it was so clean." With the loading machine "you couldn't hear and you couldn't see." Erwin ran a gathering motor—called a pull 'n place—for the first loading machine in his mine and remembered that it was so dusty that "you would have to reach out and feel to tell when your car was full. They had a man standing there with a water hose, but that was just like pouring water in this creek out here as high as it is."

Along with speeding up the pace of production, there was pressure to keep the machine running at all times. Erwin remembered well the new work schedule after the switch to mechanical loading:

They had a timekeeper on each section. He would sit right there and clock you, to see how long it would take to load the car and switch it out. And if you wasn't fast enough, son, you didn't have a job. He came in with an old dollar watch and sat down—that's all he done, he sat right there. He'd sit there and you were supposed to come in, hit the machine, load the car, switch out, and be back to that machine in three minutes. He would put down every second that machine wasn't running. A lot of times you would wreck and if you were too long putting that car back on [the track] they'd get another brakeman who could put the cars on. You worked under a strain and you worked hard because you knew a man sitting there has a watch on you, and you knew what they could do with you.

Wylie Erwin pointed out that when it came to the actual loading of coal, the machine failed in one important way. The machine loaded not only the coal but all the slate and other unwanted material shot from the face. The skilled hand loader had always prided himself on sending clean coal to the surface, which he did by picking out the impurities and setting them aside before loading his coal. And some hand loaders believed that their skill in mining clean coal would protect their jobs against competition from the machines. George Korson in his book *Coal Dust on the Fiddle* recorded an interesting song in this connection, "The Coal Loading Machine."

Chorus

Tell me, what will a coal miner do?
Tell me, what will a coal miner do?
When he goes down in the mine,
Joy loaders he will find.
Tell me, what will a coal miner do?

Stanza

Miners' poor pocketbooks are growing lean,
Miners' poor pocketbooks are growing lean,
They can't make a dollar at all,
Here is where we place the fault:
Place it all on that coal loading machine.

Now boys, I think I have a scheme,
And I'm sure that it's neither rude nor mean.
We will pick our bone and refuse,
Then we'll know our coal is clean,
Then we'll outdo the coal loading machine.[18]

A coalfield poem written in Kentucky expressed the hope that the Joy machines would be short lived because they could not mine clean coal.

> Here is to Old Joy a wonderful machine,
> That loads more coal than any we've seen.
>
> Ten men cut off with nothing to do,
> Their places needed for another Joy crew.
>
> Fifty cars a day is the goal they have set,
> With coal and slate together they will get it, I bet.
>
> The bosses all smile to see Joy at work,
> And keep him well oiled, he never will shirk.
>
> He tears up the bottom, tears up the track,
> And never gets tired for he has a steel back.
>
> He loads lots of coal and very cheap too,
> But when offered for sale the dirt won't do.
>
> We hope they will dock him the next day at work,
> And cut him off for loading so much dirt.
>
> We will pick out a spot with plenty of room
> Where Joy can rest till the day of doom.[19]

For the coal operator, the solution to the problem of dirty, machine-loaded coal was simple, if not costly. Wylie Erwin pointed out that the company for which he worked found it necessary to build a facility on the surface for cleaning impurities from the coal. And this is precisely what happened throughout the coalfields in the wake of the mechanization movement. Elaborate cleaning and preparation plants began to dot the hillsides as hand loading disappeared.

Mike Murphy, a West Virginia coal miner, was a hand loader for nine years until his mine converted to mechanical loading in the early 1940s. He remembers that earlier the company had brought in a Joy 7BU to load some slate from a roof fall, but, he noted, "when it first came there a factory man came to teach somebody to operate it, a bunch of the foreign born, a bunch of coal loaders ran the man out. They chased him down the road. They did, yes sir, 'cause it was going to take their jobs. They ran him down the road with clubs and everything else. It was a Joy Manufacturing Company representative. I suspect if they had caught him they would have killed him. He was taking their jobs. That one machine, it would take a lot of jobs."[20] Murphy made his own adjustment to the loading machine by quitting face work and applying for a maintenance mechanic's position, a job he held until he retired. Admittedly, he was making good money as a hand loader; his father, also a loader, told him he was "crazy to trade that for a mechanics job which only paid $7.14 a day." It was not an easy decision because "hand loading is an awfully nice job, you don't have any boss. If you load a couple of cars and want to go home, just go home. You can come back the next day and clean it up." But he "saw what was coming" and decided to try for the mechanic's job. Others, like his father, who had loaded by hand all their lives did not make the adjustment as easily. "There weren't too many of the hand loaders who got into machinery. A lot of them just quit coal mining. Quite a few left and went to other places where they were still loading coal by hand. That's all they knew, was hand loading. They went to what they call 'dog holes' over in Preston County [West Virginia]."

Murphy made the important observation that it was the hand loaders who stood to lose the most from mechanical loading. The day men, or "company men," already were paid a daily rate and "it didn't make any difference to them about the machines." At the time the mine changed over to mechanical loading, "the hourly people just about equaled the piecework people." Sabotage was one way some miners responded, Murphy admitted. As a mechanic he was called in when a piece of machinery broke down.

> I remember one time especially. A man called in and said that he didn't have any lights on one side of his loading machine. They had two lights on the loading head and two on the discharge boom on each side. Well, what happened is that this guy had ripped one of his lights off by letting a car hit it, a guy pushed a car up and it took the light and blew the fuses. A boss sent me in to fix it up. I put a new fuse in and hooked the wire together where the light used to be [so the other lights would work]. Well, that made the operator mad: "By God, I'll show you what I'll do." And he ran that thing against the rib and tore off the left front light. That used to go on a lot, tearing stuff up.

His job as a mechanic also gave Murphy an insight into the process by which the company made its decision to purchase certain types of mine equipment. "The equipment company that gives the biggest kickback . . . gets the job," he said. "We've gotten some awfully poor machines because the guys [superintendent and maintenance foreman] has gotten a deep-sea fishing trip, one thing or another, off of these companies and then the mechanics had an awful time with it." They wasted a lot of money on poorly built equipment. "I remember once they got four Jeffrey shuttle cars, which was the most do-nothing piece of equipment there ever was."

With mechanical loading, the mine was reorganized. "When we went to mechanical sections, the bosses went down from 120 men to 22 men," Murphy remembered. And under the new system, the section bosses were on a sort of piecework system. "He's required to get all the coal he can, and lots of times they take short circuits. They'll tell a man to do something without regard to safety," Murphy explained. Even with the reorganization of work into small crews, each with its own boss, the mine workers retained substantial control over the pace of production. The section bosses who didn't get any production "were the ones that the men didn't like. If he's arrogant, if he thinks he's a lot better than they are and lets them know it, they show him who's boss by cutting his production."

When asked how the company went about selecting persons to run the loading machines, Murphy said "that was something the company didn't know what to do about it." The factory men came in to oversee the assembly of the machine, which had to be taken into the mine in pieces and then put together before they could demonstrate its operation. At that time the company had a policy of giving a man ninety days to learn how to run the loader but, Murphy said, "I told my boss that's too much time. If a guy can't learn to run it in one day, he's never going to learn to run it. It wasn't that difficult to run." The union took the position that "the oldest man was entitled to the job but if he didn't want it the next one would get it," although apparently that was not enforced.

Retired coal miner U. G. Jordan worked as a hand loader when he first took a job in the mines in 1926. When the mine installed a loading machine, Jordan asked for and was given the job of running it. "I started in mechanical mining on the Myers-Whaley loader, one of the first of its kind in West Virginia, and then in 1930 ran the Joy 5BU loaders. Later I operated the 7 and 11 BU and other loaders," Jordan said.[21] The Myers-Whaley machine "had a shovel up front where it had a drive like a railroad engine, like the wheels on a locomotive. It went up and scooped up the coal and threw it back on a conveyor, which carried it back into a car." Jordan believed the Joy loader was far superior to others on the market, although the early Joy models had serious mechanical problems. Comparing the three loading machines available in their mid-1930s, Jordan said: "When the Goodman and Jeffrey companies came out with their machines they could load as much coal as the Joy loading machine, but they couldn't compete with Joy cost-wise on account of having to lay track for them and do special things for them which you didn't have to do for the Joy. Then when they came out with the shuttle car, that done away with the track altogether and just left the Goodman and Jeffrey out."

Jordan was able to explain in detail many of the problems encountered by coal companies that tried to mechanize their mines in 1920s. He also understood that mechanical mining dramatically altered the work process by concentrating the work force into small crews of mine workers, each of which was supervised by the newly defined management position of section foreman. In the following interview, Jordan explains some of the impact of the introduction of new technology into the mine.

What were some of the problems in going from hand to machine loading?

JORDAN: None of the coal mines were ready for mechanical loading when they started. They had developed their mines for hand loading. Their track was just thrown together with none of it set up and bonded for power, and when they put this big machinery in they had to go back and lay all their track—better track and heavier track—and get set up so transportation could be speeded up. Most mining to that time had been done by horses and mules, maybe a haulage motor, but they just weren't ready for mechanical mining when they started . . . and the mines weren't laid out for it. . . . They would start a loading machine and load a cut of coal here and they might have to tram a quarter of a mile before they could get to the next cut. . . .

We had a lot of top [roof] problems back then, and when they went from hand-loading timbering to machine loading timbering, they got a lot of men killed. They just didn't understand taking care of it [the roof] at this high speed [of mining]. In the changeover from hand loading to mechanical loading there were a lot of foremen who wouldn't even accept it, didn't want it at all. Most of the foremen were older men and you know, the older you get the more you resent change . . . and until the coal companies got young foremen trained up they never really made a success out of mechanical mining. The older men just didn't want to put the time into it, and a lot of them quit rather than go ahead and do it.

One thing mechanical mining brought in was shortage of ventilation. We had a lot of trouble with men getting sick on bad air . . . three or four a day, down sick on smoke, puking up old green slimy stuff. It was poison off the powder is what it was. [The company doctor went underground to see what the trouble was and when he came out] he told the company, "There's got to be something done. Those men can't work under that condition!" So the company fired him, and he went to Charleston and raised such a stink in the Department of Mines down there that they came up there and made a thorough inspection of it and it cost the company a million dollars to sink a shaft down through the top of the hill to get ventilation into that mine. It was finished up about 1934. . . . The mines just weren't ready for mechanization when it started.

How did the machine change men's jobs?

JORDAN: It changed it a lot. It changed it from a man getting paid for how much work he did [in hand loading] but when they went on the machine he just worked so many hours and got paid so many dollars. When he was loading coal by hand, the harder he worked the more money he made. In hand loading you were your own boss, you worked as hard as you wanted to work. For instance, I would get up at five o'clock . . . then I had two miles from the outside to where my place was. I would walk in there and bug-dust my cut and drill it [the face was undercut by machine] and shoot it and be ready by the time the motor crew came at 7 o'clock with my cars. I could load whatever I wanted to load, but I usually averaged 6 to 8 cars—two-ton cars—and if I would clean my place up the second day, which I would do, take two days to clean my place up . . . if I got done at 2 o'clock I could go home.

How did the mining cycle change with the new loading machine?

JORDAN: When they put the Joy loader in at Carbon Fuel, they started to plan for mechanical mining. They would drive four headings in a breast and while the cutting machine was in one, the Joy would be in another, the timbermen would be in another, and the drill crew would be in another. So we got it worked out on a cycle; everybody knew where he went next and such as this.

What size was the work crew?

JORDAN: About thirteen men back at that time, then later on they got it down some, depending on the condition of the mine. For instance, one mine would have bad top and they would have to have more men to do the timbering. A mine which had clean coal wouldn't have to have the "gob sows" [to shovel slate].

Was it common to have two shifts at that time?

JORDAN: Yes, that is, where you had mechanical mining going. They had their money invested in machinery and it would run where a man wouldn't be able to work both day and night. Now, some mines did work hand loading on both shifts but it had to be a big mine with a lot of development. Those mines had motors to haul the coal rather than horses and mules. But the machine made the difference. In fact, some of the mines went to three shifts after they got the machines.

What about the work crew of thirteen men, did they have a foreman?

JORDAN: Yes, there was a foreman with each crew of men. They had to have it that way in order to comply with state mining laws. . . . We still had a lot of accidents because everything had stepped up from a slow pace to fast pace and everybody was not quite with it yet.

The foreman was there for safety, but he must also have been there to keep men working?

JORDAN: That's right, he was more of a pusher than he was a safety man.

How was it decided who would run the new machines?

JORDAN: The superintendent says, "He goes on it," and that's all there was to it. That's the way jobs were given at that time. Whoever the superintendent wanted to have he give it to them . . . no seniority or no nothing. . . . If you quit a job and lived in a company house, you had to move and that's all there was to it, so they controlled what you did.

How did the miners feel about the loading machine?

JORDAN: Well, some places they accepted it readily but other places they didn't. At Carbon Fuel the men accepted it because it was a new mine and they just started it with the loading machine. At the C & O Fuel mines they [the men] didn't have any choice to accept it or not because they all lived in company houses. They did what they was told to do and that's all there was to it. If they told you not to beat your wife, you didn't do it. And you traded at the company store back at that time.

For the last half of his mining career, Jordan was a section foreman for various coal companies, a job created by the new loading machine technology. There was usually one section foreman or "boss" for each crew of twelve to fourteen men and it was a job requiring special skills. The section boss was always (by law) an experienced miner, who had to have an understanding of the state mine safety laws and had to be able to manage the men working under him. Generally speaking, the coal operators saw the section boss as someone whose primary responsibility was to maintain a fast pace of production, to see to it that workers no longer motivated by an incentive pay system would put forth their best effort.

The three miners interviewed shared the view that the introduction of the loading machines had an adverse impact on working conditions in the nation's bituminous mines. They mentioned the increased speed of production with stopwatch control, the loss of traditional skills, which had given the miner a sense of independence found in only a few other industries, the increased supervision that came with the reorganization of production into crew work, the loss of certain incentives with the change to a day rate of pay, and the restrictions on certain freedoms, such as the right to leave work early. Putting the mines on multiple shifts was a change that also affected family schedules and community life. Of course, most miners were able to make individual adjustments to the new ways, but these interviews speak of resentment and resistance. It is not surprising that miners failed to share the view that the new technology meant progress.

Job Safety and the Loading Machine

If there was an advantage that tipped the scales in favor of the new technology from the miner's perspective, it was the supposed improvements in health and safety conditions the technicians claimed would follow from the use of loading machines. The claims, however, turned out to be off the mark. What's more, mechanization of the mines introduced new hazards to the workplaces, hazards that continue to make mining one of the most dangerous of all industries.

Putting large machines to work in constricted areas was, in itself, a hazardous thing to do, and many lost-time accidents occurred when miners were pinned against the rib or knocked in the head by the boom of a loading machine. Machines were rarely engineered with the operator's safety in mind—miners' feet and hands were not protected from open gears, chains, conveyors, and other moving parts. Compounding the problem of men and machinery working together in a confined area was an inadequate lighting system, made even worse by increasing levels of machine-created dust. Since the loading machine needed more work room than hand loaders, when production pressures were great, the temptation was to neglect roof-control procedures, especially near the face, where a majority of roof-fall accidents occurred. Mining engineers argued that the more rapid rate of mining with mechanical loaders made it possible to mine out a room and retreat before the roof had a chance to settle and fall, so that the new technology should reduce roof-fall accidents. While that may have been an advantage of the system, in many coalfields the more rapid rate of mining liberated more methane gas, which combined with higher dust levels to create conditions conducive to major disasters. And the use of electricity to power the new machinery increased the likelihood that such disasters would occur. Indeed, the very pace of production under the new system became a source of mine accidents, as speed and continuous operations were necessary to make the more capital intensive methods economically feasible. Finally, the higher levels of dust associated with mechanical mining created a new occupational disease—coal miners' pneumoconiosis, or black lung.

Many of these health and safety problems eventually were resolved, or partly so, by the application of new technology. Better ventilation systems were developed to reduce methane dangers, rock dusting was perfected to reduce the danger of coal-dust explosions, roof bolting was initiated to improve roof control, and spraying water and wetting agents was used to allay coal dust at the face and in haulage. These systems, however, involved costly additions to the unit price of coal, costs incurred with reluctance in this highly competitive industry. For example, the value of rock dusting had been determined by U.S. Bureau of Mines experiments before World War I, but as late as 1940 only 9.1 percent of the mines, with 55.7 percent of underground tonnage, regularly used rock dust.[22] As the mechanization movement grew, it did to some extent create its own logic for the promotion of safer mining practices. With the growing investment in loading machines and other equipment, mine owners developed strong incentives to protect their equipment. Failure to commit appropriate funds for an adequate ventilation system could, for example, result in a gas explosion capable of destroying hundreds of thousands of dollars of underground equipment. A poorly supported roof could fall, burying a loading machine and interrupting production in a whole section of the mine. Even discounting the loss or damage of machinery, such interruptions in themselves were costly and needed to be avoided.

Protection of machinery would, of course, go a long way in providing a safer workplace, but the responsibility for the safety of the men operating the new machinery was not clearly understood in the transition period. Some argued that it was a management responsibility to provide a safe work environment. Others said that it was the worker's responsibility to work safely. A third point of view held that mechanical loading was a safer mining system than hand loading, so the problem would solve itself as the industry adopted the new technology. And a final opinion held the fatalistic view that mining was inherently dangerous and little could be done to make it as safe as other industries.

The industry's forum for much of the debate over the mechanization-safety issue was the American Mining Congress, an association of company executives, mining engineers, equipment manufacturers, and public mining officials. In 1928 the Mining Congress established a national committee on mechanized mining to research, publicize, and promote mechanical loading and other new technologies. As an adjunct to the mechanization committee, a safety subcommittee was established to investigate and report on the specific relation between mechanization and mine safety. Each year, coal operators and others presented papers to the Mining Congress meetings, and these papers, in turn, were reprinted in the organization's annual *Yearbook on Mechanization.* At first the tone of the safety presentations was quite positive, that is, the industry spokesmen praised mechanical loading as a mining method that would reduce workplace hazards. After the 1929 meeting one Mining Congress official summarized the safety presentations by reporting that "a review of the safety papers and discussions shows a rather unanimous agreement in cause and effect—the effect being the very material reduction in the accident rate over hand loading."[23]

The workplace reorganization associated with loading machines involved an increase in the number of mine foremen and more or less constant supervision of work at the face. In 1929, the vice president of the Pittsburgh Coal Company explained how this new labor process would, or should, improve the industry's safety record. He said that "to secure the efficient operation of mechanical loading devices it has been necessary to increase the number of face bosses."[24] He said this resulted in more frequent inspection of roof conditions and other safety hazards, "and with the concentration of work and the reduction in number of working places it has been possible for the places to be maintained in a more safe condition than in hand loading." Furthermore, "usually the men are working in pairs and can be required to comply with instructions of bosses more promptly than when they are loading by hand." According to this coal company official, safety would improve with mechanization because the reorganized production process would allow for greater discipline of the work force through increased supervision.

The safety director of the Pocahontas Fuel Company of West Virginia reported in 1929 that in the three years since his company had installed twenty-five loading machines of the Jones Coloder type, the frequency and severity of lost-time accidents had been cut by half or more. And the greatest advantage of mechanical loading over hand loading was the reduction in accidents from roof falls. "Our records indicate that we have effected a reduction from this cause of over 50 percent," the safety director said.[25] The difference showed up more in pillar removal than in routine face work, because rapid machine loading in recovering pillars permitted the crew to work continually under comparatively new roof, "which is a desirable feature of robbing, inasmuch as the atmospheric conditions attack newly exposed slate roof, causing it to become dangerous over a period generally required by hand loading."

Unfortunately, the individual success stories reported at the American Mining Congress meetings were not translated into an improved industry safety record of the same magnitude. And during the 1930s, the papers on mine safety shifted their focus from specific reporting to general persuasion. In 1933 a Wyoming mine inspector found it necessary to caution the industry to weigh carefully the true costs of moving too rapidly into mechanical loading. "If by loading coal mechanically the hazards are increased and injuries and fatalities are more frequent, it would be very evident that the purpose of these installations has been defeated, as any reduction in the cost of coal, if brought about at the expense of human life, is not justified," he wrote.[26] One writer after another urged the industry to take the safety question seriously and to find ways to improve safety in the mines. Attempts were made to persuade coal operators to put forth more effort than previously on the grounds that "safety pays."

Some safety advocates went so far as to estimate the actual savings that could be realized from a commitment to safe underground operations. In 1937 for example, it was estimated that "the direct and indirect cost of accidents constitutes 10 to 15 percent of the total cost to the mine operator of putting coal on the railroad cars at the mine."[27] The point was made quite emphatically by the vice president of a large coal company:

> Mines are working for months and large properties in some instances for years without a lost-time accident. If this is practicable, and evidently it is as it is being done, it is possible to improve production costs directly to the extent that accidents can be eliminated. Consequently, the realization that mines can be operated with few, if any, accidents is of great practical importance. If it may be assumed that practically all accidents are preventable, the question then may be asked—does it cost less to remove the cause of an accident or stand the cost of compensation, the attendant confusion, property damage, and losses to production arising directly and indirectly from it? The answer taught by experience is that the price of working dangerously is more than any mine can afford to pay.[28]

Even if the argument had been a convincing one, economic conditions were so depressed in the late 1920s and early 1930s that few operators could afford the additional expenses needed to make their mines safe. "One of the outstanding contributory factors at this time which should be eliminated in order to assist materially in reducing accidents is the cutthroat competition in the selling of coal. Prices at the mine are entirely too low to permit a reasonable margin of profit, a part of which should go into the upkeep and improvements of the mines," reported the state mine inspector of Virginia in 1927.[29]

It is not necessary to review the whole history of mine safety in the period from the early 1920s to the 1940s, although that is an interesting history in itself. In this discussion of the impact of mechanization on safety, some observations of a more general nature are appropriate. Underlying most safety work in the period—the coal executive's comments above notwithstanding—was a general belief that mining was inherently dangerous and could never be made as safe as other industries.[30] Even the miners' union reflected this view. "Coal mining will never be a safe occupation. Secrets of Mother Nature are not all known and the unexpected will always happen," the *UMWA Journal* asserted in 1932.[31]

One frequently expressed belief of the operators was that miners tended to be a careless lot of workers. Others believed that miners actually liked to take chances. In fact, one operator was convinced that taking chances was basic to human nature so he reasoned that he could reduce mine accidents by giving miners an alternative gambling method. He offered door prizes at monthly safety meetings, believing that if his workers were given an opportunity to take chances outside the mine they would be less likely to do so when they got underground. Finally, the view was expressed by some in the mining literature that miners were basically stubborn and would refuse to obey orders, even if these were safety orders aimed at their own protection.

Given these notions about human behavior, it is not surprising that the focus of company safety measures emphasized more the role of the individual worker rather than the importance of improving working conditions. It was necessary to persuade, educate, cajole, and even discipline the mine worker to work safely for his own benefit, many coal operators reasoned. A wide variety of programs evolved during the period: "safety first" campaigns, safety awards such as those given by the Joseph A. Holmes Safety Association, safety bonuses for foremen and for miners, safety contests, safety education programs, and safety meetings.[32] The program at the Pennsylvania Coal and Coke Corporation reflects quite clearly this predisposition on the part of mine management to see individual carelessness as the principle cause of accidents.

> It was realized from the first that to be successful one had to reach the individual and make him a responsible person in this safety movement. With this in mind, a small book of rules was devised, containing abstracts from the state mine laws and additional company safety rulings. These were distributed to each employee with the distinct understanding that they must be read until each one had a good knowledge of what his particular job required in the way of safeguarding himself and his fellow workman. The rules were also discussed at the various meetings, and in addition the foremen and assistants were instructed to ask each workman, on making their periodic inspections, to answer some simple safety questions. Naturally, some of the men thought the whole thing was just another stunt and treated it lightly, if at all, so disciplinary measures had to be used, varying according to the accident infraction of state mine laws or company rulings. Such infractions are becoming less every day.[33]

The safety record for coal mining generally improved during the period from 1930 to 1948 (table 5). The number of fatal accidents per million man-hours of exposure at work fell from 2.39 in 1930 to 1.35 in 1948. Similarly, the number of nonfatal accidents dropped from 83.75 per million man-hours at the beginning of the period to 56.28 at the end of the period. There is a serious problem, however, in using these injury rates for establishing long-term trends. The bureau had admitted in 1949 it had so much difficulty in obtaining accurate data on the number of hours worked, especially in the early part of the period when workdays were of irregular length and time clocks were rarely used, that it makes the results "so undependable as to be almost fantastic. . . . Comparing these calculated or estimated figures of the past with the more nearly accurate data of the present is the acme of folly if there is a really sincere desire to obtain factual data as to the progress of safety in coal mines."[34]

The bureau apparently had no problem in obtaining accurate data on

TABLE 5

**Injury Rates in Mechanical Loading for
Bituminous Coal Mining, 1930 – 1948**

	Accidents per Million Man-Hours		*Percent of Underground Coal Loaded Mechanically*
	Fatal	*Nonfatal*	
1930	2.39	83.75	10.5
1931	2.01	79.98	13.9
1932	2.21	72.58	12.3
1933	1.63	68.87	12.0
1934	1.80	69.39	12.2
1935	1.87	71.47	13.5
1936	1.85	65.62	16.3
1937	2.00	68.05	20.2
1938	1.97	63.47	26.7
1939	1.80	60.52	31.0
1940	2.20	61.28	35.4
1941	1.77	58.93	40.7
1942	1.84	60.21	45.2
1943	1.58	57.79	48.9
1944	1.41	56.02	52.9
1945	1.32	56.52	56.1
1946	1.28	58.81	58.4
1947	1.45	57.32	60.7
1948	1.35	56.28	64.3

Source: Forrest T. Moyer, G. D. Jones, and V. E. Wrenn, *Injury Experience in Coal Mining, 1948,* Bulletin No. 509, U.S. Bureau of Mines (Washington, D.C., GPO, 1952), p. 90. The first year the bureau collected complete data on both fatal and nonfatal accidents in coal mines was 1930.

the number of fatal coal mine accidents, but nonfatal accident reporting was an entirely different matter. Some companies did a good job of reporting all accidents, but others neglected to report accidents unless compensation payments were made or a hospital visit was recorded. "This is believed to be one of the many reasons for the wide fluctuations in nonfatal injury records and in data on a man-hour of exposure basis," the bureau reported.[35] Further, the nonfatal injury rates are combined rates, including underground mining, surface operations, and strip mining. The fatal accident rates in combination will yield a long-term downward trend as employment shifts from underground mining to the relatively safer strip mining. The measure also suffers from the fact that all lost-time accidents are recorded as single accidents regardless of their severity; that is, all accidents are recorded as single accidents regardless of the number of days of work actually lost. (In the mid-1940s, the bureau made an effort to correct this deficiency by publishing an index of severity, but no long-term trends are available for evaluating the impact of mechanical loading.)

These statistical problems aside, a comparison of the trends of injury rates and the progress of mechanical loading does not, unfortunately, suggest a very close relation, one way or the other. For example, the early 1930s experienced a drop in mine accidents, but the rate of technological change was nearly constant, and in 1932 and 1933 technology actually dropped. After 1935, when the percentage of mechanically loaded coal began to increase quite rapidly, the fatality rate held steady and even increased in several of the years. It was only after 1942, when the industry was 45.2 percent mechanized, that the fatality rate began a perceptible and consistent decline.

The Bureau of Mines, which usually took the position that mechanical loading was more dangerous than hand loading, credited the 1941 Federal Coal Mine Inspections and Investigations Act with effecting the improvement in the industry's safety record during the 1940s. In a review of the transition period to mechanical loading; the bureau pointed out that the general trend of fatality rates was upward during the nine-year period from 1933 to 1941, but in 1942 when federal mine inspections got under way "the trend was reversed, and the downward trend has been generally maintained since 1942 despite the unfavorable factors and influence during the war years."[36] Furthermore, the bureau reported, "in 1942, the trend in nonfatal accident rates started abruptly downward to a level never obtained previously and the favorable trend is being maintained." While this assessment may have been self-serving, it does point out that the bureau was not in agreement with those industry spokesmen who were saying at the time that mechanization alone would improve mine safety. In fact, in several of its published reports the bureau went on record with the opposite view: that mine mechanization introduced new health and safety hazards to the workplace.

In a paper presented to the 1930 annual meeting of the International Association of Industrial Accident Boards and Commissions, Daniel Harrington, chief safety engineer of the U.S. Bureau of Mines, addressed the isssue of miner's safety under mechanical loading. Although the process was in its infancy at that time and sufficient data was not available for definite conclusions, Harrington told his audience that when the new technology is installed and operated "with reasonable safeguarding of the mine and its workers" it could give good results in safety. But, he emphasized, "there seems to be a decided tendency to take it for granted that mechanized loading is automatically safe; hence safety is given little or no consideration in the installation or in the operation of these newer methods and there is much reason to believe that safety has been lessened rather than enhanced by them. This is indicated to a certain extent by the fact that the latest complete figures on death rates per million man-hours of exposure show that these rates have increased in the two most highly mechanized coal-mining states, Illinois and Wyoming."[37] Focusing on roof fall accidents, the primary cause of coal mining fatalities, Harrington said, "It is significant that this increase in fatalities from fall of roof and coal during the period 1924–1928 took place in those activities in mines most directly affected by the new mechanized loading systems, hence there is good reason for the inference that the influence of the new systems was in the direction of increasing the hazards from falls of roof and coal."[38]

On another occasion Harrington, presumably speaking again for the U.S. Bureau of Mines, listed twenty specific ways that mechanical loading, as being practiced in the late 1920s, made mining a more hazardous occupation. He argued that operators were assuming that concentrated mining with machines was safer, so that "common sense precautions looking to the safety of the mine and the miner" were frequently overlooked.[39] Hazards he charged to mechanical loading included the operation of electrical motors near methane-liberating faces and the increased dust level from conveyors and loaders. Frequent blasting during the working shift, loaders tearing out props and cribs, and increased machinery noise that prevented workers from hearing the slight warning sounds generally given before a roof fall were additional hazards associated with mechanical loading. Furthermore, Harrington was skeptical of the principle advantage claimed by the proponents of mechanical loading: "One of the safety advantages claimed by adherents of the newer concentrated systems is that of more intensive supervision; yet in many instances the work is placed in charge of some young electrician, mechanic, or engineer who knows little, and cares less, about haulage, timbering, blasting, ventilation, etc., though he is intensely interested in the electrical or mechanical details of the equipment."

Roof-fall accidents had been the most frequent cause of death for miners during the hand-loading period and continued to be the major hazard in underground mining in the period of transition to mechanical loading (table 6). At the end of the period, a detailed study of the causes of roof-fall accidents was made by the Bureau of Mines. The study

TABLE 6

**Principle Causes of Fatalities in
Underground Bituminous Coal Mining, 1923 – 1948**

Cause	Number	Percent of Total
Roof fall	16,702	54.9
Haulage	5,955	19.6
Gas or dust explosions	4,053	13.3
Explosions	788	2.6
Electricity	1,317	4.3
All other	1,641	5.4
Total	30,450	100.0

Source: Forrest T. Moyer, G. D. Jones, and V. E. Wrenn, *Injury Experience in Coal Mining, 1948,* Bulletin No. 509, U.S. Bureau of Mines (Washington, D.C., GPO, 1952), p. 75.

confirmed the suspicion that the new technology was fraught with dangers, especially from collapse of the mine roof. The study revealed that 74 percent of all roof-fall fatalities occurred within twenty-five feet of the working face and that a sizable majority of those fatalities occurred in the relatively small area between the last permanent roof support and the face, the average length of which was thirteen feet. Next, the study found that half of all roof-fall fatalities took place where coal was loaded mechanically, although fewer men were engaged in this work than in hand-loading face work. From this study the bureau concluded,

This proves that mechanical operations are, to a considerable degree, the more dangerous from the standpoint of roof falls, notwithstanding that much closer supervision is possible and is maintained in such operations. These facts very definitely indicate management failure in providing sufficient roof support at working faces. It should be noted that any increase in concentration of employees due to mechanical loading causes an equal increase in the destructive potentialities of each fall of roof.

Therefore, a comparable increase in expenditures on roof-support installations in such operations would be justified from an economic as well as a humane standpoint.[40]

A partial solution to the problem of roof support for safer mining came in the 1940s from a technological breakthrough known as roof bolting. In this system, holes were drilled into the roof and steel rods one inch in diameter were inserted in the holes. The rods—often called pins—were threaded at one end and slit at the other end. They were anchored at the back end of the hole by driving the slit end of the rod over a steel wedge, which expanded the end of the rod to anchor it. The rods were placed under tension by tightening nuts on the threaded end on a load-bearing plate at the collar of the hole. The purpose of this operation was, as it is today in mining, to bond several thin strata of rock to create a beamlike structure that could span a larger open space. Roof bolting had been in experimental use for many years in both metal mines and coal mines before the first discussion of the practice found its way into mining literature in 1943. In the belief that roof bolting would provide a safer workplace, the U.S. Bureau of Mines in 1945 assigned engineers to study roof bolting. Soon thereafter the bureau began to promote the practice.

The industry showed increasing interest in roof bolting during the 1940s, and by 1949, when wartime steel shortages had been overcome, 200 mines were reported to be using this system of roof support.[41] At least two important economic considerations in roof bolting influenced management: the savings that might accrue from lower accident rates and the significant advantage resulting from the increased freedom of movement of machinery in timber-free work areas.

Haulage hazards continued to be the second most important cause of mine accidents during the transition period when coal mines were shifting to mechanical loading. An increased pace of production with mechanized loading and a need for coordinated production put strains on existing haulage systems, which could be met only by increased speed of movement and increased capacity of mine cars and motors. "The constant cry of mine officials for speed in production is a factor against safety," a Wyoming mine inspector warned in 1933.[42] It was only gradually that mine owners revamped their underground rail haulage systems to accommodate the increased production from the new loading machines. Conveyor systems, which became increasingly important with the introduction of mechanical loading, were generally a much safer method of moving coal to the surface.

Gas and dust explosions, the third most important cause of fatalities in the mines, have an interesting and gruesome history of their own in the period of transition to mechanical loading. Not many of the fatal explosions were directly related to the use of mechanical loaders,[43] but changes in mining practices frequently contributed to this danger. Blasting practices, for example, were revised with machine loading in two ways. First, because the efficiency of the loader depended on adequate supply of loose coal, there was a tendency to use a heavier charge of blasting powder in each hole to dislodge more coal.[44] This practice increased the chances of a "blown-out shot," which could cause a minewide explosion. Second, as noted above, the pressure for more production under mechanized mining increased the frequency of blasting while men were still in the mine. This practice was compounded as double-shifting became commonplace. The Centralia, Illinois, mine explosion on March 25, 1947, for example, caused the deaths of 111 miners from improper blasting with men in the mines.[45]

Improvements in blasting practices eventually reduced these dangers but not before many miners had lost their lives from mine mechanization. Electric arcs were an ever-present danger on the early loading machines, which were not equipped with enclosed, or flameproof, electric motors. Some operators were unwilling to pay the extra costs of machinery with enclosed motors, and in addition, in the early stages of the mechanization movement, these special motors were protected by patent rights held by the established machinery companies. "The companies are very reluctant to grant the use of these devices to any person who may some day develop into strong competition," one coal operator noted in 1925.[46]

The role of electricity as a cause of fatal accidents is not fully explained by the 1,317 deaths between 1923 and 1948 shown in Table 6. Many of the explosions were directly caused by electricity. A U.S. Bureau of Mines study of 403 explosions in the sixteen-year period from

1929 to 1944 revealed that 179, or 44.4 percent, were caused by electricity.[47] And explosions of electrical origin caused 1,067, or 56.8 percent, of fatalities in the sixteen-year period. The study concluded, among other things, that "the indiscriminate use of open-type electrical equipment must be curtailed and the ventilating systems improved considerably" if there were to be further reduction in the number of explosions. The data show a decline in explosions near the end of the sixteen-year period, leading the authors to make the following observation: "As more mines are mechanized each year, it might be expected that the number of explosions initiated by electricity would increase. As this has not happened, it appears that some definite benefits are being shown as results of recent improvements in the observance of obvious safe practices, such as adequate ventilation, testing for gas, and restricting the use of nonpermissible electrical equipment. More careful observance of these precautions is necessary if the number of explosions initiated electrically in a year is to be reduced."[48]

The Problem of Coal Dust

If debate continued over the net effect of mechanized mining on some aspects of coal mine safety, there certainly was no question that the new technology affected miners' health by increasing coal dust in the mines. "These machines, while they do not make enough fine coal to affect the market value, do make a large quantity of fine flour-like dust," complained a central Pennsylvania coal operator in 1925, and "this dust is made in the worst possible place, namely, at the face."[49] Attempts were made from a very early date to reduce dust levels by spraying water at the face as the coal was loaded, but it did not succeed in reducing the dust danger. "We found it impossible to run enough water over a place to keep this dust down; at times we had the places so wet the men complained, but the machines were still surrounded by a haze of dust," reported another coal operator in the same publication. Coal dust thus generated created a serious safety hazard and a major health threat to miners.

As far as the safety hazard was concerned, as early as 1909 U.S. Bureau of Mines experiments demonstrated that coal dust could propagate a mine explosion.[50] "Deposited on surfaces from which it can be swept readily into the air in a dense cloud, coal dust is a grave potential explosion hazard," the bureau continued to warn the industry. The bureau's experimental work also demonstrated that dust explosions could be prevented by the proper application of finely ground rock (usually limestone), called rock dust. For rock dusting to be effective it had to be applied regularly and in sufficient quantities, but it was difficult to convince the industry to undertake this practice. As late as 1940 the bureau was still trying to persuade coal operators to take rock dusting seriously. In its review of major mine explosions in 1940 and 1941, the bureau reported that "had rock dusting to prevent propagation of explosions been in effect in all these mines, the death toll undoubtedly would have been reduced greatly and possibly one or more of the explosions would have been prevented."[51]

Coal dust was not generally recognized as a respiratory health problem during the early years of the mechanical loading period. "Miners' consumption" disabled many miners over the years, but there was a tendency to confuse the disease with silicosis, the lung disease found among metal miners and tunnel workers. There was also a belief—later proven wrong—among some mining men that rock dust contributed to lung damage of coal miners. The coal-dust hazard in mechanical mines was not unknown, however, as the following remark made by a coal operator in 1936 suggests:

Many operators have come to a belief that in addition to the explosion hazard due to coal dust at working faces in coal mines, there is a health hazard in breathing of enormous numbers of particles of fine coal dust; and coal mines may have lost the services of underground workers, especially machine men, due to illnesses brought about by breathing dust. It was found that when shoveling very dry coal at a room face of a certain coal mine, the worker was breathing four to five billion particles of dust in every cubic meter of air taken into his lungs, and in another place five to eight billion dust particles per cubic meter of air were being breathed by a machine runner when undercutting without use of water.[52]

In 1940, the Bureau of Mines cautiously pointed out that "when in suspension in mine air, coal dust is considered by some to be injurious to the health of the miners; undeniably it reduced visibility and comfort at working places."[53] Not until a 1936–41 investigation of pulmonary disease among coal miners in South Wales was it recognized that coal miners' pneumoconiosis was a disease distinct from silicosis.[54] And it was not until the mid-1960s that black lung became recognized as a compensible disease under workers' compensation laws. Dust continued to be a problem in mechanized mining operations even when large quantities of water were used at or near the face, but for many years it failed to attract sufficient attention to warrant public concern or protective legislation. It was without question one of the most serious adverse consequences of mechanical mining systems and became worse with the introduction of continuous mining machines in the late 1940s. The quality of working life—the quality of life itself—deteriorated for thousands of the nation's coal miners who had to breathe the dust created by the new loading machines and other mining equipment.

CHAPTER 5

Miners' Response to Technological Change

Without doubt, miners understood that the loading machine would eliminate many underground jobs and that it would destroy the traditional freedoms they had enjoyed as hand loaders. They may not have anticipated the adverse impact the new technology would have on their health and safety, but they soon learned how dangerous underground machinery could be and how injurious to their lungs machine-created dust could be. While some miners accepted the changes wrought by the new technology and made the most of it, others resisted the change. Their opposition took many forms. There was individual resistance: some quit the mines and sought other employment, others stayed on but refused to operate the new machinery to its full capacity, and yet others engaged in outright sabotage. More importantly, there was a collective response, as mine workers organized themselves, first through local unions and then through affiliation of their locals with others to form a national union. It was through these organizations that miners hoped to achieve economic security and to protect their interests during the industry's move to mechanize.

Few, if any, groups of organized workers have not faced technological change at some time. Most unions, therefore, have found it necessary to adopt policies to deal with the employment impact and the changes in work processes brought about by new technologies. Some union policies were designed to obstruct change; others were aimed at controlling it; and some actually encouraged the adoption of new technology, at least in the unionized sector of an industry where it was hoped a competitive advantage would protect jobs by eliminating those marginal firms that failed to adopt the new ways.[1] The relation between union policies and technological change is a complex one, and the effect of union policies on the diffusion rate of innovation varies from industry to industry and from one time to another.

For union policies—whatever they might be—to be effective, they had to be incorporated into agreements negotiated with and enforceable through management. Furthermore, national union policies had to be compatible with the basic interests of the members and with the goals of local unions, or the national union had to be in a position to make locals respect the agreements negotiated at the national level. There are, then, three basic questions that arise in considering the relation between unions and technology. First, how does a union establish policies and bargaining goals relating to technological change? Second, how effective is the union in translating these objectives into contract language? Finally, can the union meet the terms of the contract and establish internal discipline and loyalty among its constituent parts? The aim of this chapter is to examine the early responses of miners to the introduction of machine methods of mining, to explain the origins of the United Mine Workers' mechanization policies, and to point out ways that miners acting in concert affected the rate at which technology was applied to coal production.

The Struggle to Unite

Perhaps the first recorded collective action on the part of bituminous coal miners involved several local strikes in the Cumberland, Maryland, field in the early 1850s. Without formal union organization, these job actions were spontaneous expressions of protest over threats by the mine owners to cut tonnage payments to pick miners. In 1859, the Monongahela Valley miners struck for the installation of scales to determine the amount of coal each miner produced. This strike spread to most of the mines in western Pennsylvania before it ended in failure for the miners. During the same decade, miners in Ohio formed local unions for mutual aid and protection, and in Illinois local unions were organized and "made use of voluntary restriction of individual production as a means of regulating working conditions."[2]

The first national union of coal miners, the American Miners Association, was founded in 1861 when local unions in Missouri, Illinois, Ohio, and Maryland met to establish a uniform wage scale. Basic to the organizational structure of the association was the idea that the locals in each state and the mines they represented would be divided into districts based on a common market for coal. In each mining district, a district union or association was established, with its own constitution and its own elected officers. The American Miners Association did not last more than a few years, but the internal structure of this industrial union—with its local unions, district associations, and national federation—was the structure assumed by the United Mine Workers of America years later. Through the years, however, conflict within the union continued over the relative authority of the three levels of organization. One historian noted that the coal miner has always "been suspicious of centralized control of his union and insisted on a generous degree of district autonomy," but the early AMA leaders soon developed the position that, for their union to be successful in the highly competitive coal industry, national interests should be sovereign over local interest.[3]

After the American Miners Association collapsed in 1867 after a series of unsuccessful strikes, no interstate organization of miners appeared again until 1873. Under the leadership of John Siney, a new national miners' organization was formed, bringing together both anthracite and bituminous workers. It was called the National Miners Association and seemed to meet the miners' needs for federated activities. By 1874, the new union boasted 25,000 members, with locals in all the major coal-producing states. The rapid growth of the new organization was attributed to the fact that it was able to give financial support to local unions whose members were on strike. At the same time, however, Siney sought to remove the strike weapon from local control by denying benefits to locals that struck without sanction from the national executive board. But Siney and the national officers could not control the actions of local unions, nor could the organization sustain the demands made on it for financial strike support. Only three years after its formation, the National Miners Association collapsed during a wave of strikes brought on by poor coal markets and widespread wage cuts.[4]

After the failure of the second attempt at forming a national organization, local unions of miners remained active in several fields, notably the Hocking Valley of Ohio, the Pittsburgh district, and the southern Illinois area. These independent locals not only survived during the hiatus between the collapse of one national movement and the beginning of the next, they were able to protect their members and to lend financial and strike support to the railway workers in the national rail strike of 1877.[5] During the late 1870s, the Knights of Labor began organizing local assemblies of miners in several mining districts, including some of the fields where local unions already existed. A rivalry between the two types of labor organizations emerged, a rivalry not entirely resolved until some time after the formation of the United Mine Workers in 1890. It is important to note that in these early years the collective strength of miners resided in the local union and that efforts at building a national union began as federations of locals.

In 1882, representatives of several Ohio local unions met in Columbus and organized the Ohio Miners' Amalgamated Association. This assembly of local unions developed into a viable statewide organization, with its strongest locals in the Tuscarawas Valley and the Hocking Valley. It seems that these locals were powerful enough to win concessions upon demand from the operators during the early part of the 1880s. Ohio mine union official and historian Chris Evans wrote that in the Hocking Valley, "it was the custom to watch closely the action of the thermometer, and no matter how often it pointed downward an advance was asked for every time the thermometer demonstrated its increased severity."[6] That is, when cold weather approached, the demand for coal increased, and miners asked for and obtained wage increases. The job control enjoyed by pick miners at that time was translated into local union bargaining power.

Early Union Response to Mechanization

The Ohio miners union was important to the issue under study because it was the first organization in coal mining to question the use of machinery. An Ohio company, the Jeffrey Manufacturing Company, first manufactured the cutter-bar-type undercutting machine in 1877 and installed it in several Ohio mines. It was introduced on an experimental basis in the Hocking Valley mines, a union stronghold. From the beginning, the miners did not look very kindly on this development. And they must have let it be known that they would take direct action against the use of the machine, for it was reported that the company engineer who first took the undercutter equipment into the mines for demonstration purposes "took a gun for his own protection and slept beside his charge."[7]

It is not clear from the record of this period why miners objected to the Jeffrey machines. They may have feared losing their jobs if machine production replaced manual methods, or they may have sensed that the machinery might increase the pace of production and reduce some of the craft control they had traditionally enjoyed. It also must have been clear to them that the undercutting machine could pose a threat to the strength of their local unions. By the admission of one industry spokesman, the installation of the coal cutter was initiated in the 1800s more for its "moral effect in combating the organization of pick miners than for its value as an expense reducer."[8] William N. Page, a prominent West Virginia coal operator and mining engineer, writing in 1894, expressed the opinion that undercutting machinery was introduced "not so much for its saving in direct cost as for the indirect economy in having to control a fewer number of men for the same output. It is a weapon with which to meet organized skilled labor and their unreasonable demands. . . . As the machine does the mining, the proportion of skilled labor is largely reduced, and the result is found in less belligerence and conflict, a sufficient inducement though the direct costs be the same."[9]

Organized worker resistance to mechanization in Ohio, however, took the form of protests over new wage scales rather than over questions of job loss or dilution of craft control. The dynamics of the struggle between miners and management over the wage-mechanization issue was outlined in detail by the Ohio Bureau of Labor Statistics in 1880 when it reported on developments at a mine where the first undercutting machine was introduced. The report read:

> Some three years ago the Straitsville Central Mining Co. introduced in their mines a machine worked by compressed air to do the "bearing in" or under-cutting of the coal. The machines required two men to work them, besides the miner to knock down and load the coal. The miners who followed the machine were paid at first 35 cents per ton, when the price paid for regular mining was 50 cents per ton. This price was afterwards reduced to 30 cents per ton. When the price per ton for coal mining advanced, the miners following the machine also demanded an advance, and it was agreed that the price for mining after the machine should be three-fifths of the regular mining price. In August, 1880, the company desired to make a change, and offered to pay $2.00 per day for miners to follow the machines; the offer was accepted by some of the regular miners, but they soon became dissatisfied, and a mass meeting of miners was held and the men were instructed to quit work, the claim being that they were working at 25 percent below the regular wages. The company then advertised for men, and some 25 were secured who went to work. At the end of the week, the miners in the vicinity held a mass meeting at the mine of the company; the men at work were invited to attend, and did so; the result of the meeting was

that the new men left in a body, their expenses being paid by the miners, and the company paid the price, three-fifths of the regular mining price, the men being idle about two weeks.[10]

In this case, the operator, in seeking to take maximum economic advantage of the new machinery, tried to lower the wages of those who followed the machine to a level below that which the miners felt was appropriate. (It is also interesting that the company wished to put miners on a day wage rather than continue the practice of payment by the ton. This issue would reappear decades later.) The miners had the power, through concerted action, to force the payment of a higher wage and thereby to reduce management's economic incentive for mechanization. When the operator sought to employ other men who were willing to work at the reduced rate, the displaced miners were able to thwart this effort to break their control. Other operators in the Hocking Valley found themselves in a similar situation when they tried to introduce the cutting machine. Local unions of miners were too strong at that time to allow the use of this new technology.

In 1884, the Hocking Valley coal operators were determined to free themselves of worker control of what they considered to be their rights as managers of the mining enterprise, that is, the right to instal labor-saving machinery free of interference from informal customs or negotiated contract language. They decided on an all-out attack on the unions by first announcing a wage cut so large the miners were provoked into a walkout.[11] Next, the miners' strike became a lockout as the operators posted notices: "All miners in the employment of this company are hereby discharged and notified to remove their tools from the mines immediately."[12] Thousands of strikebreakers were imported under the protection of the Pinkerton Detective Agency, machinery was installed, and the mines were gradually reopened on a nonunion basis.

The prestigious trade publication *Engineering and Mining Journal* reported on the strike in September 1884, leaving no doubt in the minds of the readers as to the operators' objectives:

> Some three months ago, the coal company determined to make the issue with its men and work its mines by improved processes, let it cost what it might. . . . The first move was to empty the mines. For this purpose, a reduction was ordered of from 70 to 60 cents a ton for mining. The result was as anticipated. The miners, drivers, and every body else went out on strike. . . . The mines cleared, the company at

once put in the new machinery and set it safe in position before the
move was understood by the strikers. The green men were taken to the
mines on special trains, guarded by Pinkerton police armed with Win-
chester rifles.[13]

The union miners held out for nine months before being forced back to
work by economic necessity. On their return to the mines, union loyalists
were forced to sign yellow dog contracts, in which they agreed not to
participate in union activity while in the company's employment.

In the wake of the Hocking Valley lockout, mechanization of coal
undercutting progressed rapidly. Within five years, 12.9 percent of all
Ohio coal was mechanically cut, and within twenty years, over two-
thirds of the state's total underground production was undercut by
machines. In 1905 it was the most highly mechanized state in the nation,
with a ratio of mechanical undercutting twice the national average.[14]
The union-busting strategy worked well for operators in the Hocking
Valley. And while it may have been the first, it was certainly not the last
time this particular strategy was used by coal operators to break the
control that miners possessed through their local unions.

How was it possible for the Hocking Valley coal operators to bring in
unskilled men as strikebreakers and expect them to take over the jobs of
skilled miners? If it were true that it took years for a miner to learn how to
mine coal in a "practical and workman-like manner," how was it possible
for labor agents to round up men off of the street corners of the large urban
areas and put them to work mining coal? Part of the answer lies in the
cutting machine itself. To the extent that this machine did in fact reduce
the skill requirements for the job, it was possible to hire those with less
skill at mining. This, however, was not a major consideration. More
importantly, the answer must lie in the questionable manner in which
coal probably was mined by the strikebreakers.

Much of the skill of the experienced miner lay in his ability to mine
coal safely. His experience taught him how to listen for the roof "working," and his years working at the face taught him where to place his
shots, how much powder to use for each shot, and where to place his
timbers. Proof does not exist, but it is quite likely that the greenhorns
used as strikebreakers in the coalfields did not mine coal safely and
endangered their lives in the process. And it is quite possible that they did
not mine the coal very efficiently. Perhaps that was not important to the
operators, if the miners' union could be broken. When blacks were

imported from cities in the South to take the jobs of striking miners in southern Illinois, the state Bureau of Labor reported that it was done "in the belief that their ignorance of organization, and habits of submission, will compensate for the inferiority of their work."[15]

The Formation of a National Union

The Hocking Valley experience taught miners an important lesson. Local unions and even groups of locals in isolated coal fields could not survive a frontal attack by a determined management. Miners needed a national organization to strengthen their bargaining power. Meeting in September 1885, delegates from local unions in seven coal-producing states, many of whom had been keeping in touch by mail, met in Pittsburgh and formed a new association for mutual aid during economic strikes, for joint political action, and for education of miners across the coalfields. They called the new organization the National Federation of Miners and Mine Laborers, and in the preamble to their new constitution the miners carefully described the reasons for joining together. They recognized that local and state organizations had done "much toward ameliorating the condition of our craft in the past," but conditions were rapidly changing. "Our wages are no longer regulated by our skill as workmen, nor by the value of the products of our labor . . . and our standard of workmanship is fast being lowered," the preamble pointed out. Continuing, it read:

> We know this to our sorrow. Hence, while approving of local organiza-
> tions, whether secret or open in character, we are convinced that by
> federating under one general head our powers for good would be in-
> creased and a speedy betterment of our common condition follow. In a
> federation of all lodges and branches of miners' unions lies our only
> hope. Single handed we can do nothing, but federated there is no
> power of wrong that we may not openly defy. The cry of distress which
> arises from members of our craft in all sections of the country demands
> us to act, and act at once. Then, let us organize and agitate for liberty
> and living mining rates and for justice to our craft.[16]

The need for a federation of miners also grew out of the mid-nineteenth century expansion of transportation facilities, which had created a truly national market for coal. Railroads opened the Chicago market, for example, to West Virginia and Ohio coal, whereas in an earlier time Illinois and Indiana operators dominated this market. Intense price competition followed this development of national coal markets, with the result that coal prices were forced down toward the cost of production. In turn, this market pressure on prices forced coal operators to seek ways to keep their costs of production as low as possible or to find ways to increase the productivity of their miners.[17] These impacts of a national market on local working conditions prompted the founders of the National Federation of Miners to say in their preamble that, while local and district unions had been able in the past to improve conditions for miners, they were no longer capable of doing so. Theirs was a call for a national union to meet the needs of miners faced with a national coal market. "It is the object of this federated movement to establish a system of mining rates, placing all competitors upon a basis of equality throughout the different market districts," one federation official noted.[18]

Machinery in the mines was not considered a central issue for this early union of miners, although the national officers recognized it as a problem requiring "serious attention." Job losses as machines replaced men and the frequent lowering of wages upon the introduction of cutting machines were recognized as adverse impacts of mechanization. "The introduction of machines into our mines has greatly increased . . . and as a result many of our miners have been thrown out of employment. The prices paid in many places where machines have been introduced have seriously affected the prices on pick mining," wrote Chris Evans, executive secretary of the federation.[19] However, the federation did not adopt any particular bargaining policy, urging instead that the union's executive board "collect such information as will enable us to deal intelligently upon these questions when presented."[20]

In 1886, the coal operators in the Central Competitive Field (Illinois, Indiana, Ohio, and Pennsylvania) were invited by the union to attend a joint conference for the purpose of discussing conditions in the industry and of finding ways to stabilize coal markets. The union's goal was a straightforward one, to eliminate from competition the single largest cost factor—wages—by obtaining an agreement from operators across the country to establish and abide by a standard wage level. At first the operators were reluctant to attend such a conference, but after several attempts by the union at organizing such a meeting, a sizable number of operators did come together. Out of the deliberations at this joint conference came an agreement for a uniform scale of tonnage rates for the four states for a period of one year. The National Federation is credited with having negotiated the first interstate collective bargaining agreement in the coal industry. Success was short-lived. The northern Illinois operators found that they could not pay the agreed scale and still remain competitive with the southern Illinois operators who, by virtue of thicker coal seams, were better able to mechanize and to thereby mine coal at lower cost. The northern Illinois group pulled out of the agreement and, for nearly the same reasons, were soon followed by the Indiana operators. By 1889, the Ohio and Pennsylvania operators also broke the agreement, so that the joint conference program collapsed.

The Birth of the UMWA

The breakup of the joint conference came at a time when the National Federation was confronted with a threat to its jurisdiction and membership by the increasingly popular Knights of Labor.[21] Officials of the two organizations soon realized that union rivalry worked in the operators' interest and was destructive of the welfare of miners. In January 1890, the two unions effected a reconciliation and merger, creating the United Mine Workers of America. The constitution adopted at the time of the merger established the objectives of the UMWA as follows: (1) to secure earnings "fully compatible with the danger of our calling and the labor performed," (2) to establish a system of payment in "lawful" money, (3) to establish safe mining practices, (4) to demand the eight-hour day, (5) to provide education for miners' children, (6) to seek favorable legislation for the protection of miners' health and welfare, and (8) "to use all honorable means to maintain peace between ourselves and employers; adjusting all differences, as far as possible, by arbitration and conciliation, that strikes may become unnecessary."[22]

To promote these objectives, the constitution established a union structure that gave the national union jurisdiction over all its affiliated bodies. A national convention of the union was empowered as the supreme governing body of the union; between conventions, an executive board consisting of the president, vice-president, secretary-treasurer, and four other elected officials was given the authority to establish policy and run the affairs of the union. The 1890 founding convention of the UMWA also set a dues structure, established a defense fund for the support of union members engaging in an approved or "authorized" strike, agreed to a wage scale, which the union would seek to incorporate into contracts with coal operators, and finally, elected John Rae, a former Knights of Labor official, as president.

Under the structure of the UMWA, miners belonged to local unions, one of which was chartered at each mine site, and the locals were grouped into district unions and subdistrict organizations. An effort was made to define subdistricts by the boundaries of particular coalfields, that is, by geographical areas with similar geological characteristics; district union jurisdictions tended to conform to state boundaries. Pennsylvania, with three district unions for the soft-coal industry and one anthracite district union, was an exception to this practice. Much of the history of the UMWA in its formative years was bound up with histories of the district unions, especially the strongly organized districts of Ohio (District 6), western Pennsylvania (District 5), Illinois (District 12), and Indiana (District 11). Each district union was an autonomous unit, with the right to elect its own officials, to hold its own conventions, to establish policies affecting its members, and to negotiate district labor agreements.

The industry's basic collective bargaining structure evolved soon after the formation of the new organization and paralleled this union structure. Wage scales and basic standards were established by an interstate agreement, while separate district and subdistrict agreements were negotiated to cover the wide variations among the coalfields in mining methods, work rules, and geological characteristics of coal deposits. In some situations, where special physical conditions and local practices dictated, supplemental agreements were negotiated at individual mines. This many-tiered structure continued to characterize collective bargaining in the industry until the 1930s when bargaining authority shifted from the local and district unions to the national union.

During the 1890s, the UMWA tried to reestablish an interstate framework for bargaining by making several attempts to revive the joint conference idea begun in 1886. Even though they met with the new union in 1891 and 1892, operators in the Central Competitive Field (CCF) were reluctant to participate in bargaining at this level. Hope for collective bargaining of any kind waned in 1893 as a national depression intensified cutthroat price competition, forced a reduction in wages, and increased the jobless rate among miners. The UMWA's national executive board decided in 1894 to try to remedy the problems of excess supply of coal and low prices by calling a "general suspension" to reduce coal stockpiles. Even though the union had only 13,000 members at the time, labor conditions were so bad that 125,000 miners walked off their jobs in response to the call. The strike lasted for eight weeks and was successful in forcing a number of CCF operators to the bargaining table, where a wage scale was adopted. This agreement soon collapsed, however, because a continuation of depressed conditions in the industry made it impossible for the operators to pay the scale and stay in business.

By 1897, wages and working conditions throughout the coalfields had deteriorated so much that union officers announced another industrywide strike. The UMWA *Journal* explained that the basic cause of the shutdown was "the constant reduction in wages through several years, which had brought the miners and their families to the verge of starvation."[23] Tonnage rates, cut by as much as 40 percent over the previous four years, and shortened workweeks had made miners truly desperate for some remedy to the situation. At the time of the call for a strike, the UMWA claimed only 9,700 members, but within days at least 150,000 miners had walked off their jobs to support the strike. Nearly 70 percent of the coal production in Pennsylvania, West Virginia, Ohio, Indiana, and Illinois was interrupted by the stoppage, and the enthusiasm among the miners in these states was so high, it prompted one observer to say that "a new solidarity seems to have been born."[24] The strike lasted twelve weeks and ended in victory for the miners when the operators in the Central Competitive Field agreed to meet with the union to negotiate a uniform wage scale.[25]

A joint conference of operators and union representatives was held in Chicago in January 1898, at which time agreement was reached on an interstate scale of mining rates, or "prices" as they were referred to at the time. Several other issues were settled at the same time, most notably the establishment of an eight-hour-day, six-day-week schedule for all mining operations. While this concession by the operators was hailed as victory by the union leadership, it is questionable whether the rank-and-file miner viewed it as such. Mine workers who were paid by the day, called company men, may have welcomed the reduction in hours, but the miner who loaded coal probably saw the eight-hour day as a limitation on his freedom.[26]

This interstate, or joint, agreement was recognized at the time as a turning point in the industry's history and was referred to as a movement. In the years that followed, joint wage conferences were held and contracts signed each year until 1912, when negotiations were put on a two-year schedule. The two-year contract remained the practice until 1924, when a three-year agreement was signed. It is not particularly important to trace the collective bargaining gains and losses during the period of the joint-scale movement—that is, from 1898 to the early 1920s—but it is necessary to explain some of the union policies and practices that were emerging at this time, since they had a direct bearing on the introduction of machinery into the mines.

With roots in the earlier miners' unions, the principle of the inviolability of the contract became firmly established by UMWA leadership during this early period. In exchange for improved wages and working conditions, union leaders promised the operators continuity of operations during the term of the agreement, and for many of them, maintaining the sanctity of that promise sometimes became a moral issue. Union leaders agreed, via the bargain, not to call a strike or to sanction one should it occur in violation of the joint agreement.[27] The first explicit joint statement of policy concerning the inviolability of the contract was made at the 1902 scale conference: "We recognize the sacredness and binding nature of contracts and agreements thus entered into, and are pledged in honor to keep inviolate such contracts. . . . Such contracts or agreements having been entered into, we consider ourselves severally and collectively bound in honor to carry them out in good faith in letter and in spirit, and are so pledged to use our influence and authority to enforce these contracts and agreements, the more so since they rest in the main upon mutual confidence as their basis."[28]

So strongly did the UMWA honor this principle that UMWA President John Mitchell refused to support a proposed sympathy strike of soft-coal miners during the 1902 anthracite strike on the grounds that the bituminous agreement was still in effect and could not be broken. He told a special miners convention that "a disregard of the sacredness of contracts strikes at the very vitals of organized labor."[29] While it is true there were other considerations involved, Mitchell made it quite clear that he intended to stand by the contract.[30] He told the soft-coal miners, "we believe our interests in the community of which we are a part and our obligations to the operators, with whom we have agreements, require that we shall not inaugurate a general suspension of work in the coal trade. *They may destroy our union but they cannot make us violate our contracts.*"[31]

Development of a Formal Grievance Procedure

In the years between the first interstate agreement in 1898 to the mid-1920s, the UMWA leadership upheld the principle of the sacredness of the contract by not authorizing a single strike during the term of an existing agreement. Union officials frequently spoke of this record with pride.[32] Over the years, the national leaders were not, however, successful in promoting the idea of contract sanctity among the rank and file. Local and district strikes, common in the industry from a very early date, occurred frequently during the period of the joint-scale movement. Local strikes, referred to as "wildcat," "outlaw," "petty," or simply "unauthorized," were a continual embarassment to the UMWA in its interstate bargaining with the operators. And in an effort to reduce the incidence of local strikes, the union cooperated with management in developing a procedure for the peaceful settlement of local disputes.

The first grievance procedures appeared in district agreements before the turn of the century. For example, the Indiana district union negotiated a dispute settlement procedure in 1898 that contained a no-strike pledge: "It is further agreed that if any differences arise between the operators and the miners at any pit, a settlement shall be arrived at without stopping of work. If the parties immediately affected can not reach an adjustment between themselves, the question shall be referred to the president and secretary of the United Mine Workers of America representing district No. 11, and the president and secretary of the Coal Operators Association of the same district, whose action shall be final."[33] Grievance procedures very similar in form to the one currently in use in the coal industry were negotiated in other districts in the first few years of the new century, and arbitration was introduced as a final step in dispute settlement procedures in Pennsylvania as early as 1906.

By 1910, a highly formalized grievance procedure had evolved as an alternative to local direct action in the Central Competitive Field. Many disputes over rates of pay for dead work and yardage, distribution of turns, discipline and discharge of employees, dockage for loading dirty coal, and other locally specific issues were resolved through this procedure, the specific intent of which was "to obviate the necessity of independent action by either party." Disputed issues growing out of the introduction of cutting machines and other mechanical devices that affected local working conditions also were subject to the grievance procedure, making it a factor affecting the rate at which technological change could take place in the industry.

The Illinois state agreement, typical of those in effect in the Central Competitive Field, contained a procedure with six or seven steps, ending in final and binding third-party arbitration. In step one of the Illinois agreement, an aggrieved employee was directed to discuss his complaint with mine management; failing to obtain satisfactory resolution of the complaint, he would then ask the union pit committee to discuss the grievance with mine management. If these parties could not reach an agreement on the issue, the grievance moved upward to subdistrict union officials and a higher level of local mine management. Next, unresolved grievances were handled by district officials and representatives of the coal operators' association. If a grievance involved an issue of general applicability, a special commission of union and operator officials would be appointed to seek agreement. This commission took testimony, heard arguments on the merits of the grievance, and produced a written document specifying the settlement. If the commission members could not come to an agreement, they tried to agree in writing on the essential facts of the case and the reasons for their failure to settle. This document was then submitted to the "joint executive board," composed of the executive boards of the district union and the coal operators' association. Finally, if the joint executive board failed to reach agreement, the grievance would be submitted to an arbitration board (assuming both sides agreed to arbitrate).[34]

The Pit Committee and the Local Union

This grievance procedure worked well at settling a large number of disputes, yet local work stoppages continued to be a "vexatious" problem for UMWA leaders, who wanted to maintain the integrity of the contract, and for operators, who needed continuity of production.[35] Early in the joint-scale movement, the two sides tried to find ways to limit the control that miners exercised through the strike weapon and to limit the power of the local union grievance committee through which the collective voice of miners was expressed. The mine committee, called the pit committee, is as old as the industry itself and was found in all union mines as well as many nonunion mines. Elected by the mine workers at each mine and paid out of local union dues for time spent on workers' concerns, the pit committee had far-reaching power to affect the day-to-day operation of the mine.

Pit committees kept waiting lists of local miners looking for work and expected the mine foreman to hire from that list. In the days before union dues were checked off by the employer, the pit committee would stand at the mine mouth on days when dues were to be paid and refuse entrance to miners who did not pay their dues. Pit committeemen frequently intervened in the assignment of workplaces and challenged prices established by the mine foremen for dead work and yardage. At the turn of the century in some Illinois mines, the pit committee had the power to sanction or deny the scheduling of overtime work. And in matters pertaining to mine safety, the pit committee was a protector of the workers' interests. For example, if an operator wished to change the type of blasting powder used in his mine, he had to file with the pit committee a written notice of his desire to do so and state the reasons supporting the change. To validate its control, local pit committees frequently called for a work stoppage, a call traditionally answered without hesitation.[36]

With the introduction of the undercutting machine, the pit committee helped formulate local work rules governing the use of the machine and then enforced these rules. In a report by the U.S. Commissioner of Labor, operators complained bitterly about work rules that reduced the productivity of machinery they had put to work in their mines.[37] Some rules limited the number of loaders working with a machine, and others limited the number of runs a machine could make in each shift of work. These local union restrictions of output ran afoul of state and national UMWA policies, however, so a conflict often arose between the rank and file of the union and the leadership of the union. An Illinois district union official made an interesting observation in this connection: "The union was prepared to do anything possible to remedy the 16-run rule of the machine runners, if it could have secured any evidence that the rule was made by the (local) union. . . . The rank and file of the union, knowing their officers to be opposed to restriction, kept their restrictive agreements to themselves and concealed them . . . from the State union officials."[38]

Local unions and occasionally subdistrict unions retarded the rate at which machinery was installed by refusing to negotiate a wage scale that would make the new technology profitable. Each time a cutting machine was sent into a mine, a new tonnage rate had to be negotiated for the mine workers who loaded the coal after the machine. A local union could block the use of machinery altogether if the parties could not agree on this "machine differential."[39] Or, if the machine differential were not set low enough the operator would find that the rate of return on his investment would be insufficient to justify its continued use. The numerous complaints of operators found in the Commissioner of Labor's report are evidence that this was a common occurrence at the turn of the century.

No mention was made of the pit committee in the first interstate agreement negotiated in 1898. By 1901, however, operators began insisting on very specific regulations restraining the power of these local committees. Employers were successful in persuading UMWA negotiators to agree to the insertion of the following paragraph:

> The pit committee in the discharge of its duties shall under no circumstances go around the mine for any purpose whatever, unless called upon by the pit boss or by a miner or company man who may have a grievance that he cannot settle with the boss, and as its duties are confined to the adjustment of any such grievances it is understood that its members shall not draw any compensation except while actively engaged in the discharge of its duties.[40]

The published proceedings of the joint convention, as interstate negotiating sessions were called at this time, shows how strongly the operators felt about the control exercised by the pit committee and the urgency of their desire to limit that control.[41] One operator told the convention that "in some cases the pit committee has practically taken charge of the mine. . . . We have no desire to limit the legitimate duties of the pit committee, but in many cases they have exceeded their legitimate powers, and we want to prevent that sort of thing in the future." Another expressed the opinion that "in nearly every case the pit committees have gone beyond their bounds. I believe you cannot get anything too specific in there to get your pit committee down to business." In discussing this problem, the operators complained frequently of the "radicalism" of the pit committee, but they did not mean this in any political sense of the term. A radical pit committee was one that trespassed on what management thought of as its prerogatives. "There is not a miner or an operator in this room," one operator claimed at the 1901 convention, "that does not know that there are certain pit committees in various localities in the state who deem it their business to run everything."

In following years, further limitations were placed on local pit committees by interstate agreements and also by district agreements. In 1904, a provision in the coal agreements specified that the committee at each mine would consist of no more than three members. And constraint was placed on the pit committee by a clause that provided for the removal of any committee member who violated the contract: "Any pit committeeman who shall attempt to execute any local rule or proceeding in conflict with any provision of this contract shall be forthwith deposed as committeeman."[42] After the turn of the century, operators obtained further protection against the pit committee and local control by the insertion of a clause in a few contracts stating that the right to hire and discharge and the direction of the working force were management's responsibilities. This precursor to the modern management's rights clause meant that the pit committees could no longer see to it that union supporters found jobs in the mines.

These limitations on the traditional rights of the pit committee suggest that the effectiveness of the UMWA leadership in bargaining with the industry depended not just on verbal commitment paid to the sanctity of the contract, but, more importantly, on its willingness to cooperate in weakening local control. Further evidence of this cooperation was the UMWA's attempts to discipline local unions, pit committees, and rank-and-file miners who caused strikes in violation of the agreement. In 1906 in Illinois, the district union agreed to contractual language that fines would be imposed on "any employee or employees guilty of throwing a mine idle or of materially reducing the output of a mine."[43] Further, the UMWA on occasion used its constitutional authority to revoke the charter of striking local unions that refused back-to-work orders from union officials.[44] Some district unions even suspended from membership individuals who "willfully threw the mine idle."[45]

In their struggle to unite, coal miners faced a contradiction imposed on them by the competitive nature of the coal industry. It was clear to them at an early date, when coal markets became national in scope, that they needed a strong, centralized organization that could negotiate interstate agreements, providing them with a living wage. At the same time, it was important for miners to maintain the strength of their local unions and their representatives on the pit committees to protect their daily working conditions and preserve the "miners' freedoms." The history of the United Mine Workers is better understood if this contradiction is kept in mind. Certainly, the union's mechanization policies were affected by it.

Before closing this chapter on the origins of the miners union, one additional factor should be mentioned that helps explain the context within which the union's history evolved after the turn of the century. The operators who signed the 1898 Central Competitive Field agreement fully expected the UMWA to extend organization to the unorganized coalfields where lower wages and prices gave nonunion mine owners a competitive advantage. Under constant pressure from these operators, the UMWA spent large sums of money and directed much of its energies in its early years to union organizing campaigns. However, the economic advantage to remaining nonunion was so compelling for many operators that they made every effort to keep their mines union free. As a result, violent confrontations between mine workers and mine owners over the issue of union recognition occurred frequently throughout the unorganized fields from the late 1890s to the mid-1930s. While the UMWA was committed to upholding negotiated contracts and to peaceful settlement of issues arising under these contracts, the union found it necessary to engage in open economic warfare, if not outright armed conflict, to establish itself in some sections of the industry.

CHAPTER 6

The Union and Mechanization

THE GROWTH of coal output in the last half of the last century and for the first twenty years of this century was quite phenomenal. Spurred by the steel industry's demand for coking coal and the increasing use of this mineral in the nation's coal-fired steam boilers, production of bituminous coal increased from 43 million tons in 1880, to 212 million at the turn of the century, then to 569 million tons in 1920. Employment in underground coal mining paralleled this output expansion, as the number of coal mine workers increased from 100,207 in 1880, to 304,375 in 1900, and 639,547 in 1920.[1] This growth was not, however, on a straight-line trend. Coal sales were quite sensitive to shifts in the general level of economic activity, so that during these early years the industry experienced several major downturns in output and employment. World War I and immediate postwar years saw coal demand reach unprecedented levels, with employment reaching an all-time high of 704,793 in 1923.[2]

Soon after this peak in demand and employment was reached, coal markets began to shrink as the nation shifted from wartime production to peacetime. At about the same time, coal began to feel the impact of the growth in demand for substitute fuels such as oil, natural gas, and hydroelectric power. Technological improvements in the burning of coal also began to reduce the nation's overall demand for coal during the mid-1920s. As these factors were taking their toll, the coal industry was dealt a final blow when the nation's economy slipped into the Great Depression of the 1930s. By 1932, employment and production were pushed down to a level not seen in the industry for thirty years. It was not until the early 1940s that the industry finally recovered. Thus, from the

126

early 1920s to the outbreak of World War II, the coal industry was in an almost chronic economic depression.

The United Mine Workers' policies and programs relating to the question of mechanization of mining and, more specifically, the question of the use of the loading machine evolved within, and was shaped by, these economic realities. In the growth period before and during World War I, union leaders were not so much fearful of the threat to jobs posed by machinery as they were concerned with establishing credibility with the coal mine owners and with the public. It seems that from the beginning of the union, the national leadership feared that any hesitancy they might show about the use of machinery in the mines would be interpreted as standing in the way of progress. Later, when the industry's economic fortunes turned downward, the machinery issue became central to the industry's very survival. In this and the chapters to follow, the history of the union's involvement in the mechanization of mining is reviewed, but it is important to remember that the job control that the miners enjoyed and the local union control of an earlier period helped shape that history in very fundamental ways.

The 1917 Washington Agreement

On April 1, 1916, the UMWA and the coal operators in the Central Competitive Field signed a two-year agreement that provided for a three-cent-per-ton increase for mining coal, universal adoption of a run-of-the-mine payment system, a 5 percent increase in wages for day labor, and the elimination of certain geographical wage differentials. Acceptance of the mine-run system marked the end of a long struggle by the miners to eliminate the abuses inherent in the practice of calculating tonnage payments on the product after it had passed across a sifting screen.[3] The victory for the miners, however, may have resulted more from the changing technology of coal utilization than from their own bargaining power. Coal-fired boilers then being developed would burn the smaller sizes of coal, thus providing a market for what had formerly been a waste product. (This development also eliminated the need to screen the coal.)

Following the signing of the 1916 joint-scale agreement, the full effect of the war in Europe was felt in the U.S. economy. The cost of living rose rapidly, and because of wartime demand, coal prices advanced substantially. For the miners, wartime meant more opportunity for employment, but their higher incomes were quickly absorbed by higher consumer prices. The operators, on the other hand, were able to realize increasing profits but were soon faced with labor shortages, especially as the war had effectively cut off immigration. The wartime conditions therefore created a situation in which nonunion operators were bidding for labor by offering special bonuses and other inducements while the miners with a union contract were becoming increasingly dissatisfied with frozen wages. Union miners began a series of wildcat strikes to force their employers to pay the bonuses that nonunion operators were paying, thus threatening the joint contracts between the operators and the UMWA.[4]

This pressure from the ranks forced union officials to call for a meeting with the operators, a meeting that was held in April 1917. The operators agreed to pay an increase of $0.10 a ton to coal loaders, but the concession failed to bring stability to the industry. Wartime labor shortages became more acute and living costs continued to increase, with the result that both miners and operators ignored their contractual obligations. At this point, under the Lever Act, the federal government intervened by fixing the price of coal at $2.00 a ton and by arranging a meeting in Washington of the operators and miners under the auspices of the wartime Fuel Administration. The result of this meeting was an agreement dated October 6, 1917, providing for a $0.10 per-ton advance for miners and $1.40 per day for day labor. Most important for this discussion of the history of the union's policies relating to mechanization was the automatic penalty clause inserted in this Washington agreement.[5]

The penalty clause was not new to collective bargaining in the coal industry for, as noted earlier, it had been incorporated in some district agreements prior to 1917. For the first time, however, it became part of the Central Competitive Field agreement, to which agreements in other fields were tied.[6] Significant also was the fact that the Washington agreement was in reality a tripartite document, with the U.S. Fuel Administration being the third party, a development that put the federal government squarely in the middle of a labor-management conflict in the industry for the first time. With the insertion of the penalty clause, the federal government became party to a new form of industrial discipline. The first paragraph of the Washington agreement left little doubt of the government's interest in a settlement. "The following agreement," it read, "is entered into with the hope and belief that the advance in wages will result in an increased production of coal and the abolition of local strikes."[7]

Typical of the automatic penalty clauses inserted into district agreements was the one found in the Colorado agreement, stating that any union officer or member who caused a mine to be shut down over any dispute "shall have deducted from his earnings the sum of One Dollar ($1.00) per day for each day or part of a day they remain idle."[8] In the Illinois agreement, the employer was to collect the fines by deductions from the miners pay envelopes and turn them over to the Red Cross. The Washington agreement imposed a fine on any employer who failed, in the event of a strike, to collect the money from his employees. Some district agreements provided a penalty for any employer who locked out his miners over a local dispute, but this penalty was not mandated by the Washington agreement. It was clear from these agreements that an effort was being made to restrain local unions of miners when they expressed themselves in opposition to the policies of the national union.

It was not long before miners began to show their resentment of the punitive actions permitted against them. In January 1918, the penalty clause became a central issue in the Illinois district election. A month later, debate over the clause lasted more than two days at the International Convention. Passive acceptance of the penalty clause as a temporary wartime measure turned to open hostility by the rank and file at the war's end. And in August 1919, the penalty clause provoked a month-long wildcat strike throughout Illinois.[9] Further, revocation of the provision was one of thirteen demands by miners in a nationwide strike in the fall of 1919. Opposition continued at many levels within the union, but the penalty clause became an accepted part of national union collective bargaining policy in the years to follow and remained so for thirty years, until it was removed from the national agreement in the early 1940s.[10] It was, however, more symbolic of a union-management effort to discipline the work force rather than an effective means for curbing the right of miners to strike.

The national trade journal, *Coal Age,* reported that the first time the penalty clause was used in Illinois it created hard feelings among the miners. An employer in central Illinois assessed his miners the prescribed penalty after they walked off their jobs in protest of a change in work practices. This employer had announced a new checkout system at his mine, whereby a miner was required to hang his identifiation card in the office on leaving the mine. The miners opposed the practice because it would enable the company to determine when they left the mine and thereby make it more difficult to leave work early. They walked off their jobs but soon returned under protest, at which time the employer announced that they would be fined. The journal reported that "it is certain that the men will resist the infliction of the automatic penalty. They are laying the foundation for such resistance now by claiming that instead of striking they were locked out by the company on their refusal to comply with the new order."[11] Employers soon learned that any attempt on their part to collect the fines prescribed for a work stoppage would result in another work stoppage. Local control, therefore, rendered the penalty clause ineffective.

The 1920 Bituminous Coal Commission

A strike in October 1919 by 425,000 miners—the industry's largest to that date—halted approximately 75 percent of the nation's soft-coal production. The miners were demanding a substantial wage increase to protect them from skyrocketing consumer goods prices that had occurred in the two-year period since the Washington agreement. At issue also were demands by the miners for a shorter workweek, time-and-a-half payment for overtime for day men, and the elimination of the wartime practice of working the mines on a double shift. These three demands involved a reduction in hours, which, the miners argued, would help solve the unemployment problem they were experiencing as a result of the cessation of hostilities in Europe and the cutback in demand for coal. The miners also demanded abolition of the automatic penalty clause. They had assumed, from what the national union officers told them, that the penalty clause was a temporary measure.[12]

These demands had been formulated by delegates to the union's national convention in September, and when presented to the operators' association they were immediately rejected as being "extravagantly excessive and impossible of acceptance." Before the strike date of November 1, 1919, the secretary of Labor engaged John L. Lewis, acting president of the union,[13] and Thomas Brewster, president of the Coal Operators Association, in a conciliation session hoping to find a way to avoid a nationwide coal strike. When this meeting failed to bring about an amicable settlement, President Woodrow Wilson issued a public statement in which he characterized the proposed strike as a grave and legal wrong against the government and the people of the United States.

Using the wartime Lever Act, which outlawed any strike activity threatening both intrastate and interstate commerce, Wilson instructed the attorney general to obtain an injunction against a coal strike. Under pressure from the courts, from the president and from Congress, the union leaders called off the strike on November 11. But the miners refused the back-to-work order from their president and kept the mines closed. The unauthorized work stoppage continued until mid-December and ended only when the government moved to institute contempt proceedings against certain miners and district officials. The miners also were influenced to return to work by President Wilson's promise to appoint a commission to study the miners' demands and to make recommendations on the demands.[14] Mine workers clearly controlled the industry at this point. But they would not defy the courts, on the one hand, and they believed, on the other, they would get White House support if the public understood the strike issues.

Within a week after the strike ended, the president appointed a commission consisting of H. W. Robinson, Rembrandt Peale, and John White and charged them to investigate all of the issues involved in the strike and the general economic problems of the industry. Hearings were held and a report submitted on March 10, 1920. Actually, two reports emerged from the commission, a majority report signed by Robinson and Peale and a dissenting report by former UMWA president John White that reflected the union's position. White offered a strong justification for the miners' wage demands and supported the cause of shorter hours. He was, however, silent on the demand for elimination of the penalty clause. And when Peale, speaking for the operators, argued that the officers of the international union should be "required to assume responsibility for enforcing the terms" of their contracts in the various districts, White agreed. He said, "We can see no logical reason why a greater responsibility should not be exercised by the miners' international organization over the subordinate branches."[15]

The Commission's Recommendations on Mechanization

The question of mechanization was brought before the commission by the operators, who presented a list of counterclaims to the miners' strike demands. In item six of a seven-point program,[16] the operators asked:

> 6. That the commission in its award provide for the introduction of devices or machinery which may serve to reduce the cost of coal and consequently the cost to the public for which there is no scale of wages in the then-existing contract.

At this late date, more than forty years after undercutting machines were first introduced, the operators were still faced with opposition by miners to the use of undercutting machines. By 1920, 60.7 percent of all coal was undercut mechanically, (see appendix table A), but the refusal of locals and subdistricts to negotiate machine rates continued to be such an obstacle that the mine owners sought support from this presidential tribunal. The majority report cited it as a serious problem: "It is recognized by the commission that the introduction of machinery and devices can be prevented by the mine workers by failure to agree upon the rates, terms, and conditions under which the machinery and devices are to be used." The majority report then made lengthy recommendations pertaining to the mechanization question, as follows:

> 4. That pending the joint district agreement between the miners and operators covering a fair schedule of rates for piecework or tonnage operation of any new device or machinery, the right of the operator to introduce and operate any such new device or machinery shall not be questioned, and his selection of such men as he may desire to conduct tests with or operate such device or machinery shall not be in any way interfered with or obstructed by the miners or their representatives, provided the wages offered are at least equal to the established scale rates for similar labor.
>
> The operator shall be privileged to pay in excess of the established scale rates of pay without such excess pay being considered as establishing a permanent condition for the operation of said device or machine.
>
> After the device or machine shall have passed the experimental stage and is in shape to be introduced as a regular component part of the production of coal, then for the purpose of determining a permanent scale of rates (such rates to continue until the joint scale conference above referred to fixes a scale) for operating such device or machine, the mine workers may have a representative present for a reasonable time to witness its operation, after which a schedule of rates

shall be determined by mutual agreement, which scale shall be concluded within 60 days after a fair test has been made.

The test will disclose the labor-saving in the cost of producing coal, out of which labor-saving the mine worker shall receive the equivalent of the contract rates for the class of work displaced, plus a fair proportion of the labor-saving effected.

In like manner new or untried systems of mining; for instance, long wall, retreating long wall, or the panel system may be introduced by the operator for the purpose of conservation, increasing production, the lessening of cost, or in the interest of safety without his right to make such change being abridged: Provided, however, that for this class of work the mine worker shall in the same manner receive the equivalent of the contract rates for the class of work displaced, plus a fair proportion of the labor-saving effected.[17]

A close reading of this statement, to which the operators' representative concurred, reveals that the mine owners may not have been as much concerned with the cutting machine as they were with entirely new types of mining machinery and mining systems. It will be remembered that developmental work on mechanical loading machines had been going on in the years immediately prior to the war and continued, notably at the Jeffrey Company, during the war. And at the time the commission was holding its hearings, it was no secret that the Pittsburgh Coal Company, the nation's largest, was having success with four Joy loading machines, which had been installed in one of its mines on an experimental basis.[18] The statement did not specify any particular type of mining equipment but referred simply to a "device or machine." A detailed plan was proposed, however, for establishing wage rates for operators of new machinery. It is interesting to note that the commission proposed a floor under wages so that mine workers affected by new machinery would receive "the equivalent of the contract rates for the class of work displaced." Although the amount was not specified, the operators also agreed in principle that the mine workers on new machinery should receive "a fair proportion of the labor-saving effected." Since the operators proposed a parallel set of principles in the event of the introduction of new mining systems such as long-wall mining, it seems quite clear that the stage was being set in anticipation of major technological developments in the industry.

The union's position, as expressed in John White's minority report, was to reject outright the extended discussion on the issue in the majority report and to propose quite briefly the following substitute:

> Labor-saving machinery: The operators have the right to install labor-saving machinery at any time, and such machine work not now covered by this agreement shall be governed by such scale as the miners' and operators' representatives may determine.[19]

If this was the union's policy toward mechanization, it was little more than a policy of expediency, to allow the problems associated with mechanization to be solved at the local and district levels. The policy—or nonpolicy—did reflect the reality of local control and the reality of the internal structure of the union, which at that time had not been sufficiently centralized to weaken the authority of its subordinate units and the power of the rank and file.

In his report, White reiterated the UMWA's position on the machine question, namely that "the United Mine Workers have always been favorable to and have never opposed the introduction of machinery or labor-saving machinery in the operation of the mines."[20] He went on to cite the increase in the number of machines in unionized territory and then tried to demonstrate the savings operators had realized upon installing machinery. In all cases, he was referring to the cutting machine and seems quite oblivious to the fact that the operators, as suggested in the majority report, had something else in mind. Nor did he respond to the operators' suggestion that when new machinery is installed a union representative would be permitted for a "reasonable time to witness its operation," so that a scale could be negotiated. Why the union failed at this point even to consider a constructive policy toward mechanization is not known. It may have been that White was unaware of the potential threat to jobs and working conditions of the new loading machines, or it may have been, as suggested above, that a hands-off policy was the only realistic one the international union officers could take at that particular time.

When the Bituminous Coal Commission reported its findings in March 1920, it awarded twenty-four-cent advance in scale to both pick miners and to those who loaded after an undercutting machine. A dollar-a-day advance was recommended for day workers, and when these awards were later incorporated into the Central Competitive Field and outlying districts agreements, miners wages were at record high levels.

The central Pennsylvania wage agreement, for example, established the
following basic rates:[21]

Per Ton Scale

Pick mining	$1.14
Machine loading	$0.77

Inside Day-Wage Scale

Motorman	$6.10
Spragger	$6.00
Tracklayer	$6.00
Tracklayer helper	$5.77
Timberman	$6.00
Timberman helper	$5.77
Inside day laborer	$5.77

It is somewhat confusing for this labor agreement to specify a "machine
loading," rate, because it did not mean that a rate was established for a
loading machine operator. The term machine loader, in common use at
the time, was the designation for the miner who loaded coal that had
been undercut by a cutting machine.

The general terms and conditions of earlier agreements were carried
forward in the CCF agreement and in the various district and subdistrict
agreements made in 1920. The much-disliked penalty clause was carried
forward without change, and the traditional work rules negotiated over
the years were also to be found in the new agreement. Mechanization was
dealt with in mixed fashion; some agreements ignored it entirely, while
others made passing reference to the Bituminous Coal Commission's
report. The CCF and the Illinois agreements made no mention of the
issue, and the absence in the central Pennsylvania agreement of any
mention of it prompted one coal trade journal to note, quite propheti-
cally, "If anybody thinks up a thing that will dig and load the coal without
human energy they will have to start non-union, for there is no provision
for this sort of thing in the Central Pennsylvania contract."[22]

In a few other agreements, such as the one negotiated in northern
West Virginia, the contract introduced the mechanization issue by the
following language:

The majority report of the Bituminous Coal Commission regarding the
introduction of new machinery is adopted. The joint boards will agree
upon a commission for making any necessary tests.[23]

In Harlan County, Kentucky, the question was more directly addressed in that the contract gave the operators unilateral authority to instal machinery:

> The right of an operator to change from pick to machine basis, or from machine to pick basis, or change the type of machinery or appliance for any purpose, when he desires to do so, shall not be questioned. [24]

And in the George's Creek field of Maryland, the 1920 miners' contract contained this provision:

> The operators have the right to install labor-saving machinery at any time and such machine work not now covered by agreement shall be governed by such rates as the miners' and operators' representatives may determine. [25]

Within a few weeks after the signing of the 1920 agreements, opposition to its terms developed across the coalfields. The day men in particular were dissatisfied with the $1.00 increase they received and, later in the summer, led a series of unauthorized strikes in Illinois and Indiana. Under pressure from these strikes, the operators, who at the time were enjoying a temporary improvement in coal markets, met with the union and renegotiated day wages. The operators conceded an increase of an additional $1.50, bringing the daily rate up to $7.50. Ironically, the renegotiated contracts continued the penalty clause, although it had been largely ignored during the 1920 strike period. [26]

By the time these contracts expired in the spring of 1922, the operators were experiencing serious financial problems resulting from declining sales and falling coal prices. The industry's overexpansion in capacity was compounded by a national recession in 1922, and many operators let it be known in negotiations that they would demand wage reductions instead of agreeing to wage increases. To support their hardship claim, the operators published data showing that wages in some nonunion fields were as much as 56 percent lower than the union scale. And they claimed further that, if wage concessions were not made, union mines would lose markets for their product and miners would lose jobs. Other operators took an even harder line when they announced that they were absolutely unwilling to meet with the national union for any purpose but were willing to negotiate at the district level. Others said that they would bargain with their own employees on a mine-by-mine basis.[27] Miners were thus caught in a contradiction not of their own making. When it came to wages and other economic considerations, they needed a strong national union that could speak for them with one voice; they needed union solidarity to prevent wage reductions that would follow from local bargaining as operators played one local against another. At the same time, it was important to maintain the control that they had through their local unions and pit committees in order to protect basic job rights and working conditions.

The Union Responds

At the expiration of the old agreement on March 31, 1922, the union called a strike, which quickly spread throughout the coalfields. At issue was more than a question of money: some operators expressed the view that the time had come to eliminate the interstate bargaining structure in which they had participated for many years. The union, on the other hand, was committed to preserving interstate bargaining and to a "no-backward-step" wage policy. The strength of the commitment to these principles indicated that the strike would be a long one and would involve a sizable part of the industry. By the first of August, the U.S. Department of Labor estimated that 610,000 of the 795,000 mine workers employed before the strike had walked off their jobs.[28] Although both sides remained adamant in their positions, the public became increasingly concerned as the fall heating season approached with coal stockpiles severely reduced.

Several bills and resolutions were introduced in Congress calling for an investigation of the industry, compulsory arbitration was urged by some, and one U.S. senator proposed that the federal government take over and operate enough coal mines to prevent a coal shortage.[29] In mid-August, John L. Lewis extended an olive branch to the operators by inviting them to meet in Cleveland to discuss ways the strike might be settled. The operators agreed, and at the meeting the two sides were able to reach an interim agreement stipulating that, in exchange for a resumption of work, the operators would send representatives to a joint-scale committee meeting, at which a new interstate agreement would be negotiated. Following the Cleveland meeting, the strike was officially called off, and mine workers returned to work. It was not until the spring of 1923, however, that a new, one-year labor agreement was negotiated and ratified.

Local Agreements and Workers' Control

At the district, subdistrict, and local levels of the union, labor agreements also were negotiated for a one-year term. These agreements continued the tonnage rates and the basic wage of $7.50 a day that had been won in 1920. In addition, these agreements carried forward the negotiated work rules and other terms found in prior agreements. A year later, the 1923 agreements were extended without significant modification in what became known as the Jacksonville agreement. If little new appeared in the labor contracts at this time, they were no less important in the history of collective bargaining in the industry, because they marked the beginning of the end of an era for coal miners. The agreements of the hand-loading period came under increasing pressure as management moved to mechanize the mines, to increase discipline of the work force, and to extend management's rights and prerogatives. A review of two subdistrict agreements made in this period will establish an appreciation for why some miners a decade later lamented their loss of job rights and why they petitioned their union at that time to seek a restoration of the worker's control they once enjoyed.

The 1923 subdistrict agreement between the UMWA and the operators of the Hocking District of Ohio is a good example of a typical contract in the early period before the introduction of mechanical loading.[30] Mining rates were established at $1.12 per ton, run-of-the-mine, and the day rate for most inside jobs was $7.50. An eight-hour-day provision for day or company men was continued from earlier agreements, and eleven unpaid holidays were set aside. Under the terms of the agreement, the operators were bound to provide a "square turn" (i.e., an opportunity for each miner to receive an equal number of empty mine cars), while the miners agreed to mine clean coal and "produce their coal in such a way as not to increase the percentage of fine coal." Many other details were included in the contract, such as payment for slate removal, establishment of a standard room width, rules governing work on idle days, and the conditions under which call-in pay was to be awarded. The settlement of disputes was left to an informal arrangement under which a matter would be taken up by the mine superintendent and the mine

committee. There were no restrictions on the rights of the mine committee and, most interestingly, there was no provision for grievance arbitration. Although the standard no-strike and penalty clause inserted in all
coal labor agreements since 1917 was included in the Hocking Valley
contract, it is likely that grievances not settled in the informal procedure
in fact resulted in a local work stoppage.

The Hocking Valley contract is noteworthy as much for what was left
out of it as for what it contained. There was no discipline and discharge
provision nor was there any form of a management's rights or management prerogatives clause. It is clear from this contract that workers
exercised considerable control over the labor process, so much so that the
mechanization issue was not even mentioned. There was not even a
reference to the 1920 Bituminous Coal Commission report and its recommendations on technology. And all this was happening in the shadow
of the Columbus plant of the Jeffrey Manufacturing Company, the
world's largest producer of mining machinery.

In northern West Virginia, a coalfield organized only a few years
earlier, a labor agreement was signed in the spring of 1923 similar in many
ways to the Hocking District agreement, although it also differed in
important ways.[31] The similarities related to wages, holidays, and basic
work rules relating to hand-loading coal, while the differences suggested
new trends in labor-management relations in the industry. For example,
a well-defined grievance procedure contained an arbitration provision for
"a final and binding award." That this new procedure was intended to
serve as a substitute for local strikes is implied in the arbitration clause,
which stated that "in all cases all parties involved must continue at work
pending the investigation and adjustment" of grievances. And 'if any
employee . . . refuses to work because of any grievance . . . [he] will be
subject to dismissal without recourse at the option of the company." The
mine committee, which "shall consist of three men, all of whom shall be
American citizens," was responsible only for the adjustment of disputes
"that the mine boss and miner or miners have tried but are unable to
adjust." It was specified that the mine committee "shall have no other
authority or exercise any other control, nor in any way interfere with the
operation of the mine." There was the further admonition that "the mine
committee shall under no circumstances go around the mine for any cause
whatsoever unless called upon by the mine foreman or by the miner or
dayman who may have a grievance that he can not settle with the mine
boss, and then only to investigate that grievance with the parties in-

volved." Unlike the Ohio agreement, the northern West Virginia contract included an Irregular Work section aimed at disciplining individual miners who absented themselves from work for two days or more "unless through sickness."

For those who have worked under or who have knowledge of modern wage contracts in the coal industry, this 1923 agreement will sound quite familiar. One important difference, however, should be pointed out. There was no allowance, either implicit or explicit, for the introduction of new technology. New machinery might have been introduced under a management's rights clause, but none existed at that time. The closest thing to it was a provision under the Hire and Discharge section, which read as follows:

> The operator or his superintendent or mine foreman shall be respected in the management of the mine and the direction of the working force.[32]

Nor did the contract contain any reference to the use of machinery. Even the clause appearing in the 1920 Fairmont, West Virginia, agreement, which said, "The majority report of the Bituminous Coal Commission regarding the introduction of new machinery is adopted," was missing from the 1923 contract.

While it is purely conjecture, it is reasonable to conclude that the operators wanted to drop the commission's recommendations suggesting that wage rates for machinery operators be negotiated locally. After introducing a new arc-wall cutting machine in 1920, the Fairmont coal operators consulted with union officials to establish a wage scale, as recommended. But it took almost two years before agreement could be reached and the machinery installed.[33] The operators were convinced that their workers, acting through their local union representatives, were simply trying to stall or halt completely the use of labor-saving equipment. A summary of this situation by the U.S. Bureau of Labor Statistics at the time tended to support the operators contentions:

> The many obstacles interposed by the workers to the introduction of labor-saving machinery result indirectly in restriction of output. The United Mine Workers of America is on record as favoring the introduction of labor-saving machinery. Actually, however, when a labor-saving machine is to be introduced there are violent objections on the

part of the men. These objections express themselves very often in a demand for rates which, if paid, would eliminate all saving brought about by the new machine, thus causing a distinct loss to the extent of the additional investment. The Arc-Wall case is typical of the situation."[34]

The 1922 U.S. Coal Commission

Public concern with the coal industry went beyond the inconveniences brought about by the lengthy 1922 strike. There was growing evidence at this time that the industry was moving rapidly toward economic disaster. For example, in its 1923 annual report, the U.S. Department of the Interior summarized conditions in the following manner: "The salient features of 1923 and the years immediately preceding may be summarized in a word. The number of employees and the output per man have been increasing and with them the potential capacity. The demand has been stationary or even declining. The average time worked has therefore been decreasing, and with it prices have tended to fall."[35] Both the 1922 strike and the general state of the industry prompted President Warren Harding to recommend to Congress that a special investigating commission be established to study the industry and make suggestions for its economic reorganization. In asking Congress to deal in this manner with the pending industrial crisis in coal, the president said, "I am speaking now on behalf of mine workers, mine operators, and the American public. It [a commission] will bring protection to all and point the way to continuity of production and the better functioning of the industry in the future."[36] Following this presidential request, Congress set up in October 1922 the U.S. Coal Commission and charged it with the duty of investigating all phases of production, transportation, and distribution of coal and "all organized or other relationships among operators and miners with a view to recommending remedial legislation."[37] (It was not the first, nor would it be the last, time that a president and Congress responded to a crisis in coal by appointing a fact-finding commission.)

Some statistics on the industry in the early 1920s will indicate the seriousness of the problem confronting the new commission. High wartime prices and special market conditions in the immediate post–World War I period stimulated expansion of production in existing mines and encouraged the opening of many new mines. Full-time mining capacity, which had grown by 82 million tons in the five years from 1913 to 1918, increased by 254 million tons in the five years from 1918 to 1923. The number of operating mines increased from 8,319 in 1918 to 9,331 in 1923.[38] Never before had the nation been in a position to mine so much coal. Unfortunately, however, this potential was not matched by an increase in demand for the fuel. On the contrary, the demand for coal was experiencing a decline, because competing fuels such as oil and natural gas were taking over traditional coal markets.

In addition, technological improvements in the utilization of coal, such as the development of the by-products coke process and the redesign of steam locomotives, reduced demand. When the average number of days worked in the industry dropped from a wartime high of 249 days to 179 days in 1923, it was an early-warning sign for miners and operators. The downward trend in prices, from $3.75 a ton on the average in 1920 to $2.68 a ton in 1923, also indicated that the quantity of coal produced exceeded the demand. And when coal prices and number of days worked failed to rise with an upswing in the national economy in 1923, it became quite clear to everyone that there probably were "too many mines and too many miners" for the industry's well-being. In this economic context, the U.S. Coal Commission was directed to formulate long-run policies for stabilizing the industry.

Although the UMWA progressives, such as District 2 President John Brophy, hoped the commission would make recommendations that would support their program for nationalizing the mines, John L. Lewis apparently expected very little from it. There were no union representatives on the seven-member board, as there had been on the 1920 commission, and while most of the members might have been considered neutral in their attitudes toward the labor movement, more than one was considered to be antiunion.[39] After eleven months of study, the commission published its findings that detailed the extent of the irregularity of operations, the overexpansion of the industry, and the destructiveness of the industry's competitive market structure. The deplorable conditions under which many miners lived and worked, especially in the nonunion fields, was documented along with many other aspects of the industry, such as collective bargaining relations, structures of the UMWA and the operators' associations, management practices, engineering problems, and railroad rate structures. While the study still stands as the most thorough one ever made of the industry, the final recommendations of the commission were quite disappointing to both the operators and the union. Labeled "vague, platitudinous, and occasionally even meaningless," by one scholar, the recommendations were frequently contradictory.[40] And as might be expected, "such trivial recommendations received the fate they deserved from operators, union and government, absolute neglect."

The commission's study of underground mine management is important to this review of the union's mechanization policies because it demonstrated that the technology for mechanical loading was scientifically well advanced and economically viable. Several mines that had been using mechanical loading equipment for a few years were examined and contrasted with hand-loading mines. The conclusion was that the cost of mining a ton of coal could be reduced by as much as 30 percent by using the new technology.[41] While noting that a decrease in human labor for any given production level would follow, the commission pointed out that, with the use of a machine loader, many of the duties that the hand loader traditionally performed passed over to day men, or company men. A division of labor and specialization of tasks followed from efficient use of the technology: "Such work as timbering, laying track in rooms, cleaning up after the loader, and removing rock or slate, is necessarily done entirely by men who can be specifically trained for it. Furthermore, these men work in a small area and under constant supervision of the foremen, which is impracticable where individuals are scattered in work places widely apart. Consequently they can be more effectively employed and at correspondingly lower unit costs."[42]

After detailing the advantages to be gained from mechanical loading, the commission's report dealt with the problems associated with the transition. It was pointed out, for example, that loading machines were not adaptable to thin seams of coal and that machine loading might not be so profitable where considerable slate was found mixed with the coal. Significantly, the commission claimed that the union itself was an obstacle to the introduction of machinery: "A handicap in the development of loading machines has been not merely the overcoming of mechanical and physical difficulties but also the opposition of the union, which has opposed their introduction or has attempted to attain so high a rate of pay for operating the machines as to invalidate a large part of their value from the economical standpoint."[43]

The operators, in a brief submitted to the commission, also charged that, while the UMWA claimed to support mechanization, its wage and other policies at the local level tended to restrict the use of new equipment. They noted that introduction of labor-saving devices is specifically permitted in almost all joint agreements but "while they do not object to the installation of the machines, as such, they do adopt a number of methods to make the installation of machines unprofitable to the operator and to prevent him from cutting down his force of laborers."[44] The central Pennsylvania operators offered specific examples of the union's opposition to introduction of labor-saving machinery and expressed the view that finding the ways and means for mechanizing the industry was the single most important question facing the U.S. Coal Commission. These operators summarized their feelings about the UMWA's mechanization policy in the following manner: "It is our opinion that if the United Mine Workers controlled the mining industry 100 percent, there would never be another machine introduced in the mining industry. It is only by the force of economic pressure, due to the introduction of labor-saving machinery in non-union fields, that they are finally accepted in the union districts of the United States at this time."[45]

The UMWA's response to these charges of obstructing technological change came in the form of a letter written to the commission reaffirming a position taken publicly by former union president John White. In bold letters for emphasis the union wrote to the commission:

> THIS UNION NEVER HAS OPPOSED THE INTRODUCTION OF ANY KIND OF
> SAFETY OR LABOR SAVING MACHINERY, METHODS OR DEVICES WHERE IT
> IS PROVED THAT SUCH MACHINERY, METHODS OR DEVICES MAKE FOR
> THE SAFE AND THE MORE EFFICIENT PRODUCTION OF COAL. WHAT THE
> UNION DOES INSIST UPON IS THAT WHEN SUCH SAFETY OR LABOR
> SAVING MACHINERY, METHODS OR DEVICES ARE INSTALLED THEY SHALL
> BE OPERATED BY UNION MINERS; AND THAT THE MINERS SHALL HAVE
> SOMETHING TO SAY ABOUT THE RATE OF WAGES THEY ARE TO RECEIVE
> FOR SUCH WORK.[46]

This appears to be the only input the union made to the commission on this issue. However, it published a short pamphlet titled *The United Mine Workers and The United States Coal Commission*, in which it answered many of the commission findings. And the pages of the *UMWA Journal* were used to respond to others of the commission's recommendations. But the letter quoted above seems to be the only response it made to the charges of obstructionism.

Based on its perception of the importance of bituminous coal to the nation's economic welfare, the U.S. Coal Commission's final report urged two reforms for the industry, both to be conducted under "fishbowl" conditions of public fact finding and supervision. The first recommendation called for a readjustment of railroad freight rates "to express the true relation of cost to service." The goal of this reform was to eliminate the discriminatory rate differentials that made it possible for southern Appalachian coals to compete with Illinois, Indiana, and Ohio coals for the Great Lakes trade. The second reform the commission proposed was the consolidation of mining companies by "removing the existing legal barriers to such an economic arrangement." In calling for a relaxation of the antitrust laws, the commission asserted that "the consolidation grouping, or pooling of bituminous mining operations should not only be permitted but encouraged, with a view to insuring more steady production, less speculative prices, better living conditions, more regular employment, and lower costs."[47] The necessary protection of the public interest could be assured, the commission asserted, by requiring federal supervision of the financial structure of any coal consolidation, in much the same way that transportation legislation required supervision of railroad mergers.

Although the UMWA tended to belittle the findings and the recommendation of the U.S. Coal Commission, both the freight rate proposal and the consolidation plan were important parts of John L. Lewis's scheme for rationalizing the industry. And the idea of allowing "grouping or pooling" of mining interests formed the basis of the union's stabilization proposals that were later incorporated into the New Deal industrial recovery programs of the early 1930s. The progressives in the union were disappointed that the commission failed to support the idea of nationalization of the mines but welcomed the recommendations of federal fact finding and public involvement in reviewing the industry's performance.

By way of assessment, it can be said that President Harding's special investigating commission had little or no direct impact on legislation affecting the coal industry. Its report, which enthusiastically supported the introduction of mechanization and scientific management for the more rational production of coal, and its program for the consolidation of capital to increase control over the market both tended simply to justify what was already taking place in the industry in the mid-1920s.

The Jacksonville Agreement

The UMWA's successful strike in 1922, by preserving the $7.50-a-day wage and proportional tonnage rates, increased the confidence miners had in the union and led to an expanded membership of 445,000 by 1923. With the power that a larger membership and a bigger treasury gave him, Lewis demanded that the existing scale be extended for four years when he met with the CCF operators early in 1924. After a lengthy meeting in Jacksonville, Florida, the operators reluctantly agreed to renew the contract, but for only a three-year period, ending April 1, 1927. This pact, which came to be known as the Jacksonville agreement, stated simply, in two short paragraphs, that the wage-scale contract in existence for the Central Competitive Field would be carried forward and that the district and subdistrict agreements then in effect would be extended "without further negotiations."[48] The UMWA *Journal* hailed the contract as "the best ever negotiated with the CCF operators," and it reported that union miners ratified the agreement by a vote of 164,858 to 26,253.[49] While the Jacksonville agreement may have been the best the union could have negotiated under the circumstances, it is misleading to think of it as an improvement over prior agreements. It was, in fact, only a continuation of existing agreements. Even the $7.50-a-day wage, which became so closely identified with the Jacksonville accord, was negotiated two years before that date.[50]

Following the signing of the agreement in Jacksonville, the union began negotiating with operators in the outlying districts and was successful during the spring of 1924 in reaching an agreement with operators in northern West Virginia, central Pennsylvania, and in several western states. For example, after two weeks of bargaining in Baltimore, the union and the Northern West Virginia Coal Operators Association signed a three-year contract covering 28,000 miners. From the beginning it was apparent that depressed market conditions would make the wage issue a critical one and that many operators would resist paying the wage and tonnage scale that had been negotiated in more prosperous times.

While the CCF operators agreed to the $7.50 scale, it became increasingly difficult for the union to impose this wage on operators in some of the outlying districts. The operators in the Kanawha District of central West Virginia would not agree to the Jacksonville scale and broke off talks when the union refused to consider a reduced rate of pay. The Kanawha operators claimed that the nonunion mines were paying less than $5.00 a day. *Coal Age* reported that "the fact that non-union Kanawha operators are paying much lower wages than fixed in the Jacksonville agreement presents union producers with a difficult problem, as it will be impossible for them to compete with the non-union mines if the 1922–1924 wage scale is paid." In western Kentucky, the Liberty Coal Company refused to consider the Jacksonville scale and shut down its union mine. And, in a move that anticipated events that would follow in many coalfields over the next several years, this company announced that it would reopen the mine if miners would accept the wage level that had existed in 1917. Some of the union miners accepted the cut in pay, but others refused, so the company imported nonunion men from other states and evicted the loyal union miners and their families from company-owned houses. Violence followed as union miners attempted to protect their jobs. But the mine was kept open with scabs under the protection of state police.[51]

John L. Lewis was committed, both politically and philosophically, to maintaining the wage scale agreed to at Jacksonville regardless of the slump in coal sales and prices.[52] The 1924 miners' convention had endorsed the no-backward-step policy, so Lewis was able to say that he was duty bound to carry out this policy. But he firmly believed in the policy anyway, for he saw in high wages a way to bring stability to the industry. He reasoned that high labor costs would force operators to put management of the mines on a more efficient basis, to consolidate their operations, and to instal labor-saving machinery, especially mechanical loaders. Once established on a more efficient and modernized basis, Lewis argued, the union mines could easily reverse their competitive disadvantage and drive less efficient firms out of business. While many might suffer in the short run from this Darwinian program, Lewis was convinced that both the union and the industry would prosper in the long run. In May 1925, when the union was on the brink of disaster, he told a reporter that "we expect losses, perhaps heavy losses, but we are confident of victory in the end."[53]

The ink was barely dry on the labor agreements in some outlying districts before operators began to warn the union that they could not operate profitably under the Jacksonville scale. Union mines in many fields were reported to be closing because they could not compete with output mined in nonunion districts. In some areas where union mines were forced to close, union miners were reported accepting work in nearby nonunion mines, which were operating on the 1917 scale.[54] By midsummer 1924, the first outright abrogation of the Jacksonville agreement took place in the Oklahoma coalfields. Individual operators withdrew from the operators' association and claimed that they were not legally or morally bound as individual companies to a contract signed by the association. The editor of *Coal Age,* outraged by this blatant act of bad faith, asked rhetorically, "Who is sinning now?"[55] After years of chastising the UMWA for being unable to prevent striking local unions from violating the contract, he labeled the Oklahoma operators' strategy an "evasion." He wrote, "It is not possible for this paper to support [the Oklahoma operators] who, as members of their operators' association, were definitely committed to the Jacksonville Agreement, but who, in order to evade the obligation of the contract, withdrew from their association and opened their mines on a nonunion basis with wages at the 1917 level."

As the fall of 1924 approached, the economic situation became increasingly desperate for many operators, especially of small- and medium-sized firms. Production figures showed that the nonunion fields were capturing an increasing share of the market, while in the union fields most mines were working a shortened workweek or closing down altogether. In November, Joseph Pursglove, owner of several mines in northern West Virginia, told Lewis that "something must be done or all the men who are operating union coal mines are going bankrupt. . . . All the union operators are in bad shape financially and it certainly will not be a good thing for the industry as a whole . . . for these men to go bankrupt."[56] When members of the Northern West Virginia Coal Operators Association asked Lewis to meet with them to consider a wage reduction, he agreed to meet but warned them in advance that "there will be no modification of that scale now or any time until the term ex- pires."[57] He explained his reason for this hard-line position by saying that, if wages were lowered in the union mines, "the non-union crowd would merely make another cut in the wages of their miserable workers and the same relative condition would obtain." Lewis intended to en- force his no-backward-step policy.

CHAPTER 7

Evolution of the UMWA's Mechanization Policy

THE INTRODUCTION of collective bargaining to the coal industry not only offered protection against much of the economic exploitation of miners, but it also codified many customary work practices and local work rules, which in turn protected both the income and craft autonomy of miners. The square turn, which assured all miners an equal number of empty cars during each shift of work, was formalized in most union agreements throughout the coalfields. This prevented management from favoring the more productive workers. Work rules relating to timbering, shooting, loading, pushing cars, and all other aspects of the traditional miner's job were formalized in local union contracts. Restrictions on the hiring of new employees were negotiated in some of the union fields; dead work payments were formalized, and even promotion and transfer rights were built into some of the early labor agreements.

Local agreements containing language pertaining to work rules and customs protected the craft autonomy of the miner and, at the same time, made it difficult for management to instal labor-saving machinery or to introduce scientific management practices. In fact, management's rights clauses, which would have given mine owners the contractual authority to alter the production process, were missing from most of the early coal contracts. That these work practices and work rules were anathema to management was obvious from their testimony before the 1922 Coal Commission, in which they charged the union with "restriction of output."[1] They also pointed out, as noted earlier, that the UMWA may have endorsed the advantages of mine mechanization but it was unable to enforce its national policies on its constituent local and state organizations. What good was a national union policy, they asked, if the UMWA could not discipline its membership to accept it?

As we trace the evolution of the UMWA's policy toward mechanization, it is important to keep in mind that, while a national union policy supporting new technologies was being formulated, it was business as usual at the mines. Job control and local union control could slow the introduction of labor-saving machinery, affect the type of new machinery introduced, and even prevent its introduction altogether. Before the coal industry could mechanize, union policies notwithstanding, workers' control had to be weakened.

John Mitchell's Business Unionism

The successful 1897 strike, which led to the joint conference of miners and operators and the 1898 Central Competitive Field Agreement, was directed by UMWA President M. D. Ratchford and Vice-President John Mitchell. Within a few months after signing the precedent-setting CCF agreement, Ratchford resigned his union post to accept a presidential appointment to the U.S. Industrial Commission, and the job of running the union fell to John Mitchell, a twenty-nine-year-old coal miner from Illinois. For ten years, Mitchell presided over the miners' union and helped it grow in membership tenfold during that period.[2] He led organizing drives west of the Mississippi and brought union protection to miners in parts of Missouri, Colorado, Wyoming, and Montana. During his administration, union contracts were signed for the first time in Alabama, Kentucky, Tennessee, and other states.[3] After the anthracite coal miners were organized in 1902, the union reported a membership of 330,000, making it by far the largest union in the country at the time.[4]

As union leader, Mitchell was a very popular individual, with widespread support for most of his policies and programs. He did, however, come under attack on many occasions by the socialists within the union, who disliked his conservative policies, his business unionism, and his propensity to socialize with industrialists, financiers, and national political figures.[5] Mitchell could not deny many of the charges made against him by his critics, but defended his conservative policies and tactics as being more appropriate for solving the problems of the day than the idealism of the socialists. Mitchell promoted the use of conciliation and arbitration for settling industrial disputes. He hoped to establish harmonious relations between employers and employees, asserting that cooperation, rather than conflict, best served the interests of workers.

Above all, he believed in the sanctity of the labor agreement, treating it almost as a religious covenant. He opposed wildcat strikes and sympathy strikes, and although on occasion he found it necessary to authorize a strike against an employer who had failed to live up to an agreement, he did so under pressure from competing operators who continued to pay the agreed scale. Mitchell joined the National Civic Federation, an organization of the top business leaders in the country, and he kept the union out of state and national politics even to the point of prohibiting political discussion in the *UMWA Journal.* [6]

On the question of machinery in the mines, Mitchell also expressed a very conservative trade union philosophy, and one that influenced the thinking of John White and John L. Lewis, who followed him into the UMWA presidency. Mitchell made this philosophy public in a book he published in 1903, *Organized Labor, Its Problems, Purposes and Ideals and the Present and Future of American Wage Earners.* [7] In a chapter titled "The Right of the Machine," the UMWA president defended the trade union movement against the business community criticism that organized labor generally obstructed mechanization. While there may have been opposition in the past to machinery, Mitchell wrote, "at the present time all but a small minority of workmen are converted to the view that machinery is a necessity, to which it is foolish and unwise, if not impossible, to offer permanent resistance." He then claimed that trade unions (and presumably he was referring to his own union) "have consciously adopted the policy of encouraging inventions and the use of machinery."[8]

Mitchell was well aware of the employment impact of mechanization and the dehumanizing effect of machines that deskilled traditional craft jobs. In describing the machine impact, he wrote that "in hundreds of thousands of cases the machine drove the man from his work and in many instances substituted for patiently and painfully acquired skill the services of an untrained laborer, of a little boy or girl."[9] Where the worker retained his or her job, Mitchell understood that skilled workers "lost their positions and their only asset, their knowledge of a trade." As a skilled miner himself, Mitchell described what it meant for the worker to lose control over his tools and his job: "The old tool of the workers, like the sword of the soldier or the pen of the scholar, had been their friend, their assistant, their very own, but this new machine was a terrible, soulless monster, to which they were chained, to which they were subject, and over which they had no manner of control."[10]

Yet with all of this concern for the negative impact of technology,

Mitchell still counseled against trade union resistance. Obstructing the introduction of machinery in one plant or mine would be "to send the new machines into non-union establishments, and by means of competition of the new with the old, of the better with the worse methods of production gradually to lower and reduce the union scale," Mitchell wrote.[11] It is not clear what his position would have been if the whole industry had been organized and under union contract. Since this situation did not exist in Mitchell's day, and would not exist in the coal industry for at least thirty years to come, Mitchell cannot be faulted for not dealing with a hypothetical situation.

Even if outright resistance was unacceptable to Mitchell, he did state firmly that the union should retain control of the workplace. "While there can be no doubt that the sudden introduction of machines often works great hardship to working men, the method of securing redress is not by fighting the machine but by obtaining control of it."[12] By obtaining control, Mitchell meant that the union must fight to keep collective bargaining rights and to retain jurisdiction over any new jobs created in the process of mechanization. Writing as if he represented the views of all organized labor, Mitchell said that "what the trade unionist desires is not the prohibition of machinery but its regulation . . . The unionist demands first that machinery be introduced in such a way as to give the least possible damage to the workman, and second, that the introduction of machinery shall rebound to the direct and immediate advantage of the workman, as well as to the direct and immediate advantage of the employer." Mitchell believed that mechanization had to take place in a union setting: "Where trade unions do not exist, employers with the worst and oldest machinery and the most antiquated methods manage to eke out a precarious existence by underpaying and starving their workmen, but where trade unionism is able to enforce a definite maximum wage, these less skillful and less adequately equipped manufacturers must either introduce the modern appliances or go to the wall."

Mitchell was not faced with a crisis in coal; on the contrary, it was a growth industry during his tenure as president. But Mitchell did not understand the dynamics of market competition, and he believed that trade unions, if they stuck to the narrow goal of better wages, hours, and working conditions, could promote the interest of workers and industrialists alike. He viewed the employment relationship as a cooperative one in which factors such as mechanization, which benefited the employer, could serve to benefit the employee as well. In his book, he did not deal with the private and social costs of unemployment resulting from technological change, however.[13] That problem, it seems, was beyond the scope of Mitchell's business unionism. His influence on the evolution of UMWA policy toward machinery was nonetheless important.

The machine question does not appear to have been a burning issue at the collective bargaining table during Mitchell's time. True, the question of the differential in wages between machine miners (i.e., loaders who followed the machine) and pick miners continued to be a matter of contention between the union and the operators. Mitchell did not offer his readers an economic analysis of the role of labor-saving machinery in the coal industry, but he did promote the idea, later developed by John L. Lewis, that modernization through mechanization was necessary for the healthy growth and development of any industry. Mitchell was probably motivated to discuss the question of machinery and to develop a positive policy toward it by contemporary critics of unionism who argued that the labor movement was restricting the nation's output.[14] Whatever the motivation, Mitchell can be credited with initiating a national UMWA policy toward mechanization that remained influential throughout the period of this study, and longer.

The Socialist Alternative

Socialists in the UMWA, who attained substantial influence in the union in the years immediately following Mitchell's retirement, failed to develop specific plans for dealing with machinery in the mines, but their call for democratic control of industry through nationalization did provide an alternative to Mitchell's conservative unionism.[15] Leadership of the socialist movement in the UMWA came principally from Illinois District 12, where socialists such as John Walker, Duncan McDonald, Frank Hayes, and Adolph German held various district offices. Alexander Howat, president of Kansas District 14, was a socialist, as was John Lawson of Colorado District 15. The socialists claimed large numbers of supporters in Indiana District II and western Pennsylvania District 5 during the period from 1908 to 1913. While no exact determination can be made of the number of rank-and-file miners who considered themselves to be socialist during this period, some indication of their importance was given by John Brophy's estimate that about one-fourth of the delegates to the UMWA international conventions were socialists.[16] A review of convention proceedings of the UMWA shows that, in the years between 1909 and 1916, the socialists dominated convention activities. Frank Hayes, a socialist from Illinois, was elected vice-president of the UMWA and retained that position until 1917.[17] In 1911 and 1912, the UMWA *Journal* had a socialist as its editor.

Support in the UMWA for a program of public ownership of industry dates back to the mid-1890s. John McBride, union president, told convention delegates in 1894 that "you must bear in mind that the people must either own or control the means of production and distribution or be subjected to the dictation, as they now are, of those who do own and control these two powerful agencies."[18] During the term of conservative union leader John Mitchell, the socialist program of Eugene Debs and the American Socialist Party was frequently debated at international conventions. Most significantly, in each year between 1909 and 1923 a resolution calling for nationalization of the mines was introduced and approved by the delegates to the UMWA international convention. The UMWA's Nationalization Research Committee, chaired by John Brophy from 1921 to 1923, developed a specific program for mine nationalization; and when Brophy ran for president of the union in 1926, public ownership and democratic control of the mines were issues in his campaign.

Although not well developed before the 1920s, the nationalization program was not a Utopian scheme put forward by political idealists. It was routinely put forward by socialists in the union as a reasonable alternative for dealing with the problems of the coal industry. The pages of the union's *Journal* were open for rank-and-file debate on issues during this period. For example, when one Michigan miner wrote that machines were taking jobs and reducing the income of those who remained, a socialist miner from Illinois responded to his letter by saying that to avoid the evil effects of machinery, it would be necessary for wage earners to acquire the tools or machinery of production so "that all may become part owners of the machinery and distribution in order to receive the full equivalent of what we produce."[19] In the discussion of mine health and safety, the socialists made one of their strongest arguments for nationalization of the mines. They reasoned that as long as production was for profit alone, the miner would pay with the loss of his life or his health. Under government ownership, the coal miners, the socialists believed, would see "the dawn of a new day . . . when accidents and unemployment will decrease and the pay increase."[20]

At a time when the industry was beginning to experience some of the economic ills that were to plague it for decades to come, a good analysis of the situation can be found in some of the socialist articles and letters in the *Journal*. Part of the excess capacity found in the industry was due, they argued, to the relative decline in demand for coal caused by a better utilization of the fuel by final consumers. "More commodities can be produced and distributed with less coal than some years past," it was pointed out. And substitute fuels were beginning to reduce the market demand for coal, since "natural gas as well as artificial gas has in many hotels and homes supplanted coal." And of course, the use of modern machinery has increased the "productivity of the miners' labor power" and contributed to unemployment, irregular work, and excess capacity. Some socialists agreed with the conservative union approach that unemployment in the industry could be offset by a shorter workweek. One writer to the *Journal* said that "some relief no doubt could be had concerning the slack work and non-employment by shortening the work day and every effort should be made in that direction," but the reduction of working hours would never be a permanent solution. "Nothing short of the overthrow of capitalism can solve the problem," and then "to replace it with a society based on the collective ownership of the means of life and the tools of production and distribution."[21]

As the discussion of nationalization evolved in the union, its meaning became more clearly focused, but at the same time the socialist political influence in the UMWA began to wane. More and more, the socialists found their energies directed toward survival in their union jobs as conservative business unionism returned under John P. White and later under John L. Lewis. The centralization of power in the international union and the elimination of district autonomy, which began in the years just prior to World War I and was carried to its limits by John L. Lewis, eliminated the power base of the UMWA socialists and also made it difficult for any organized opposition to develop against incumbent national officers. There were numerous other reasons for the decline of the socialist movement both in the union and in the national political arena, but the fact remains that its influence was creative and important. In the years after World War I when the economic crisis in coal worsened, the socialist philosophy and programs reappeared in militant forms among rank-and-file coal miners.

The Nationalization Movement in the UMWA

A popular movement within the miners' union advocated that the industry could be stabilized and workers' rights protected if the mines were nationalized. This attitude had its roots in the socialist influence in the union preceding World War I. As early as the 1909 UMWA convention, delegates had passed a resolution calling for public ownership of the mines, and in the next few years progressives in the union made a concerted effort to direct union policy toward this goal. In March 1919, representatives from each district in the union were called by UMWA President Frank Hayes to a National Policy Committee meeting in Washington to discuss wartime wages and the cost-of-living squeeze on miners as well as other problems facing the industry. At this meeting Hayes proposed, among other matters, a plan for nationalizing the mines, a plan that was accepted by the policy-making committee. Further, the committee instructed the union president to draw up appropriate legislation for presentation to Congress and voted to place the issue before the membership at a special convention to be held in September 1919.

Frank Hayes had been a leading Illinois socialist before serving as vice-president of the UMWA in John White's administration, and for years he had been an outspoken proponent of nationalization of the mines.[22] He apparently saw his 1919 proposal as an expression of solidarity with the British miners, who were engaged in a struggle for nationalizing their mines. He believed, too, that since the Fuel Administration had been, on balance, a stabilizing influence in the industry during wartime, it demonstrated the positive role that government could play in correcting the economic problems that plagued the industry. Hayes believed, and several others on the union's National Policy Committee concurred, that under public ownership, geographic wage differentials could be eliminated, the work-day and workweek could be reduced to spread the work, and the wage level could be raised to protect miners against rapidly rising prices. None of these goals, Hayes argued, was obtainable under the system of cutthroat competition which characterized the coal industry.

Although Hayes thought of nationalization as a practical solution to the industry's ills, he did not have an implementation program in mind, nor did he address himself to other details, such as the protection of job rights and the introduction of machinery under nationalization. These details were important, the committee decided, and should be worked out in the UMWA's president's office before the special convention in September. Unfortunately for the nationalization program, Hayes did not remain in office long enough to carry the idea forward, and his successor, John L. Lewis, was lukewarm, if not actually hostile, to the idea.

When the special UMWA convention was called in September 1919, wage and other contract demands were the chief issues subject to discussion, but nationalization was also an important item on the agenda. Lewis, who had become president during the intervening six months, had failed to carry out the policy committee's charge to draw up legislation pertaining to nationalization for the consideration of the delegates. The new president might well have been preoccupied with other union problems when he first took over from Hayes, or he might have chosen simply to ignore the policy established by the union governing board. His failure to present a plan to the delegates did not, however, keep the issue off the floor. A rousing keynote address by Glenn Plumb, well-known Chicago attorney specializing in railway legal matters, placed the nationalization question before the delegates in a manner that assured that it would be discussed and considered seriously.

The Plumb plan for nationalizing the nation's railroads called for government purchase of railroad assets at a fair-market value and management of the system by a tripartite commission composed of representatives of the public, the workers, and the railroad managers. After his speech, a resolution pledging full UMWA support for his plan and solidarity with railroad workers received "rising unanimous" support.[23] Twelve local unions had submitted resolutions to the convention for public ownership of the mines and, after debate on the issue, the delegates unanimously endorsed a single resolution, which read in part: "We demand the immediate nationalization of the coal mining industry of the United States." This resolution also instructed the national officers to draw up legislation for submission to Congress, legislation that would involve federal purchase of coal properties and miner representation in the administration of a publicly owned mining corporation. The union's officers were further instructed to "use their every influence to bring our demand for nationalization to the attention of the American people."[24] Finally, as if to show their commitment to the plan, delegates to this 1919 convention adopted a resolution calling for the organization of a labor party that would work toward the political goal of mine and railroad nationalization.[25]

It is difficult at this distance from the event to determine the extent of support among rank-and-file miners for the reforms proposed by progressives in the union. The official proceedings of the 1919 convention reflect the fact that at least the delegates to that meeting took the issue seriously and supported it wholeheartedly. The delegates also understood that, for any nationalization plan to succeed, a long political struggle involving a commitment on the part of the national officers and alliances with other unions to form a labor party would be required. Within the next few years, however, the UMWA nationalization movement failed to pick up the momentum it needed to bring the issue before the public, although it continued to be debated within the union for a long time to come.

The nationalization movement also failed because John L. Lewis managed to sabotage it. In the months following the 1919 convention, it became apparent that, regardless of the resolutions passed by the delegates, Lewis would quietly neglect to carry them out. Later, he became openly hostile to the plan and took advantage of the national "red scare" to discredit union progressives, to strengthen his control over the administration of the union, and to direct its policies along very conservative lines.[26] It is also true that the UMWA nationalization movement was linked with a declining movement toward socialist and labor-party reforms in the national political arena.[27]

Before Lewis was able to bury the nationalization issue, however, he found it politically expedient to support the idea publicly on at least two occasions in 1921. The first occurred during his unsuccessful effort in the spring to unseat Samuel Gompers as president of the American Federation of Labor. Since Lewis needed the support of the delegates to the AFL from his own union as well as the support of other unions committed to nationalization, such as the railroad brotherhoods and the machinists, he endorsed public ownership of mines and railroads. He also came out in favor of federal old age pensions and unemployment insurance, but his courting of the left failed to win the AFL election for him.[28] Just three months later, at the 1921 UMWA convention, Lewis, as presiding officer, found himself confronted with new resolutions relating to nationalization. Because of his recent endorsement of public ownership during the AFL campaign, Lewis found himself in a position of having to support these resolutions. The convention again called on the national officers to develop a plan for government ownership and to give the plan the widest possible publicity.[29] This time, Lewis did take action in response to the convention mandate. He appointed a three-member Nationalization Research Committee and named John Brophy as chairman. In his letter to this new committee, Lewis said: "The duties of your committee will be to carry out the instructions of the international convention with reference to this subject matter and to familiarize yourselves with various phases of the problem as they be encountered

with a view of formulating practical policy to bring about the nationalization of the coal mines and to aid in the dissemination of information
among our members and the public and the crystallization of sentiment
for the attainment of such end."[30] If Lewis had hoped to pigeonhole the
whole question of nationalization, he could not have picked a more
inappropriate chairman for the committee. John Brophy, then president
of UMWA District 5, turned out to be a determined supporter of the
movement and refused to let the issue die even in the face of growing
opposition from Lewis.

Within a few months, the Nationalization Research Committee had
developed a detailed plan for the government purchase and administration of the nation's coal mines. The union published the committee's
plan in 1922 in a pamphlet titled *How to Run Coal: Suggestions for a Plan of
Public Ownership, Public Control, and Democratic Management in the Coal
Industry.*[31] In this publication, the committee dealt with the legal questions of public ownership, estimated the amount of public funds needed
to purchase all of the coal reserves and capital equipment then in private
hands, and proposed a plan for policy making and management of the
system. The committee opposed the more radical idea of worker ownership of the mines, arguing that the American worker had no interest in
socialism.

The heart of the plan for administering coal mining was the notion of
"democratic management," which meant that "coal shall be run by the
people who mine it, who apply their scientific knowledge to its problems,
who transport it, who sell it, and who use it." Miners, railroad workers,
mining engineers, and other workers would be given greater responsibility in the management of production and distribution under the committee's plan. The worker "wishes the right to make suggestions or technical
improvements, on car-pushing, on slack work, on output, and the right
to take part in carrying them out. . . . The working miner must have a
real part in the government of coal." Rational planning for production
would be possible under public ownership, the committee argued. A
permanent fact-finding agency would determine "how much coal the
people want, how much of a supply is already in stock, what is the cost of
mining coal, how much the miners get, and what the correct price is for a
ton of coal." This agency would advise a permanent federal interstate
commission of mines, whose director would be a cabinet member.

Those who considered themselves progressives in the union had
offered a concrete plan for restructuring the industry, a plan that was

particularly timely given the events that soon followed. The coal industry was entering a period of depression, which was to last for a decade and a half. At the same time, the industry was entering a new technological era with the development of the loading machine. In hindsight, there is little doubt that the tremendous social costs of unemployment and excess capacity, which were unavoidable under the existing market conditions, could have been avoided with a modicum of central economic planning and coordination that the UMWA progressives proposed. Public owner-ship and democratic control might well have stabilized production, allowed the rational deployment of new machinery, and at the same time established a decision-making system in which workers' jobs and job rights would have been secured. While the nationalization movement in the UMWA may not have had a perfect plan for stabilizing the industry and protecting workers' rights, it filled a void left by the failure of the U.S. Coal Commission to arrive at meaningful recommendations, and it certainly provided a meaningful alternative to the conservative, business-oriented policies that John L. Lewis was soon to espouse.

Lewis's Response to Nationalization

Lewis's basic policy for promoting prosperity in the industry was summarized by Ellis Searles, editor of the *UMWA Journal*, in May 1923, when he was interviewed by a New York newspaper reporter: "Shut down 4,000 coal mines, force 200,000 miners into other industries, and the coal problem will settle itself. The public will then be assured of an adequate supply of low-priced fuel."[32] As Lewis solidified his control over the internal politics of the UMWA, he felt freer to disassociate himself from the nationalization movement. For example, he refused to print the Nationalization Research Committee's program in the *Journal* and would not open its pages to debate on the issue. When one member of the committee gave a speech in New York in which he discussed the commit-tee's work, Searles criticized him in the *Journal* for publicizing a plan that had not been officially approved by the union and that had been "pre-pared largely by a bunch of Greenwich Village Reds." Brophy and the other committee members resigned in protest, and research on na-tionalization was discontinued. Although the 1924 UMWA convention again adopted a resolution strongly calling for nationalization of the mines, by that time it was nearly a dead issue. John Brophy, recalling the 1924 convention in his autobiography, lamented: "The resolution was adopted, but the national organization made no effort whatever to translate its pious generalities into activity. It was not intended, by the administration, to be a plan for further education and research, but rather as an epitaph over the grave of the nationalization idea. I kept hoping that we could reform our lives and resume the campaign, but that hope was never realized."[33]

Brophy was not quite ready to let the whole issue die. In 1926 he challenged Lewis for the union presidency and made both nationalization of the mines and the formation of a labor party important parts of his campaign platform. Lewis defeated Brophy by a vote of 170,000 to 60,000, and it is safe to say that with that defeat, the nationalization movement within the UMWA was finally put to rest. After the Brophy effort, Lewis was never again seriously challenged for the leadership position, and through his effective control of the international convention, he became the chief policy maker and sole spokesman for the United Miner Workers of America.[34] Resolutions for nationalization continued to be submitted to the union's conventions and usually were approved by a large majority of the delegates,[35] but Lewis simply ignored them. When he published a book called *The Miners' Fight for American Standards* in 1925, there was no indication that any of the ideas from the nationalization movement had influenced him.[36] On the contrary, his plan for the salvation of the industry rejected any form of public intervention into the affairs of the industry.

Lewis's Response to Mechanization

As discussed earlier, Lewis' predecessors had adopted a general policy of supporting mine mechanization. Lewis not only favored the use of new technology but believed that it was the key to long-run stabilization of the whole industry. The Lewis stabilization program was outlined in his keynote address to the 1924 UMWA convention, was promoted in interviews in various newspapers and trade journals, and was featured in the book mentioned above. Although ghost-written by the men Lewis hired as consultants, speech writers, and union publicists,[37] this book clearly reflected John L. Lewis's basic political and economic values. Writing as if he spoke for all union members and as if the nationalization movement within the UMWA was insignificant, Lewis rejected government control of the industry and supported "the operation of natural economic laws to bring about a permanent improvement."[38] He claimed that "the policy of the United Mine Workers of America at this time is neither new nor revolutionary. It does not command the admiration of visionaries and Utopians. It ought to have the support of every thinking business man in the United States, because it proposes to allow natural economic laws free play in the production and distribution of coal."

Asked by a reporter if he thought government operation or ownership could save the industry, Lewis expressed the view that free enterprise was the only system the UMWA supported. Even though delegates to the international convention continued to endorse a program of public ownership, Lewis was quoted in 1925 as saying: "The United Mine Workers, although they came out in favor of nationalization of mines some time ago, are really against such a nebulous sort of thing as Government ownership. Our American life and our American system of business has been built up around the principle of competition and the United Mine Workers believe in competition just as much as the executives who guide business."[39]

Lewis's book was an attempt to establish a new image for the UMWA, which had come under attack during the investigation by the Presidential Coal Commission in 1923 and which now was suffering from lack of public support for its refusal to make wage concessions under the Jacksonville agreement. The union's policy of absolutely no backward step on wages, even when an increasing number of union operators were abrogating the Jacksonville agreement, was justified in Lewis's book on the grounds that higher wages meant greater purchasing power for workers, which in turn was necessary for full production. "Mass production can only be maintained by a purchasing power in the home market sufficient to make it possible," he asserted.[40] High wages also were essential to providing an incentive for mechanization in the mines and, conversely, "the policy of those who seek a disruption of the existing wage structure would only postpone mechanization of the industry and perpetuate obsolete methods."[41]

The Lewis program, sometimes referred to as his Jacksonville program, was based on the belief that if the union could hold the line on wages, the operators in the union fields would be forced to instal loading machines and would, in so doing, be able to lower their costs of production and thereby drive out of business the less efficient and, presumably, nonunion operators. By this process, industry capacity would be brought into proper relation to consumer demand. Lewis also argued that freight rates charged by the railroads should be adjusted to remove the existing unfair advantages enjoyed by many nonunion operators, notably those in West Virginia and points south. Stabilization of the industry also depended on extending union protection to all coal miners, Lewis argued. "Every car of Non-union coal at present represents an intrusion into the general industrial system of a malignant influence; because this coal could not be produced and sold, as it is now, without the denial of American rights in the mines from whence it comes and without an uneconomic system of railroad favoritism to boost it to market," he claimed.[42]

Considerations of wage levels and wage structures played an important role in John L. Lewis's program for economic recovery of the industry, not to mention survival of the union and solidification of his own power and prestige in the labor movement.[43] It is interesting to note that Lewis urged that the tonnage payment system be abolished in favor of a time payment system. His argument rested on the notion that a uniform daily wage would make labor costs per unit of output higher for the less efficient (i.e., low productivity) mines and would force them from the industry. He also argued that elimination of piecework in the mines would help eliminate the source of many local disputes and would reduce local strikes. Also built into the traditional wage system were payments for various forms of dead work, which routinely created conflict and disagreement. A straight daily wage would, for Lewis, improve industrial relations in the industry: "It is Utopian to expect that such local conflicts can be entirely eliminated as long as piecework prevails and men are men."[44]

A second dimension to the Lewis wage-mechanization program for the industry was the elimination of regional wage differences, which tended, he felt, to keep too many mines, most notably the nonunion ones, in operation when they should be shut down. Over the years, Lewis kept steadfastly to his wage policy, and as he gained increasing control over the administration of the union, his policy became the union's policy. "The union's current [wage] strategy is easy to describe," one scholar observed in 1955. It has remained essentially unchanged since Lewis first tried to justify the Jacksonville scale: "By raising wage rates (and labor costs per ton) and by eliminating regional wage-rate differentials, heavy pressure to mechanize will be brought to bear on all firms, especially the relatively high-cost operations. . . . The increased use of machines will enable the union to exact even higher wage rates or shorter hours or both. Higher wage rates, in brief, encourage mechanization, which permits still higher wage rates."[45]

Lewis was, however, forced temporarily to abandon his no-backward-step, high-wage policy when an incipient mutiny among the membership in Illinois and Ohio threatened his control of the union. He had reasoned that, in his refusal to make wage concessions, the large coal operators would be forced to introduce labor-saving equipment and otherwise modernize their operations, while the smaller firms, which could not afford to mechanize, would be forced to shut down. He believed that technology, with the aid of the union's wage policy, would save the industry. It might have worked if, first, the union could have organized the whole industry and imposed a uniform wage and, second, if Lewis had been able to neutralize local control so that a wage scale for machine operators could have been negotiated and limitations on the use of machinery eliminated. Lewis was unable to do either during the 1920s. In response to rank-and-file pressure in parts of the Central Competitive Field, where coal markets and jobs were being lost to nonunion coal, Lewis reluctantly agreed to let district unions negotiate their own wage scales without reference to the Jacksonville scale. Further, Lewis relaxed his long-standing opposition to federal government involvement in the industry's affairs when, in the summer of 1928, the UMWA testified for and strongly supported passage of the Watson bill, a piece of legislation that would have exempted coal operators from antitrust laws so they could fix prices and that would have promoted industry collective bargaining. Lewis hoped at that point that the government could save the coal industry and his union.

Objections to the Lewis Plan

Mechanization was at the center of John L. Lewis's 1925 plan to stabilize the coal industry. A key element of this mechanization policy was the conversion of the traditional tonnage payment system to a daily or hourly wage rate. But on this question of a new payment system, it soon became clear that Lewis did not represent the views of all miners, especially after they realized that day wages involved more than just a new way of calculating their income; it involved a new way of doing things in the mines.

Lewis failed to address, either in his book or in response to his critics on the union's convention floor, the concealed issues behind the payment question. It is interesting to note that the industry itself was not so certain that a day wage was the only system to use with the installation of loading machines. One industry spokesman argued in 1924 that a tonnage payment system is better "because, by that method of compensation, the machines are most likely to be worked nearer to their full capacity and . . . the attendant work around a loader will be more expeditiously done."[46] But another, who clearly understood the changes the loading machines would bring to the labor process, argued that day wages were better for several reasons: "Loading machines are going to force mine operators to assume full responsibility for what goes on at the face . . . [which] means men working at the face are going to be under more direct supervision."[47] Mines could be made to function more like Henry Ford's automobile factories, with close supervision and a daily wage, one mine superintendent claimed.[48]

The day-wage system had the obvious advantage for the mine owners of limiting the returns to the mine workers who operated the new machinery, but it had the disadvantage of requiring greater supervision. After a local machine-loading scale was negotiated and several loaders were installed in a large Illinois mine in the summer of 1924, one trade journal summed up the problem very succinctly: "The job that now confronts that coal company and every other company that adopts machine loading in Illinois is the ever-present job of getting a full day's work out of men paid on that basis."[49] Several plans were suggested by various industry people for sharing the gains from productivity increases with the workers. Most of these plans involved a combination day wage, or minimum wage, and a bonus or incentive payment for production beyond a fixed standard.[50] Lewis showed no interest in any of these gain-sharing plans, preferring instead to rely on periodical wage negotiations to share in productivity increases.

At the 1927 UMWA convention, a delegate from the Belleville, Illinois, region made an eloquent appeal to the union policy-making body for a return to the tonnage payment system with mechanical loaders. His arguments on the convention floor were well thought out and were based on two years' experience with the new technology. He explained that the reason he and his fellow workers were opposed to the day wage was that it "gives the boss the right to direct every move." In other words, he said, "You have a boss looking down your shirt collar all day long."

In referring to the trade journal *Coal Age* and its advocacy of scientific management in the mines, the delegate claimed that the flat day wage "will factoryize the mine. . . . They want to make a Ford plant out of every coal mine."[51] Anticipating what was in store for miners, the delegate said emphatically, "we don't want a day-wage scale because in our opinion based on our experience, a flat day-wage scale will eventually mean a haven for efficiency experts and straw jacks and an underground hell for coal miners." Finally, the Illinois miner told the convention that he and his fellow workers objected to the day wage because it excluded miners from participating in the productivity gains created by the loading machines. But, he urged, "if we were put on a tonnage rate and the capacity of that machine is increased, our wages are going to automatically increase with the capacity of the machine." In concluding his appeal to the convention, the delegate offered a resolution that said, in essence, that the only way that miners could safeguard their "independence and prevent the factoryizing of our mines" was to "demand a tonnage rate for all cutting, loading and shooting of coal, and no day-wage scale be tolerated under any condition."

Response to this appeal came from three individuals: William Mitch, president of Indiana's District 11 and a staunch Lewis supporter, John Brophy, president of District 2 in central Pennsylvania and a long-time opponent of Lewis: and Lewis himself. Mitch said that several mines in Indiana had installed loading machines and were operating on a day-wage scale. He admitted that within his district there was a "vast difference of opinion as to what should be done" on the pay question, but he also said that he thought that the decisions should be made by the union officers whose job it is to negotiate the contract.[52] He doubted that tonnage rates were feasible, because "when you go into the problem of fixing a tonnage rate you have got a tremendous problem . . . because we have found that there are too many opinions as to what should be done." But, he told the delegates, "I think you will all agree with me when I say that the officials of this organization, the men whom you pay, are certainly going to do the very best that they can for you."

If Mitch managed to divert attention away from the issue by trying to get the delegates to defer to their union leaders, John Brophy avoided the issue altogether when he rose to speak immediately after Mitch. Instead, Brophy launched an attack on Lewis's failure to organize the nonunion fields.[53] True, Lewis had been unable to expand the union's jurisdiction into hostile coalfields, but in his failure to respond to the mechanization questions raised by the Illinois delegate, Brophy missed an important opportunity to demonstrate his concern for a problem facing rank-and-file miners throughout the industry.

Lewis then took the floor and turned the situation to his advantage.

"May the Lord save us from our alleged friends," he said. In referring to Brophy's attack, which Lewis went to great lengths to answer, he lamented that "it is an astounding situation that men who profess themselves to be leaders in our great movement should come upon the floor of our council chamber and give utterance to sentiments and to statements, every word of which brings joy to the sworn enemies of our movement and our people."[54]

Lewis's response to the "very pertinent discussion" by the delegate from Illinois was to say that the question would be discussed at the next Joint Interstate Conference "to the fullest possible degree consistent with our ability to secure consideration of it from the operators." That was it. There was no further discussion of the question of tonnage rates versus day rates on loading machines, although Lewis did use the opportunity to repeat his own position on the use of labor-saving machinery in general, a position the delegates had no doubt heard many times. He said "we stand for the encouragement of the installation of labor-saving devices and improved machinery in the mines. . . . We only ask that all of the benefits of that improved machinery be not taken by the operator entirely to himself."[55] That ended debate on the pay question, and the Lewis policy of bargaining for a day wage for machine operators became, in the years to follow, the official union policy.[56]

Lewis's diversion of convention debate on the issue did not, however, end rank-and-file support for the tonnage payment system, nor did it lessen rank-and-file concern over the impact that labor-saving machinery was having, and would have, on their jobs. Each year from 1927 until well into the 1940s, many local union resolutions were referred to the Scale Committee, under Lewis's control, which in turn ignored them. Interest in the industry for retaining at least some form of incentive pay waned in the late 1920s, so that by the time the technological revolution in underground loading exploded in the mid-1930s, the day wage and mechanical loading were inseparably paired.

CHAPTER 8

Union and Industry During The Great Depression

T̲H̲E̲ ̲Y̲E̲A̲R̲S̲ from 1925 to 1933 are an important transitional period for the coal industry. John L. Lewis increased his control over the UMWA internal affairs, although the union lost substantial membership and influence during the period. Coal operators, facing their worst economic crisis to date, began reorganizing themselves along more efficient lines and searching for ways to lower costs of production to remain competitive. The "American plan" of union busting, so popular in other industries, was applied with a vengeance in the coal industry in an effort to break the Jacksonville wage scale. At the same time, the technology for modernization was increasingly available during this period, and the industry, especially its larger firms, was determined to find ways to overcome local resistance to the use of machinery.

Breaking the Scale and the Union

Early in 1925, several coal companies in West Virginia, including Consolidation Coal Company, withdrew from their associations and announced they would reestablish the 1917 scale of wages in their mines. Day rates of pay for "company men" were reduced nearly $3.00, to $4.50, and tonnage rates were cut nearly in half, to $0.25 a ton.[1] The Pittsburgh Coal Company, the nation's largest producer at the time, had a somewhat different strategy for dealing with its employees. The company, which had closed its fifty-four mines in western Pennsylvania and Ohio in 1924 to protest the Jacksonville scale, began reopening them in April 1925 with imported workers willing to work at the 1917 wage scale. The company hired only those miners who were willing to sign a yellow dog contract, which made working nonunion a condition for employment. A company union was formed to forestall reorganization under the UMWA banner, and a private police force was employed to maintain company control in the mining camps. This union-breaking plan, referred to at the time as the Pittsburgh plan, was soon adopted by other operators in Pennsylvania, Ohio, and West Virginia. The result was that, not only were the operators able to return to a lower wage scale, but they also broke the control that miners and their pit committees had established over day-to-day operations at the mine site.

The Bethlehem Steel Company, owner of many captive mines in Pennsylvania and West Virginia, used the Pittsburgh plan to break the union and then instructed its own police force to see that union organizers were kept out of the coal camps. Control over private lives of their workers as well as over life on the job seemed to be the goal of the operators. In an interesting report to his employer, the head of the police department hired by Bethlehem in the Johnstown, Pennsylvania, area explained his role as he saw it in 1925: "The introduction of the Police Department on the Ellsworth Division, for the purpose of affording police protection during the resumption of operations on a non-union basis, has caused considerable activity of a wide divergence from that coming within the category of routine police operations. The constant vigilance necessary in the apprehension of labor agents, labor agitators, the exclusion of undesirables and the effecting of numerous arrests and prosecutions concident with the above mentioned conditions, is the natural cause of such divergence."[2]

In northern West Virginia, the UMWA attempted to forestall the wholesale abrogation of the 1924 wage scale by calling a strike, which proved to be the "most prolonged and disastrous ever waged in the State," according to former state attorney general H. B. Lee.[3] While the walkout was initiated by the union, it soon turned into a lockout by the owners. Coal operators posted notices on their bulletin boards and in the coal camps that, after a certain date, the mines would reopen only if miners were willing to return to work on a nonunion basis, to sign a nonunion pledge, and to work at a substantial reduction in pay. Breaking the influence of the union and the power of local pit committees clearly were the operators' goals, as they "employed additional mine guards, erected high barbed wire fences around their mines, posted watchmen at the gates to exclude unwanted visitors, and installed searchlights at strategic points," according to Lee, who visited the area in the spring of 1925. Miners who refused to return to work without their union found their families forceably evicted from company houses by the companies' private police forces (figure 21). Lee estimated that between 20,000 and 30,000 miners were so evicted in northern West Virginia during the mid-1920s.

The UMWA spent millions of dollars to support evicted miners and their families, with much of the money going to purchase building materials for the barrackslike structures the miners themselves constructed (figure 22).[4] Some miners and their families lived in these barracks for several years, since the struggle was a long one.[5] Eventually, the miners were forced to return to work to feed their families, but they did so reluctantly and bitterly. To this day, miners who lived through the events of that period remember it sadly as the one time in their lives when they were forced to work as scabs.

In 1925 the UMWA was justified in charging that the Mellons, Charles M. Schwab, and John D. Rockefeller, Jr., were conspiring to destroy the union. Representing Pittsburgh Coal, Bethlehem Steel, and Consolidation Coal, respectively, these individuals and their managers were in the forefront of the ruthless movement. Their objective was not simply to win wage concessions from the union, but to eliminate the union altogether in their mines in the tri-state area of Pennsylvania, West

FIGURE 21. *Coal miners' families were evicted from coal company houses, Pursglove, West Virginia. (Van A. Bittner Collection, West Virginia and Regional History Collection, West Virginia University Library)*

Virginia, and Ohio. The following letter addressed to the employees of the Pittsburgh Coal Company, dated February 17, 1927, leaves no doubt about the company's intention to run its mines on a union-free basis.[6]

To Our Men:

Don't believe any story that this company is going to sign up with the union on April 1 or any other time. This is not true and has been put out to scare you and make you unhappy.

We will never sign a scale with any union again.

We will always have open-shop mines.

The Pittsburgh Coal Company has operated on the open-shop basis for over eighteen months and will always operate that way. The open-shop plan makes it possible for us to give you men steadier work, better working conditions, and better pay, than is possible to give on any other plan.

The open-shop policy wins because it is the fairest, squarest policy. . . .

There will be steady work for you at our mines at good wages. You will be protected. Don't believe any stories that we will change.

We will never run any mine any way but shop open.

PITTSBURGH COAL COMPANY
J.D.A. Morrow, President

Some operators, not wanting to go to the extremes of the Pittsburgh plan, found other ways to circumvent their obligations under the 1924 agreement. In central Pennsylvania, the Rochester and Pittsburgh Coal and Iron Company, in a move anticipating modern corporate legerdemain, leased two of its mines to an independent operator, who mined the coal and sold it back to the owner. While the 400 union miners were given preference for the jobs under the leasing arrangement, production was carried out on an entirely nonunion basis.[7]

Another subterfuge, popular in some states, was an arrangement by which mine owners leased their mines to their own employees who, in turn, operated the mines on a cooperative basis. Coop mines were reported in Ohio, Indiana, and Illinois in 1925, with most of them working on what was called the 60/40 plan. From the sales of coal, the

FIGURE 22. *Coal miners' families constructed barracks after eviction from company houses. (Van A. Bittner Collection, West Virginia and Regional History Collection, West Virginia University Library)*

miners withheld 60 percent of the revenue to be divided among themselves to pay for their labor and supplies. The remaining 40 percent was turned over to the mine owner to cover his fixed costs and to return a profit to him.

In reporting on the cooperative movement, one trade journal, not wanting to give miners any credit for self-management, claimed that when a coop mine was established, the work force usually rehired the foreman and superintendent to run things. This journal described the experience at one mine: "These men had the sense to realize that 300 to 500 men could not possibly manage a mine by a purely democratic form of government. . . . Instead of trying to manage a coal mine by mob rule, they retained the manager of the mine."[8] While some cooperatively run mines were still in operation during the 1930s, most of them had failed for several reasons, not the least of which was opposition from the union.

The United Mine Workers was vehemently opposed to the operation of cooperative mines for practical reasons. First, since the cooperatives were devised specifically to lower the cost of coal by violating the Jacksonville wage scale, the miners so employed were put into a position of exploiting themselves and scabbing on those still working under union contract. Second, the union knew that when miners were hard-pressed to make a financial showing with their work, they would probably cut corners on safety and ignore the rules that had governed working conditions. That this occurred was confirmed by the same trade journal, which said that "all of the elaborate 'working conditions' which were written into the coal-mine wage scale . . . were eliminated by the miners themselves within a month after they began paying the cost of mining."[9] Finally, the union realized that the cooperative idea was a recession-induced phenomenon that probably would be rescinded when economic conditions improved. And this is, in fact, what happened. So opposed to cooperative mining was the union that several times it revoked the charters of local unions that had gone that route, and it imposed fines on individual union miners for working in coop mines.[10]

Industry Modernization

The determination of larger producers to break the power of the union must be viewed in the context of a broader movement in the industry to rationalize production and to stabilize sales. While small- and medium-sized firms seemed interested principally in obtaining relief from high wages during these years, the industry's giants were embarked on a far-reaching program of expansion, reorganization, and modernization.[11]

Horizontal expansion through merger and acquisition became widespread during 1924 and 1925. For example, the Pittsburgh Coal Company added eleven mines to its collection of sixty-four operations in western Pennsylvania and northern West Virginia. The West Virginia Coal and Coke Company acquired the holdings of the Main Island Creek Coal Company, giving the merged firm fifty-eight mines and making it the largest producer in the state at that time.[12] An estimated 6.2 percent of total U.S. coal production was affected by the merger movement in 1924 alone.[13] Corporate expansion took place vertically, also, as public utilities, steel firms, and other manufacturers took advantage of depressed conditions in the industry to buy coal properties at reduced prices. The number of captive mines increased during the period, with the major share being accounted for by steel firms.[14] Increased market control was the goal in some of the mergers, such as the acquisition of the Milwaukee-Western Fuel Company and the C. Reiss Coal Company by the Pittsburgh Coal Company. The three companies continued to operate as separate firms, but the purchase gave the Pittsburgh company virtual control over Lake Michigan coal trade.[15]

Internal reorganization in the large coal companies took several forms. Old-line management was replaced by younger, more aggressive individuals with engineering and scientific management experience. Production was centered in mines where the economies of large-scale operations could be realized, and those properties with less promise were permanently closed. Consolidation Coal Company, operating primarily in northern West Virginia, "through concentration of operations looking toward more economical production," reduced the number of operating mines from eighty in 1922 to fourty-four in 1927, while at the same time reporting a substantial increase in total output.[16] In a single county, the company was able to increase production by 35.3 percent between 1923 and 1927, while reducing the number of operating mines from sixteen to seven.[17] Economies of scale and an increase in the number of days worked per week explain most of the increased output, because there was yet very little increase in production through mechanization at those mines.

Early in 1925, *Coal Age* reported that Pittsburgh Coal was involved in a similar program: "This company, which has more than fifty mines in the Pittsburgh district, is embarking on a larger program of concentration of mine plants in which smaller and older mines are to be concentated into a fewer number of larger scale. These will be million-ton plants with every modern facility for cost cutting."[18] In Illinois, most of the large companies were involved in a similar course of action in the mid-1920s. "Every sound company in the state is beginning by trimming down all the mines it can, thus obtaining the best possible working time for the others. The Old Ben Coal Corporation, for instance, is now running four out of twelve mines," *Coal Age* reported.[19] National statistics on coal production by mine size show very clearly the trend toward concentration of production in larger mines during the 1920s. Class I mines, those producing 200,000 tons or more annually, accounted for 31.5 percent of total coal mined in 1922 but produced 65.2 percent of the nation's output in 1929.[20]

The merger movement, concentration of production in larger mines, and the other steps taken by the larger corporations during the 1920s set the stage for a technological revolution in underground coal mining. By the mid-1920s, there were many new developments in underground mining machinery. One trade journal reported in 1924 the development of at least thirty-six different mechanical loading devices; nine were still in the design and construction stage, but twenty-seven had operated underground with varying degrees of success. In the spring of 1924, the

American Mining Congress held its first convention, at which a full line of mechanical loading machines were exhibited for the industry, and by 1925 there was sufficient use of mechanical loaders to justify a nationwide survey by the Carnegie Institute of Technology.

There remained, however, several obstacles to widespread adoption of the new technology. Most of the new loading machines were not designed for use in low-coal seams, which ruled out their use in many fields. Another problem was financial, with firms finding it difficult to raise funds for the purchase of capital equipment when the prospects for selling their coal, at any price, were so gloomy. But even for those financially sound firms favorably situated in high coal, the owners had to deal with the problem of workers' resistance before they could mechanize. Mine workers' earlier opposition to the cutting machine carried forward to the 1920s, when many firms decided it was time to switch from hand loading to mechanical loading.

Coal Age, the most important trade journal of the period and a staunch promoter of mine mechanization, was quite explicit in defining the problem. Where mine workers were organized, they were able to block the use of mechanical loaders by refusing to agree to a wage rate for the loading machine operator. The *Coal Age* summary of the situation is worth quoting at length:

> It must be said . . . that progressiveness in engineering often is handi-
> capped by labor in such solidly unionized districts as the states of Il-
> linois and Indiana. The strong effort to introduce mechanical loaders is
> one case in point. Although the unionized Middle West is keen to use
> them, only twenty-five have ever penetrated Indiana and a bare four-
> teen in Illinois, whereas there are nearly 100 in West Virginia—52 of
> them of one make—and only a little less than fifty in Pennsylvania,
> most of these *in the non-union mines of that state.* Maneuvers by the
> operators to get wage scales fixed for loader operators have failed.[21]

It is clear from this statement that, in spite of the official UMWA position supporting mechanization, the industry viewed local union bargaining power and pit committee leadership as major obstacles. Abrogation of the Jacksonville agreement and implementation of the Pittsburgh plan of union busting meant, therefore, a great deal more than a return to a lower wage scale. Given favorable coal markets, it meant freedom from local union control and freedom to instal loading machines.

An interesting turn of events involved the union and the Hocking Valley, Ohio, coal mines. Here the subdistrict union renegotiated the terms of the interstate agreement in the summer of 1924 and made concessions that lowered mining costs without actually changing the Jacksonville wage scale. While sticking to the union's no-backward-step policy on wages, these Ohio mine workers agreed that the removal of slate would be the miners' responsibility. They also agreed to reductions in dead work charges, which further lowered costs and helped the mine owners remain competitive.

Most importantly, the Hocking Valley concessions involved a change in the miners' position on the installation of machinery. A clause inserted in this Ohio agreement read: "Men may be employed on new types of mining machinery at a temporary arranged wage between officers of the sub-district and operators introducing said new machinery as a test which will be used to arrive at a permanent scale for the working of said new machinery."[22] The inclusion of this provision, which not only permitted the installation of loading machines but permitted a "temporary arranged wage" for machine operators, indicated that in some areas miners, faced with the threat of unemployment, decided to change their position on machinery.

Paradoxically, miners agreed to the use of "labor-saving" technology in an attempt to save their jobs. Coming in the form of a concession during very difficult times, the new contract language also indicates that the introduction of labor-saving machinery in fact depended more on local conditions and less on the policy of the international union.

The Midwest Unionized Fields

The strategy of the Illinois and Indiana operators in the Jacksonville agreement years was to continue dealing with the district union, which had been entrenched there for many years, and to attempt to retain their rapidly declining share of the coal markets by lowering costs through modernizing their operations. They stuck with the Jacksonville scale, but by the end of 1924 coal from western Kentucky and other fields that had returned to the 1917 scale was passing through their states on its way to Chicago and other lake ports. The effect of this competition was to throw 30,000 miners in Illinois out of work and to reduce the workweek to two or three days for the remaining 50,000. Given these conditions, it is not surprising that a local agreement allowing the introduction of loading machines and establishing a machine operator's wage was signed at a large mine in this state.

In July 1924, the miners at the Orient no. 2 mine owned by the Chicago, Wilmington and Franklin Coal Company ratified an agreement that established a wage of $10.07 a day for operators of the Joy and the Myers-Whaley loading machines. While not the first contract in the industry to establish a wage scale for loading machine operators, this agreement was negotiated to be "the die in which all future wage agreements for machine operation probably will be cast." It was also heralded by the industry for another reason: "The most agreeable thing about it is that it puts machine loading on a per diem instead of a tonnage basis—and that in the citadel of unionism, Illinois."[23] *Coal Age* Washington correspondent reported that "official Washington" regarded the development as "an unexpected but highly gratifying surprise."[24] His assessment of the situation points out how important he perceived the agreement to be for the whole industry: "Opposition to the employment of machinery in coal mines long has been regarded as one of the sinister things which could be laid at the door of the union. The Illinois membership of the UMW has been regarded as the most reactionary element in that organization. That it should be willing to take this progressive step is regarded as making certain the universal application of this policy." The author of this article noted that the concession did not come too soon for the thousands of unemployed in the moribund Illinois coal industry. The mines in that state were operating at only 25 percent of capacity. Now, he reasoned, Illinois coal, by virtue of lower production costs, could begin to compete with coal from other fields where operators had broken the Jacksonville wage agreement.

To those who foresaw this Illinois development as a breakthrough in traditional resistance to new machinery, it was unfortunate that the accord was short-lived. First, the mine workers who had been operating the undercutting machines became dissatisfied with their rate of pay and instigated a strike. After this was settled, the company became increasingly upset with the manner in which the new loading machines were being operated. Apparently, the men running the loaders engaged in a little "soldiering." According to a company spokesman, the men resented the changes brought about by the machinery and refused "to load the cars to capacity or to do their utmost to obtain a good tonnage." The *Coal Trade Bulletin* referred to the miners' resistance as "Russian communistic sabotage," and argued that the miners did not know what was in their own best interests.[25] "A brave attempt was made by capital to put in machinery that would enable southern Illinois to stay in the market despite high wages and severe competition. Labor failed to appreciate this effort." The company announced, only three months after they were introduced, that the loading machines would be removed, and production resumed on a hand-loading basis.

While the record is not available to document why the miners at the Orient no. 2 mine refused to cooperate with management's drive for greater productivity, one possible explanation emerged at the 1927 UMWA convention. It seems that, although the $10.07 a day wage was substantially higher than other pay rates at the time, the loading machine operators felt they should be paid on a tonnage basis so that they could benefit from the substantial productivity increase the company would realize. As noted above, one Illinois delegate to this convention complained that the loading machine made a "factory" of the mine and increased the amount of supervision over the work crews. For these and perhaps other reasons, the miners at Orient no. 2 were effective in blocking the introduction of new technology in 1924, even though the official UMWA policy, supported by the district and subdistrict unions, was to support mine mechanization.

General economic conditions for the coal industry continued to deteriorate during 1925 and 1926, with some major disruptions within the industry beginning to appear during this time. By 1927, the Jacksonville agreement existed in name only in most of the nation's coalfields. Only in Illinois and Indiana were operators still paying the $7.50-a-day Jacksonville wage, and they were finding it increasingly diffcult to retain their customers even though their mines were some of the most efficient in the country. In other fields, the operators had returned to the 1917 scale, or to an even lower one, and had reduced their coal prices accordingly. With lower priced coal, these nonunion operators were able to encroach on markets traditionally held by the Illinois and Indiana producers, with the result that these states began to lose their relative share of the coal trade.

Operating on a nonunion basis gave operators the advantage of continuity of production, which helped them win customers away from the union fields where strikes sometimes occurred. George W. Reed, president of the Illinois-based Peabody Coal Company, said in 1928 that "an important factor in the loss of business to these [nonunion] districts is the uncertainty of production through a long record of strikes and suspensions."[26]

Proof of the nonunion advantage is found in the production data for each state. In the five years between 1923 and 1928, the Illinois share of total U.S. production dropped from 14.1 percent to 11.0 percent, while at the same time West Virginia's share, for example, increased from 21.0 percent to 26.6 percent.[27] The Peabody Coal Company spokesman claimed that the Illinois and Indiana operators "cannot survive under a continuation of a scale that is so far out of line with those paid in competing districts." Nor could they compete successfully unless they could increase productivity through modernization of their operations and at the same time assure their customers uninterrupted production. In Illinois, the operators got all three items: a wage cut, a negotiated agreement on mechanization, and a four-year labor agreement.

The loss of markets to the southern nonunion operators made the Illinois operators uncooperative, if not hostile, when the UMWA demanded a renewal of the Jacksonville scale in the spring of 1927. The union announced that it would stick to its no-backward-step policy and expect the operators to continue paying $7.50 a day. The operators countered with a demand that wages be reduced and put on a sliding scale tied to coal prices. With neither side willing to compromise on the wage question, the union issued a strike order for April 1, 1927. Union miners throughout the Central Competitive Field were called on to support the walkout, with the result that 200,000 miners in Illinois, Indiana, Ohio, and western Pennsylvania walked off their jobs.[28] After several months, consumer stockpiles of coal began to diminish, so that by early autumn coal prices began to rise. Given this favorable turn of events, the operators in Illinois and Indiana agreed that if the miners would return to work they would pay the Jacksonville scale, at least until March 31, 1928. This temporary agreement also called for the appointment of a commission, made up of two union officials and two operators, to study the Illinois situation and to make recommendations for a permanent settlement.[29]

When this commission made its report to a union-management meeting in February, 1928, it reported that Illinois coal was fifty to seventy-five cents a ton too expensive to compete with nonunion coal. The commission then recommended a general wage reduction, a wage scale for miners employed on "mechanical devices," and changes "in the working agreement which contemplate better control of the miners by the producers."[30] The commission said "it is the wage rates and unnecessarily restrictive conditions that can be wisely adjusted." For example, "there are many mines where a removal of limitation on machines or output would permit tonnage men to earn on a substantially lower wage rate the same amounts they have been earning under the Jacksonville scale." Even when faced with these recommendations, Lewis remained adamant in his refusal to agree to a wage concession. Undoubtedly, he was in agreement with the other recommendations relating to mechanization, but he held fast on the wage issue. Once again the result was an impasse.

Upon termination of the temporary agreement on March 31, 1928, Lewis again called a strike.[31] This time neither the walkout nor the hard-line wage policy was well received by the rank and file miners. Several large locals rebelled from the national union and took the unprecedented action of signing local agreements so their impoverished members could return to work. Miners representing seventy-eight locals met in May at Belleville, Illinois, to denounce the officers of the Illinois district union and the Lewis wage policy. *Coal Age* claimed it was "the first step in a nationwide movement to oust John L. Lewis,"[32] a movement that seemed confirmed when 2,000 miners in nothern Illinois actually broke away from the UMWA and formed a rival union, called the Northern Illinois Mine Workers Union. This new union began negotiations with the operators and later signed an agreement calling for a $5.00-a-day wage and $1.20 a ton for pick mining.

It was apparent that these Illinois miners, whose commitment to union solidarity had rarely been questioned, were desperate for jobs and were determined to protect what they perceived to be their own interests, irrespective of the policies and goals of the UMWA. The rebellion was not limited to Illinois. At Bellaire, Ohio, 300 miners representing forty-two locals met in May to find ways to regain their jobs. They passed a resolution calling for Lewis's resignation as president of the United Mine Workers.[33] The extent of the insurgency movement has not been fully documented, but it was of sufficient importance to force Lewis to call a special meeting of the union's National Policy Committee to consider which course of action should be taken. As a result of this high-level meeting on July 18 1928, Lewis announced that the UMWA was abandoning its policy of strict adherence to the Jacksonville scale. Henceforth, each district would be free to negotiate its own contracts "upon a basis mutually satisfactory."[34]

The movement to oust Lewis picked up momentum after 1928 and continued to grow during the early 1930s. In Illinois, the opposition to Lewis expressed itself in the formation of rival unions; first, the Reorganized United Mine Workers of America appeared in 1930–31 and then the Progressive Mine Workers in 1932. Lewis finally won the power struggle in Illinois in 1933 when he removed the district officials and put the district under trusteeship.[35] From that point, Lewis was able to formulate union policies largely without opposition and could negotiate and sign labor agreements without the necessary ratification by the membership. (From 1933 until his retirement in 1958, Lewis exercised unchallenged control over the administration of the UMWA.)

Before the end of the month, after district unions were released from strict adherence to the Jacksonville scale, Illinois operators and UMWA District 12 officials met to negotiate a settlement of the strike. The union representatives, with thousands of their members out of work and with others working under maverick agreements, found themselves in a disadvantageous bargaining posture. By the first of September, the union made some major concessions and agreement was reached. The $7.50 daily wage was reduced by 18.7 percent to $6.10 and the tonnage rate from $1.08 to $0.91.

However, the operators insisted on more than a wage concession. They demanded and obtained changes in work practices to increase productivity and they got a statewide wage rate established for loading machine operators and helpers. They also insisted on the right to hire without having to rely entirely on the local union's waiting list. The union agreed to the following language: "the operators will employ members of the UMWA when available and when in the judgment of the operator the applicant is competent." Further, the operators wanted a more formalized and more consistent grievance procedure, so the union agreed that a permanent arbitrator would make the final and binding decision. Finally, the operators demanded that the terms of the contract be binding for a long term. The termination date they settled on was March 31, 1932, making this contract the longest yet in the industry's history.[36]

UMWA Authorization of Mechanization

It is noteworthy that this 1928 Illinois agreement marked the first time a major subdivision of the union had agreed to terms that removed the obstacles for full-scale mechanization of the mines. Practically, it cleared the way if the contract could be imposed on local unions and on the miners who had to operate the machines. The agreement stated:

"The right to install mechanical loaders and conveyors of all types is recognized," and that payment for loading coal with such machinery shall be on a tonnage basis "if practicable."[37] The union and company representatives were not, however, able to arrive at acceptable tonnage rates of pay for machine operators, so a commission was appointed to "study various conditions surrounding the use of such machinery," and to "arrive at a tonnage basis of pay." In the meantime, the following scale of wages was established:

Men loading coal on conveyors	$8.04
Men employed drilling and shooting	$8.20
Cutting machine operators and helpers	$10.07[38]
Mechanical loading machine operators	$10.07
Mechanical loading machine helpers	$9.00
Men employed at the face as members of loading machine crew	$7.50

Either the commission was unable to arrive at a tonnage rate for loading machine operators or the rate agreed to was unacceptable to the miners, because the practice of paying a day rate to men who worked with machinery continued without change. For whatever the reason, day rates became the established practice in the industry, so much so that when the 1932 contract was negotiated, tonnage rates were not even mentioned. Only hand loaders continued to be paid by the ton, and as they were replaced by machinery, incentive systems of pay disappeared.

The new contract, which Lewis wholeheartedly supported, was submitted to the membership of District 12 for ratification, and it passed by the narrow margin of 26,838 to 25,497.[39] Many miners, anxious to return to work, were willing to accept a pay cut and were willing to accept the concessions permitting employer-controlled mechanization.

Once the 1928 agreement had been ratified, the Illinois operators wasted no time in placing orders for machinery to load their coal. Annual reports from the U.S. Bureau of Mines reveal how rapidly the transition to mechanized mining took place in the state and, by contrast, how retarded the movement was in a nonunion state such as West Virginia (table 7). The jump from 13.3 percent in 1928 to 59.4 percent in 1931 was clearly a result of the mechanization agreement. For a short while it appeared that, by agreeing to the installation of loading machines and to a wage scale for machine operators, the Illinois mine workers had saved their jobs. State coal production increased from 46,848,000 tons in 1927 to 60,658,000 in 1929, and the state's share of the national market inched upward from 9.0 percent to 11.3 percent in the same period.[40] Unfortunately, the Illinois recovery was short-lived. As the national economy declined in 1929 and 1930, the demand for coal slumped, and production in all the coalfields dropped dramatically.

It is important to note that the mechanical loading devices that the Illinois operators ordered, however, were not the Joy loader, Goodman shovel, or others of the fully mechanized types then available. In surprisingly large numbers, they placed orders for the simple pit-car loader, the inexpensive, inclined conveyor that moved the coal from floor level to mine car with minimum effort of the mine worker. In addition to their low cost—some cost only $700 in 1928—the pit-car loaders increased labor productivity without major changes in the labor process and without increasing the need for more supervision. The pit-car loader did not increase productivity as much as the mobile loading machines, but their use did offer an opportunity for the miners to clean the coal of refuse before it was sent to the surface. This advantage obviated the need for expensive cleaning and preparation facilities on the surface.

It has been argued that the pit-car loader was a transitional form of technology, preceding the mobile loaders manufactured by Joy and others. In a strictly mechanical or engineering sense, this obviously was not the case. Fully mechanized loaders had been on the market for years by 1928 and were readily available and technically feasible for use in the high-coal seams of Illinois. The pit-car loader may have been transitional in the sense that it changed the labor process very little in a state where

TABLE 7

**Underground Bituminous Coal Loaded Mechanically,
Illinois and West Virginia**
(%)

	Illinois	West Virginia
1928	13.3	1.7
1929	33.0	2.0
1930	48.0	2.3
1931	59.4	2.2
1932	57.1	1.3
1933	58.9	1.2

Source: U.S. Bureau of Mines *Mineral Resources,* selected years (Washington D.C.: Government Printing Office).

opposition to mechanization had been widespread. The Illinois operators desperately needed increases in productivity in order to retain their shrinking markets. With full mine mechanization blocked by restrictive local practices and uncooperative mine workers, the pit-car loader may well have been the only form of mechanization the Illinois operators could undertake at that time.[41]

Although the mine worker using a pit-car loader in his room was no longer paid a tonnage rate, the day-rate schedule in the 1928 agreement was supposed to be temporary, pending agreement on tonnage rates. Even though payment by the day altered a practice as old as mining itself, there were some advantages to the miners in using these conveyors, and these advantages changed attitudes toward the use of machinery. First, the day rate for loaders was $8.04, an amount substantially higher than the $6.10 negotiated for timbermen, trackmen, and other inside day labor. Second, it was claimed by the operators that the pit-car loader would enable the mine worker to load twenty tons of coal per shift with the same effort it formerly took to load ten tons. If this increase in productivity meant that Illinois could recapture some of its lost markets, it meant more work for everybody, or at least regular employment for those who were rehired. And third, the pit-car loader did not materially affect the manner in which coal was mined. The mine worker retained much of his traditional job control, and he continued to work mostly without supervision. The freedom of the miner to leave work at his discretion was, however, discouraged by many operators, who began docking the men a fixed amount if they came out of the mine before the end of the shift.[42] For miners, the loss of this freedom must have been offset by the other advantages, principally the opportunity for more work without a substantial change in job content.

CHAPTER 9

Government Intervention in the Industry

Economic CONDITIONS in the nation's coal industry shifted from bad to worse as the national economy slumped in the early 1930s. As business in general declined, coal output fell from a peak of 573,366,985 tons in 1926 to 309,709,872 tons in 1932. This cutback in output was accompanied by a decrease in the number of men employed from 593,647 to 406,380 during the same period. The average number of days worked per year fell from 215 to 146 and, at the same time, average hourly earnings of coal miners fell from $0.76 an hour to $0.50 (see appendix table C). Interregional competition intensified, with the result that prices continued to be cut, in some cases to levels below the cost of production. The average price of a ton of coal was $2.06 in 1926, but was only $1.31 in 1932,[1] and in that year only 16 percent of 1,900 reporting coal companies had a net income after taxes.[2]

The times were incredibly difficult for mine workers and operators alike. Many solutions were offered for the industry's ills. As Irving Bernstein noted in his book *The Turbulent Years*, the Great Depression made everyone an economist: "Panacea makers set busily to work and found large audiences for their concoctions."[3] And it is not surprising that the means by which order eventually emerged from the chaos involved methods that the government, the industry, and John L. Lewis would have found absolutely unpalatable in less desperate times.

Industry Self-Regulation

A concrete plan for stabilizing the industry was proposed by the National Coal Association in December 1931. The plan called for the formation of sales agencies in each of the coal-producing districts for

185

the purpose of eliminating interfirm price competition and for promoting the use of coal through joint advertising. Under the plan, individual coal operators would agree to sell their coal exclusively through the sales agent and, in the event that total demand fell, each producer would curtail his output in proportion to his original share of the region's output. There was, of course, a serious question as to whether this price-fixing and output restriction proposal would be legal under the nation's antitrust laws. The NCA legal counsel argued that the plan did not violate the antitrust laws as long as no effort was made to coerce or compel recalcitrant producers to subscribe to the plan.

The NCA anticipated many problems in obtaining sufficient cooperation in this highly competitive industry, yet urged adoption of the sales agency idea because "it will tend to the stabilization of bituminous coal production in the respective districts, and will develop for the operators a fair return on the capital invested and for the employees a better return in earnings."[4] If this industry self-help plan worked, it would have the obvious advantages of improving profit margins for coal producers and of establishing a business climate conducive to investment in new mining technology. A hidden agenda item was the association's hope that, if the sales agency plan worked, it would forestall the growing pressure for legislative intervention into the economic affairs of the industry.[5]

So eager were the operators in the southern high volatile field to escape the pattern of destructive competition that had driven coal prices below the cost of production, that they moved quickly to implement the NCA marketing agency idea. They organized a firm called Appalachian Coals, Inc., and vested it with the responsibility of selling the coal of all of its affiliates. Within three months of its formation in early 1932, 147 coal companies in southern West Virginia, western Virginia, and eastern Kentucky had committed their tonnage to Appalachian Coals. The combined output of these operators amounted to 73 percent of the total commercial production in the southern field.[6]

The Justice Department immediately raised questions concerning the legality of the organization, since its admitted purpose was to restrict competition and to limit output. In a landmark decision in March 1933, the U.S. Supreme Court ruled that the activities of this sales agency did not violate the Sherman Antitrust Act.[7] The Court reasoned that the formation of a sales agency eliminated the destructive aspects of coal markets and improved the economic health of the industry. In this new and much more flexible approach to the issue of restraint of trade, the

Court seemed to reflect the general public's loss of faith in unrestricted competition. As an economic system for the allocation of resources, the competitive model had so clearly failed for the coal industry that it is understandable why the Supreme Court might approve a plan that offered some hope for the salvation of the industry, even though it involved collusive price fixing and output restrictions. Following this favorable decision, plans were made in many of the coalfields for similar sales agencies, but their economic role was largely overshadowed by the regulatory legislation enacted by Congress in the spring of 1933.[8]

Government Regulation

The experiences of World War I's Fuel Administration with industry control were important in the formulation of a government strategy for management of the coal industry.[9] All of the studies made of the coal industry during the 1920s, notably the U.S. Coal Commission investigation, offered recommendations for stabilizing the industry. In 1922, then-Secretary of Commerce Herbert Hoover proposed a plan to attack the problem of excess capacity in the industry by financially penalizing mines that worked less than full time and by using the funds to compensate owners of less efficient mines for closing their operations. Hoover, at this early date, also proposed cooperative district associations that would sell coal for their members.[10] Most of the plans for industry stabilization focused on the problem of excess capacity and destructive competition. Only a few of the proposed remedies dealt with the long-term growth of the industry in the face of increased rivalry from competing fuels.

The movement by progressives within the UMWA for nationalization was discussed in chapter 7. Events, it seems, were converging in such a way as to vindicate those who believed that the market economy was an untenable way for organizing the nation's productive resources and those who believed that public ownership and control of industry were necessary. As early as the spring of 1928, John L. Lewis—a lifetime Republican, a union leader more conservative than most, and a vocal opponent of the nationalization movement within his own union—became convinced that his laissez-faire program for industry survival would not work and that the only remaining hope for the industry and for his union lay with federal government intervention. Lewis's chief economist, W. Jett Lauck, is credited with working out the details of a program that would give the union the bargaining power necessary for negotiating a nationwide wage scale and that would give the operators a means for ending destructive price competition.

When the UMWA plan was introduced as a bill in Congress by Indiana's Republican senator, James E. Watson, it met with a cool reception from coal industry lobbyists and supporters. While the industry certainly approved of exempting operators from the antitrust laws so they could organize price-fixing sales agencies, it objected vociferously to those sections of the proposed legislation that required operators to bargain with the union, established the miners' right to a checkweighman, and abolished company scrip. The Watson bill died in committee; it was reintroduced in 1929 again without success, because prevailing economic philosophy still resisted the federal government's assuming a direct role in the affairs of a competitive industry.

In 1932, Lewis tried again for legislation to stabilize the industry and to promote unionism. Similar in many ways to the union's earlier proposed legislation, this Davis-Kelly bill proposed a national coal commission to license operators who sold coal in interstate commerce and to act as a public referee to assure fair trade practices in the industry. The bill encouraged the formation of sales agencies such as Appalachian Coals, Inc., and assured that collective bargaining would be established in the industry.[11] The National Coal Association attacked the bill in committee hearings, and *Coal Age* editorialized that "unionization by legislative fiat is vicious in principle and dangerous in practice."[12] The bill failed to pass, but it became, along with the Watson bill, an important influence on New Deal recovery legislation enacted in the spring of 1933.

The National Industrial Recovery Act (NIRA) became public law on June 16, 1933. The purpose of the act was "the removal of obstruction to the full and free flow of interstate commerce, promotion of welfare through organization of industry under adequate governmental supervision, promotion of the fullest use of production capacity through increased purchasing power, reduction of unemployment, improvement of labor standards, and conservation of natural resources."[13] The act included provisions to implement these aims and mandated industrial codes of fair competition for each industry. The industrial codes were to be formulated by trade associations in each industry and then presented to the president for his approval. Once approved, the codes would become the set of rules governing general business practices for each industry.

Each code was required to have a provision asserting the right of employees to engage in collective bargaining, prohibiting yellow dog contracts, and declaring that employers should comply with the maximum hours, minimum wage rates, and other conditions of employment established by the National Recovery Administration (NRA) and the president. To enforce the industrial codes, a penalty of $500 a day could be imposed for any violation and, further, the president was given the power to license industry if it became necessary.[14]

The Union Reorganizes

The NIRA codes put the federal government in the position of policing business conduct and interfering with traditional laissez-faire business decision making. Section 7a guaranteed workers the right to organize unions of their own choosing and to bargain collectively with their employers. Within one week after the NIRA became law, a union organizer in West Virginia reported on the speed with which miners flocked back to the union: "We expect to be practically through with every mine in the state and have every miner under the jurisdiction of our union by first of next week."[15] Northern West Virginia, which was only partially organized, and southern West Virginia, which had no organization at all, came under union protection as tens of thousands of miners signed union cards and were sworn in at mass meetings. By August 1, the UMWA's membership drive had successfully penetrated nearly every producing field and reached nearly every mine except the captive mines owned by steel firms.

The speed with which the UMWA was able to rebuild its membership rolls in districts where operators had worked their mines on a nonunion basis since the abrogation of the Jacksonville agreement is generally credited to the protection guaranteed to unions in the NIRA and to Lewis's organizing genius. Both factors were undeniably important, but what appears to be a nearly spontaneous rebirth of the UMWA was in fact a culmination of several years of local struggles to win union recognition. Local strikes in 1931 and 1932, many of which were initiated by miners without official union leadership, indicated that the spirit of collective action had not been stamped out by the open-shop policies of the operators. This militancy in the face of massive unemployment provided the backdrop for the successes scored by the organizers whom Lewis sent into the field in June 1933.

Why coal operators, many of whom had fought the union bitterly for years, would acquiesce at this point in history and agree to recognize the union is somewhat puzzling. The explanation lies in the fact that many apparently were confused by the Roosevelt administration and its intentions, while others were caught unaware by the whirlwind organizing drive that swept the coalfields in June and July 1933. Others actually welcomed the union. They perceived "the New Deal reforms and the unionization of the miners as an opportunity to resurrect a declining industry."[16] These operators "favored the UMW as an instrument to equalize wage rates, and they saw the New Deal's economic recovery program as a means to control prices, allocate markets, and rationalize an otherwise anarchic industry." They knew that the stability that the NIRA and the union could bring to the industry would also establish a climate for the modernization and mechanization of the mines.

A Code for Coal

Establishing a code for the bituminous coal industry proved to be one of the most difficult tasks faced by General Hugh Johnson, administrator of the National Recovery Administration. No code "gave rise to more severe struggle, more perplexities, and more procedural crises" than did the coal code.[17] The chronic problems of the industry, the interregional rivalries, and the conflicts between union and nonunion operators contributed to the difficulties. Added to these factors was a long-standing coal operator antipathy toward government involvement in business affairs. In all fairness, it should be noted that some operators supported the idea of a government-enforced code of conduct. For the most part, however, the industry's position, as expressed through the National Coal Association, was that if the antitrust laws were relaxed, industrial self-government would be sufficient to bring about the desired recovery.

Some employers did refuse to recognize the union even though their employees were signing union cards in unprecedented numbers. Pressure was put on these recalcitrant operators by "militant miners, acting on their own," who walked off their jobs. Pressure also came from the White House, since President Franklin Roosevelt was anxious for all coal operators to come to Washington to meet with Lewis and NRA officials to hammer out a code of fair competition for the industry. In August, hearings finally began, with operators from every field voicing their opinions on proposed terms of the administration's industry code. Many operators objected to the wage levels Lewis was demanding, while others opposed any restrictions on the length of the workday. Some wanted a general code for the whole industry, and a few operators argued for separate district codes to allow for different mining conditions.

Miners became impatient as these hearings dragged on through August and into September. Anxious for a settlement with a living wage, they threatened to strike and actually did so in western Pennsylvania. In September, 75,000 miners quit work in an effort to force the government, mine management, and union officials in Washington to come to an agreement.[18] This show of strength had the desired effect, because in late September the operators in the Appalachian region agreed to the terms of a labor contract that became the basis for the labor provisions of an NRA bituminous coal code.

The code was a compromise between those who wanted centralized authority and those who opted for a decentralized administration of the act—that is, between those who sought more government control and those who argued for industrial self-management.

The Appalachian Agreement

With the expressed belief that it "marks the beginning of a new era in the task of stabilizing and modernizing the economic processes" of the industry, the Appalachian agreement became effective on October 2, 1933, and expired March 31, 1934. The agreement, which covered approximately 70 percent of the U.S. bituminous output, soon was extended to other districts, so that the whole industry began working under a union contract that had the full force of federal NRA authority behind it.

Praising the coal code as a great experiment in "tri-partnership of industry," the editor of *Coal Age* thought the minimum wage provision of the code was its most important feature. "Definitely pegging wages puts an end to that particularly vicious form of competition under which the wage earner was the chief victim of a frantic scramble for tonnage at any price," the trade journal proclaimed.[19]

Some operators also recognized the stabilizing influence a minimum wage and uniform benefits could bring to the industry. One northern coal operator wired Lewis soon after the code was approved: "I want to congratulate you on getting a code . . . which puts the United Mine Workers in every mine in the country which I am sure will do more to stabilize the . . . coal industry than anything which has been done in its history."[20] The important feature of the 1933 Appalachian agreement and the code provisions based on it was, for the industry, the fact that negotiated wages would be uniformly imposed across the coalfields. By taking wages out of competition, the operators could move ahead with mechanization of their mines without the earlier fear that their coal would be in competition with nonunion, low-wage coal. The higher wage level negotiated in this agreement provided an added inducement for operators to substitute machinery for traditional and hand methods.

Even though the terms of the coal code were negotiated in Washington without direct rank-and-file input and were put into effect without ratification by the union membership, the substantial wage increases and other benefits were welcomed by miners who had been suffering increasing hardships since the collapse of the Jacksonville agreement. And even though the agreement set the stage for the mechanical transformation of the industry and the loss of traditional job control, it offered miners the hope that the industry could be stabilized, the union rebuilt, and their jobs restored. Workers throughout the industry were faced with the same problem the Illinois miners had faced in 1928: they were desperate for a job at a living wage and were not in a position to protect the local control they had enjoyed under hand loading. In fact, the situation did not present itself to rank-and-file union members at the time as a choice. It was only later that many realized what they had given up during these desperate times.

Under the agreement and the bituminous code, geographic wage differentials were maintained, although the minimum wage levels established in all districts were many times higher than wages paid before the agreement was signed. An eight-hour day and a five-day week were established, along with the right of miners to select their own checkweighman. A grievance procedure ending in third-party arbitration was established. The long-standing requirement at some mines that employees shop in company-owned stores and live in company houses was abolished, and the payment of wages in scrip was prohibited.

With language reminiscent of the Jacksonville agreement and others before it, the Appalachian agreement said that work stoppages were forbidden during the adjustment of grievances, and in the event such stoppages occurred, the operator was prohibited from discussing the matter with the pit committee. This agreement was silent on the issue of the unpopular penalty clause, but it reappeared in the next negotiated agreement. A strongly worded Management of the Mines clause stated that the management of the mine, the direction of the working force, and the right to hire and discharge were vested exclusively in the operator, and prohibited the United Mine Workers of America from abridging these rights. While the operators would not agree to Lewis's demand for a union shop provision in the agreement, they did agree to reinstitute the practice of checking off union members' dues.

Finally, in reference to mechanization, it was implicit in the wording of the agreement that the introduction of machinery was a management right, but the question of pay was left open for negotiations at the district level of the union. The 1933 contract read, "Any change in mining methods or installation of equipment that relieves the Mine Worker of any of the above duties [i.e., drilling, shooting, cleaning, and loading of coal] and increases his productive capacity shall be recognized and a piecework rate agreed to therefor properly related to the basic rate."[21] The provision for a piece rate must have been a sop for those miners who continued to resist mechanization, for it was never taken seriously in subsequent wage negotiations.

In addition to its labor provisions, the bituminous coal code contained provisions relating to fair practices in the marketing and sale of coal. No sale of coal, for example, was to be made at less than a "fair market price," and this price was to be determined in each of five geographic divisions by either an industry sales agency, where one existed, or by regional NRA code authorities. In setting prices, the sales agencies were required by the code to consider the purposes of the National Industrial Recovery Act, the minimum wage rate, and the effect on employment, as well as the competitive position of bituminous coal in relation to alternative fuels. While prices thus established were subject to review and approval by NRA authorities in Washington, they were to be determined primarily by industry representatives rather than government officials. To prevent coal operators from circumventing the established prices in their district, the code outlawed certain common practices, such as using discounts, refunds, and special credits to encourage sales; using gifts and bribes to obtain business information; and the intentional misrepresentations of coal sizes and analyses.[22]

Establishing fair-market prices under the code turned out to be a more difficult task than industry and government officials had anticipated. So few sales agencies were in operation that ad hoc operator groups had to be formed quickly. When these groups turned for advice to NRA officials, they found that no clear pricing policies had been established. After much trial and error, a pricing system for most market areas was worked out, which raised the average price per ton of coal by 37 percent. For the industry as a whole, this increase was sufficient to cover wage increases and other variable costs, so before-tax earnings in 1934 approached the break-even point for the first time since 1927.[23] While it was far from being a perfect system, the coal code price-fixing apparatus did establish minimum prices and abated the intense interregional price competition that had created so much chaos and hardship in the industry since the mid-1920s. The reorganized UMWA was strong enough to enforce the new wage scale negotiated for the industry, which tended to create limits below which prices could not be reduced.

In the fall of 1934, a year after the code became effective, *Coal Age* reported that, while many operators were opposed to the way the NRA was administered, the industry in general was "convinced that some form of continuing price regulation and correlation is necessary to prevent a revival of cutthroat competition that robs both capital and labor of their just rewards."[24] The National Coal Association, an organization that had opposed government regulation of the industry in any form, reversed its position and called for a two-year extension of code control over prices and New Deal labor agreements.

Industry and Union Cooperation

At the time, Lewis was given most of the credit for engineering the Appalachian record and the coal code, but the source of his bargaining power was, as always, the militancy of the nation's coal miners—a militancy that expressed itself in self-organization and in disruptive work stoppages. Miners, well ahead of the union leadership, expressed their demands through collective action, and they frequently ignored union officials who sought to have them return to work. Dubofsky and Van Tine are quite emphatic on the point that it was the rank-and-file coal miners who moved history ahead in these critical years of the Great Depression. They noted the importance of this pressure from below in the following way:

> Without coal miners' loyalty to trade unionism and their willingness to walk out of the pits repeatedly, neither John L. Lewis nor Franklin D. Roosevelt could have compelled operators to acquiesce in the September 21, 1933, agreement. It was the militant behavior of coal miners, not the tough language and sharp bargaining of John L. Lewis, that threatened Roosevelt's plans for industrial recovery. However astute

Lewis may have been during his negotiations with operators, his achievements would have been minimal had miners not occasionally "blown the lid." Lewis, moreover, knew this. His bargaining achievements, he realized, flowed not from his own tactical and stategic brilliance but instead from the power exercised by masses of angry workers. Alone, Lewis was important as a labor leader; backed by hundreds of thousands of loyal followers ready to struggle for their rights, he wielded real influence.[25]

The 1934 UMWA convention held in January was a notable one. The union, which the year before had been only a shadow organization, now boasted that it represented 90 percent of the nation's coal miners. Furthermore, most of those who had joined the union were, in 1934, working under the protection of a labor agreement legitimized by federal legislation. Feeling their collective strength, the delegates to the January convention were eager to extend the gains they had won in October in order to catch up for years of deprivation. They unanimously endorsed the recommendations of Lewis's Scale Committee calling for a substantial wage increase, the elimination of the North-South wage differential, and a thirty-hour workweek. But convention delegates representing the perspective of the rank-and-file miner wanted more. They expressed concern about local job issues, many related to the new machinery being installed in the mines. A delegate from an Indiana local, for example, explained to the convention some of the problems his members faced when the operator installed Joy loading machines. He then urged the convention to adopt provisions for the gradual removal of the machinery from the mines.

Lewis, after allowing discussion on the machinery question, quietly put the issue to rest by voicing his fear that the union's image might be tarnished: "I would hesitate to see our convention take an action which might be erroneously construed by the world at large and bring upon the mine workers of the country a greater degree of criticism than the actualities of this problem would warrant." He said he feared the UMWA would be accused of wanting to "turn backward the clock of time and scrap the advances and the efficiencies made possible by modern invention in the application of modern genius."[26] When other delegates expressed similar opposition to the use of loading machines, their resolutions met the same fate. The Lewis policy was clear and he intended to enforce it; the union would support mine mechanization.

In an unprecedented move, Lewis invited J. D. A. Morrow, principle negotiator for the northern coal operators, to speak to the 1934 union convention. Morrow had long been a promoter of mine mechanization and, as president of the Pittsburgh Coal Company, had engineered the company's abrogation of the Jacksonville agreement. He is the company official who wrote his employees in 1927 that "We will never sign a scale with any union again. . . . We will always have open-shop mines." While the miners at the convention may have wondered why this archenemy of the union was invited to address them, the significance of his appearance was not lost on the industry. *Coal Age* editorialized that "no better illustration of the inherent possibilities for genuine coopera-tion between capital and labor could be asked than the appearance of an officer of the National Coal Association before the biennial convention of the UMW to discuss the common stake management and men have in the future of the mining industry."[27]

Clearly, Lewis was trying to establish the UMWA as a responsible organization, willing to cooperate with management in a businesslike manner. And cooperation between the union and some of the important operators did, in fact, occur when Lewis sat down with the industry representatives in February 1934 to negotiate the second Appalachian agreement. Under Morrow's leadership, the northern coal operators were willing to agree to many of the demands Lewis made during these negotiations. They were willing to collaborate with Lewis because they believed that the union's wage equalization demand would improve their competitive position over southern operators. Of course, for that same reason, southern operators refused to agree and held out for some time before settling.

Realizing that the union miners were prepared to walk off their jobs if the contract was not settled and that if this happened federal intervention might follow, the southern operators finally agreed, on "the last minute of the last day," to the terms of a one-year contract. The new agreement, obviously a victory for the union, called for a seven-hour day and a five-day workweek, plus a base wage of $5.00 in the North and $4.60 in the South.[28] Soon after the contract was signed by all the parties, Lewis persuaded NRA officials to make its terms part of the bituminous coal code, thus extending it throughout the coalfields. It might have been referred to as the Appalachian agreement, but it became virtually a national coal wage agreement. In this manner, with help from the federal government, industrywide bargaining was established in bituminous coal mining.

The National Recovery Administration's success in stabilizing coal prices continued through the summer of 1934, and the industry, faring better than it had for years, continued to support the coal code. In August, for example, Morrow told the *New York Times* that his company was doing better than it had since 1924 and that he thought the NRA was the best thing that could have happened to the industry: "You can call it government control, state socialism, or whatever you like. I don't care. It's the practical answer for those who have money invested in the business and for those who are employed in the industry."[29] This euphoria was short-lived, however.

During the autumn of 1934, a breakdown in NRA pricing authority appeared as some operators began to resort to traditional forms of cut-throat competition. Under pressure from large coal consumers who were seeking better prices and threatening to go to competing fuels, a few operators signed contracts at below-code levels for coal to be delivered after the expiration of the NIRA in June 1935. By midwinter, this practice had become so widespread that it threatened the entire NRA coal program. A last-minute effort to extend NRA authority over coal prices was made early in 1935 with the organization of the National Coal Board of Arbitration, an agency charged with responsiblity for resolving disputes over code prices. But this effort was too little and too late. By the time the Supreme Court invalidated the National Industrial Recovery Act in 1935, and with it industry codes, price warfare had returned with a vengeance to the coal industry.

Beyond the NRA

In the hope that special legislation aimed at the coal industry could restore stability, Lewis, backed by Morrow and other northern operators, pressured Roosevelt to support a bill giving the government more authority than the NRA had to fix prices. Within the industry, there was much disagreement over the form any new legislation should take, and when new legislation came before Congress in the form of the Guffey Act, it lacked support, principally from the southern operators. The act passed by a narrow margin in both houses because of White House pressure, which was a response to a strike "orchestrated" by Lewis during the summer negotiations for the third Appalachian agreement.

After the U.S. Supreme Court (*Carter v. Carter*, 1936) declared the Guffey Act unconstitutional, Lewis went back to Congress and secured the passage of a second Guffey Act in 1937. The new Guffey Act, titled the Coal Conservation Act, established another National Bituminous

Coal Commission with the responsibility of fixing minimum coal prices for the various coal-producing regions. When the commission promulgated a set of prices for the industry in November 1937, its authority to do so was challenged in the courts by the City of Cleveland, by almost 200 railroads, and by other large consumers. Injunctions prohibiting enforcement of the law were granted, and the commission's first round of prices was revoked.

Following this aborted effort, the commission held a series of public hearings in the hope of arriving at a set of minimum prices that would satisfy both producers and consumers of coal. As it neared completion of this task in the summer of 1939—two years after the act was passed—Roosevelt "sacked the commission" by transferring its functions to the Department of the Interior. Minimum prices were finally established in October 1940. But by then, minimum-price regulations were largely redundant because the nation was preparing for war, and coal prices were being driven up. When Congress refused to reenact the Coal Conservation Act during World War II, it marked the end of the federal government's efforts to bring stability to the coal industry through minimum price controls.[30]

When NRA code authority to set coal prices was revoked in 1935 and the industry entered a period without effective price controls, conditions were different from those that had existed ten years earlier. Demand for coal was still suffering from the double blow of a depressed economy and competition from alternative fuels. However, by the mid-1930s, the industry's workers were organized and had established a contractual relation with the industry. Under threat of federal penalties, the operators could not, or would not, attempt to break these agreements as they had the Jacksonville agreement. Price competition did not, under these circumstances, express itself in wage competition as it had earlier. In the mid-1930s, if a company wanted to lower its coal prices it had to find a means other than wage cuts for reducing costs of production—and this search quite naturally led to the use of labor-saving machinery.

The floor under wages imposed by the NRA and the Appalachian agreements contributed to the expansion in mine mechanization that began in 1935 and 1936. In retrospect, however, industrywide wage levels seem to have been a necessary, but probably not a sufficient, explanation for the increased use of mobile loaders and other forms of mine machinery in the late 1930s.

CHAPTER 10

Miners' "Freedom" Under Increased Mechanization

IN ADDITION to NRA code prices and a higher and uniform wage level, there were other economic forces converging in the mid-1930s to open the way for a mechanization movement in the nation's coal mines. Interest rates and capital costs were at historically low levels, a slight upturn in coal demand took place in 1933 and 1934, concentration of production in the larger mines had continued, and the market offered a larger selection of well-tested new machinery.[1] Yet with all of this, there was still the long-standing obstacle of local workers' control. This control had expressed itself in a refusal of local unions to negotiate specific rates of pay for machine operators and in the enforcement of work practices, such as the traditional freedom to leave the workplace at will, that limited the productivity of installed machinery. This control had to be broken, or at least weakened sufficiently, to make the use of new technology profitable.

New Deal Wage Agreements

It was pointed out in the last chapter that the collective bargaining process in coal during the mid-1930s was integrated into the New Deal recovery program, being materially affected by it and, in turn, helping shape it. Five coal wage agreements were negotiated during the first eight years of the New Deal.[2] Covering the period from October 1933 to March 1941, these contracts were referred to as Appalachian agreements, although their terms and conditions were generally extended throughout the industry. Since the mine mechanization movement began in earnest during these years, it is important to analyze these contracts to determine how they might have affected the transformation from hand loading to mechanical loading and how they reflected the changes in work relations which accompanied mechanization. The dates of the five agreements are as follows:

	Effective Date	Termination Date
First Appalachian agreement	October 1, 1933	March 31, 1934
Second Appalachian agreement	April 1, 1934	March 31, 1935, extended to September 30, 1935
Third Appalachian agreement	October 1, 1935	March 31, 1937
Fourth Appalachian agreement	April 1, 1937	March 31, 1939
Fifth Appalachian agreement	April 12, 1939	March 31, 1941

Naturally, there were many similarities between the Appalachian agreements and the labor agreements of the early 1920s. One important difference, however, was the extent to which the Appalachian agreements acted as "parent" agreements, spelling out in detail the terms and conditions of employment. By contrast, the 1924 Jacksonville Agreement and agreements that preceded it were very general in nature, establishing only an interregional wage scale. In the earlier years, specific language relating to working conditions and nonwage benefits came from negotiations at the district and local levels. This difference reflected a fundamental change in the bargaining structure of the industry, as power within the union shifted away from the local and district unions to the national office and especially to the president's office.

During the 1930s, the Illinois district union, which had maintained its autonomy longer than most, was something of an exception to this consolidation of authority in that it still negotiated at the district level many details not found in the new parent agreements. In this connection, it should also be pointed out that because of the quasi-legal status of the early Appalachian agreements, Lewis was able to sidestep the usual practice of having the miners vote on their wage agreements. While these agreements, negotiated in the shadow of the White House, contained a substantial wage increase for miners and may well have had their approval, they lacked formal ratification by the membership.

The first Appalachian Agreement established a mining rate of $.65 a ton for traditional pick mining in thick veins and $.48 a ton for loading coal that had been cut by machine. A day rate of $4.80 for timbering, track laying, and similar inside work was also established by this parent agreement. It is far from certain that the wage gains negotiated by Lewis between 1933 and 1939 (table 8), meant increases in real incomes, however, for many companies responded to the rise in their labor costs by

TABLE 8

Tonnage Rates and Day Rates Established by
Appalachian Agreements, 1933–1939
($)

Appalachian Agreement	Tonnage Rate[a]	Day Rate	
		Inside Workers[b]	Loading Machines Operators
First (1933)	0.65–0.48	4.60	—[c]
Second (1934)	0.75–0.56	5.00	(6.20)
Third (1935)	0.84–0.64	5.50	6.90
Fourth (1937)	0.93–0.72	6.00	7.60
Fifth (1939)	0.93–0.72	6.00	7.60

Source: Coal wage agreements, West Virginia Collection, West Virginia University Library.
a. Tonnage rates are given for pick mining and for loading machine-cut coal.
b. Day rates are for timbermen, trackmen, drillers, and other inside company men.
c. Not applicable.

increasing rents on company houses and on the prices miners paid at company stores. Coal operators also used the occasion to alter job content and work practices, so that coal loaders found themselves required to do more dead work for the same pay. Complaints about these practices were voiced at the union's conventions in 1936 and later in the form of resolutions submitted by local unions.[3] Typical of these resolutions is the one from a local at Pocahontas, Virginia:

Whereas, We the members of Local Union No. 6050, have had undue and unjust increased rentals for company owned houses imposed upon us since November 1, 1935, in which all Local Unions have been very active in opposing same; be it

Resolved, That this convention goes on record as opposing any further increases of any kind that will decrease the earning capacity of the miners, unless accepted and agreed to by the Scale Committee negotiating agreements; and, be it further

Resolved, That this increase be discontinued and the amount previously collected be refunded to the employees involved.[4]

In 1938 a miners' local from Switchback, West Virginia, was quite emphatic on the point:

> Whereas, The coal oprator in the last two contracts has raised our
> house rent, coal and hauling fee; be it
> Resolved, That in the next contract there will be no advance in
> house rent, coal, and hauling fee.[5]

Changes in job tasks that reduced the miners' income were explained in a resolution submitted by delegates from a mine in Red Ash, Virginia:

> We ask the great officers of our organization to use their great influence
> in trying to get pay for all slate handled by the miner, and that we get
> pay for the 5 inches that we have to move at present for nothing. We
> have always gotten pay for all slate until the last contract. We want
> this put back if possible.[6]

The five parent Appalachian Agreements did not establish a wage scale for loading machine operators during the 1930s. Day rates for operators and helpers on various types of loading machines were, however, negotiated by each of the Lewis-controlled district unions during this period, and these rates were imposed on the local unions. (It was noted earlier that a few local unions had, in fact, already agreed to a wage schedule for loading machine operators, but for the most part no negotiated wage rate for machine operators existed until the mid-1930s.)

Beginning with the 1935 agreement, the Appalachian contracts recognized that loading machines were being used in the coalfields by specifying that an across-the-board increase of $0.70 a day should be applied to existing day rates for operators and helpers. If there had been an impediment to the use of loading machines for lack of an established rate of pay, this obstacle probably no longer existed after 1935. The following 1935 pay scale for western Pennsylvania (UMWA districts 3, 4, and 5) shows that loading machine operator rates were set even for specific machines:

Operator of Joy, Oldroyd, or similar loading machines	$6.90
Operator helper	$5.86
44C [Jeffrey] operator	$6.62
44C helper	$5.86

Each of the Appalachian agreements negotiated during the 1930s contained an interesting reference to the installation of loading machines. In the section of the contracts defining pick mining and setting tonnage rates, the following sentence (as noted in chapter 9) is included:

Any change in mining methods or installation of equipment that relieves the Mine Worker of any of the above duties and increases his
productive capacity shall be recognized and a piece work rate agreed to
therefor properly related to the basic rate.

This provision nothwithstanding, piece rates were rarely used for loading
machine operators, and why it continued to be included in the
agreements remains a mystery.

The issue of a day rate or a piece rate for operating loading machines
was a hotly debated question, with most mine workers and a few mine
operators lined up against John L. Lewis and a majority of the operators.
The handful of operators who favored a continuation of some form of
incentive system believed that with a tonnage payment "the machines
are most likely to be worked nearer to their full capacity." They also knew
that close supervision at each workplace would be required if miners were
to be paid a day rate. Miners had worked with the tonnage system since
the earliest days of mining and saw in this system a method by which they
might share in the productivity gains made possible by machine loading.
They also realized that a day wage would mean a loss of another traditional freedom: they would be working under direct and constant supervision as management reorganized the labor process.[7] Lewis had been a
staunch supporter of the day wage, and this became the accepted industry
system during the 1930s.

Hours of Work

The length of the workday, a persistent issue, also was resolved by the
Appalachian agreements. The eight-hour day, which had been a part of
coal wage agreements since John Mitchell negotiated it in 1898, was
reestablished in the first agreement. The workweek was specified as five
days. In the 1934 agreement, Lewis was able to obtain a reduction in the
workday to seven hours, a provision that remained in effect until 1941,
when the industry returned to an eight-hour day. Under Maximum
Hours and Working Time in the Appalachian agreements, the following
language indicated some fundamental changes in work practices:

Seven hours of labor shall constitute a day's work. The seven-hour day
means seven hours' work in the mines at the usual working places for
all classes of labor, exclusive of the lunch period, whether they be paid
by the day or on a tonnage basis.

There are at least three noteworthy points to be made about this new language. The first is that shorter hours had a direct impact on productivity and on mechanization. The second deals with the implications of extending the coverage of the hours provision to all classes of labor. Third is the effect of the new language on the traditional freedom of the miners to leave work when they pleased. A shorter workday had long been a Lewis policy, one he promoted as a way to soften the impact of mine mechanization on the number of jobs. The workday provision negotiated in the Appalachian agreements went beyond simple work sharing, however.

A study of the impact of the 1934 hours reduction concluded that the cutback from eight to seven hours a day was immediately followed by a 10 percent decline in output per man-day.[8] To maintain the same level of output, coal operators quickly increased the number of days the mines were in operation and added unemployed miners to their payrolls. The Bureau of Mines reported that the average number of days worked by bituminous coal mines increased from 167 in 1933 to 193 in 1937, while, during the same period employment increased from 418,703 to 491,864, a 17.5 percent gain.[9] Increasing the number of days the mines operated improved the take-home pay of miners at first, and the increased employment seemed to justify the union's long-standing claim that shorter hours would mean more work for everybody. Before long, however, miners began to complain that the operators were assigning two men to a room and were transferring day men to loading coal whenever it suited them. Given the tonnage payment system with a fixed labor cost per ton, operators had an incentive to increase output by putting more loaders to work. And NRA price supports provided the motivation for each operator to expand his output.

For the men in the mines, this doubling up—or "crowding of the mine" as they called it—violated the proprietorship a miner traditionally had assumed over his room. Many complained that they could not make as much money when they were forced to share the output of their workplace. It is important to note in this connection that the Appalachian agreements dropped the language that had formalized this custom in an earlier period. The 1924 contract provision that read "Each miner shall be awarded one working place" is not to be found in the agreements Lewis negotiated in the 1930s.

In 1936 when the union met in convention, many locals sent instructions with their delegates to complain of this omission and to seek relief through the union's Scale Committee. For example, the local union from Russelton, Pennsylvania, submitted the following resolution:

> Whereas, the operators have made a practice of crowding the mine and in that way preventing the miners working at the face from making the inside basic wage.
> Therefore, be it resolved, that in our next agreement it shall be understood that we insist that two men shall have two places.[10]

By 1938 the complaint that coal loaders were suffering economic hardship became quite general, as described by a resolution from an Amsterdam, Ohio, local:

> Having regard to the unsatisfactory status of the piece rate loader under our present contract, because it contains no provision of security or assurance that piece rate or tonnage loaders will be given an opportunity to earn the equivalent of the basic scale wage each shift the mine operates; and, many employers take unfair advantage of this fact to overcrowd the mines to a point where it is impossible for piece rate or tonnage loaders to earn the basic day way.[11]

In spite of these and many similar resolutions at the two conventions, the issue was not addressed in any of the Appalachian agreements, so that the status of the hand loader continued to deteriorate. Delegates from a local union at Elkhorn, West Virginia, summarized the plight of the tonnage men in a resolution submitted to the 1940 convention:

> Whereas, Due to the authority of the mine management to hire men, often more men are hired than are really needed thus creating a crowded condition in the mine, and
> Whereas, Due to overcrowded conditions many of our old men are frequently out of a place to work and many times have to come out of the mine because of the lack of a place to work and thereby losing time and money, therefore be it
> Resolved, That the scale committee in the next Appalachian Wage Conference take some steps to correct this evil and curtail the practice of overcrowding so that loaders may have a reasonable assurance of a place to work when they go into the mine.[12]

A subtle yet important change in the wording of the Hours and Working Time provision of the Appalachian agreements extended coverage of the

eight-hour—and then the seven-hour—workday to all employees. The
1924 Jacksonville agreement had stated that an eight-hour day meant
"eight hours' work for all classes of day labor," but the 1934 coal
agreement dropped the word *day* from the hours clause. To avoid any
confusion on the issue, new language was added: seven hours work in the
mines applied to all employees "whether they be paid by the day or a
tonnage basis." For the first time in the history of the industry, mine
management was armed with contract language that could be used to
keep hand loaders in the mine for the full length of the workday.
Providing a work discipline to make output and costs more predictable,
management had solved a problem about which coal mine owners had
complained for years. But the workday meant a corresponding loss of job
freedom that miners had enjoyed since the earliest days of the industry.
With the addition of time clocks at the mines, the 1930s witnessed
changes that moved mining even further toward factorylike production.

Another sign of the changes taking place in the industry was the
operation of the mines on more than one shift. The Jacksonville agreement had carried forward the tradition of having the mines in operation
on the day shift only. When this agreement was abrogated, many
operators began a two-shift, and some a three-shift, operation. This
practice was particularly common in the mechanized mines, where there
was an economic incentive to keep machinery in operation on a continuous basis. In anticipation of the expanded use of machinery, the Appalachian agreements recognized shift work with the following language,
new to the industry:

> The operator shall have the right during the entire period of this
> Agreement to work all the mines, or any one of them, extra shifts with
> different crews.

Management Rights

The Management of Mines clause, which had been gradually inserted
into coal labor agreements in the 1920s but was usually consigned to that
part of the contract relating to the employer's right to hire and fire
employees, received elevated status in the Appalachian agreements with
a special section of its own. In addition, the wording of the management's
rights provision was altered to reflect an increase in management control
over the labor process. Whereas the Jacksonville agreement for northern
West Virginia stated:

The operator or his superintendent or mine foreman *shall be respected* in the management of the mine and the direction of the working force,"

the new Appalachian agreements read:

The management of the mine, the direction of the working force, and the right to hire and discharge are *vested exclusively* in the Operator, and the United Mine Workers of America shall not abridge these rights.

(Emphasis is added to highlight the difference between the 1924 Jacksonville agreement and the Appalachian agreements.) A second sentence inserted in the management's rights clause seemed directed at an ongoing practice that the union hoped to stop.

It is not the intention of this provision to encourage the discharge of Mine Workers, or the refusal of employment to applicants because of personal prejudice or activity in matters affecting the United Mine Workers of America.

A reading of the resolutions submitted to the UMWA conventions in 1936, 1938, and 1940 shows that blacklisting of local union activists was a frequent complaint, despite this new language.[13]

Contract Language and Mechanization

With the exception of the one line noted above, there is no direct reference to mechanical loading in the Appalachian agreements until 1937. At that time, Lewis was able to get the operators to agree to a joint commission to study "the problems arising from mechanization of bituminous coal production by the use of conveyors and mobile loading machines." The commission consisted of eight representatives of the operators, including J. D. A. Morrow, and eight union officers, including Lewis. The commission was charged with making a report of its findings of fact and its recommendations to the Appalachian Joint Wage Conference on March 14, 1939, the time set for negotiating the next labor agreement.

According to the UMWA, the operators were "non-cooperative" in making the called-for study, so the union took it upon itself to make its own mechanization study, the results of which were reported to the 1938 convention. Not surprisingly, this study confirmed that Lewis had been right all along in pursuing his high-wage and mechanization policy. In a comparison of the Illinois coalfield, where mechanization was more advanced, and the Appalachian region, where it was just getting started, the union study reported that real take-home pay of miners in the Midwest was higher than in the mountains. "In other words, it may be said that under the far-sightedness of the Union, the miners have attained, in a measure, participation in the advantages derived by the owners from mine mechanization."[14]

The study did call for some form of income protection for those miners displaced by machines, and it cited the need for increased safety measures with mechanical loading. And the study noted, as an aside, the widespread abuse of company payroll deductions for "exorbitant prices in company stores, high rent for sub-standard housing, excessive charges for inadequate medical care, etc."[15] Interestingly, the study showed that when these payroll deductions were combined with the deduction charged the hand loaders for supplies, powder, and so forth, the tonnage men in nonmechanized mines were making substantially less than day men. Whether by design or by accident, the job that had been at the center of the labor process during the hand-loading days was now being downgraded to a less desirable position. And it follows that, if hand loaders had resisted the introduction of machinery in the past, now they might welcome it.

The union mechanization study of 1938 failed to elicit any response from the operators except that in 1939 they agreed to participate in yet another Mechanized Mining Commission. The second commission was charged with identical responsibilities and was to consist of the same operators and union officials. It was to make a report of its findings and its recommendations to a joint wage conference in March 1941, on the expiration date of the 1939 Appalachian agreement. Now it was a matter of the two parties going through the motions of being concerned about the impact of mechanization.

The second commission was not even mentioned in the officers' report to the 1940 UMWA convention. In the 1941 negotiations, the mechanization issue was ignored, as the union and the operators' association fought over the North-South wage differential, captive mines, the union-shop question, paid vacations, and other issues. When the 1941 agreement was finally signed, it did contain, for the first time in the industry, a seniority clause, which read,

Seniority affecting return to employment of idle employees on a basis
of length of service and qualification for the respective positions . . . is
recognized.

And this clause made specific mention of miners who were laid off as
management introduced new technology. The agreement established a
panel or recall list with the following language:

Men displaced by new mining methods or installation of new mechanical equipment so long as they remain unemployed shall constitute a
panel from which new employees shall be selected.

This gesture of protection against the impact of mechanization must have
been a welcome addition to the language of the bituminous coal
agreements. It certainly had been called for by rank-and-file miners at the
union's conventions for many years. However, had John L. Lewis been
truly responsive to his union members' needs, he would have made
seniority rights a priority item in negotiations with the industry at a much
earlier date.

Other significant aspects of the 1941 wage agreement included elimination of the extremely unpopular penalty clause, which dated to World
War I, and the right of the miners to have on-site safety committees.
Although these committees were to be appointed by district union
presidents and were limited in authority, they represented a first step in
the direction toward rank-and-file influence in correcting mining
hazards. Again, one wonders why Lewis waited so long to incorporate
these on-the-job needs of coal miners into the union's bargaining goals.
The answer lies, of course, in what we know about his own program for
the industry, that is, his commitment to mechanization. The rights of
individual miners—job rights, safety rights, and the right to strike—were
of secondary importance to this goal. For Lewis, they were items to be
dealt with after the industry had been transformed with the new technology.

Mechanization Takes Off

In the mid-1930s there was a convergence of trends that created
conditions leading to a virtual explosion in the use of mechanical loading
machines (see appendix, table A). The reduction in the length of the

workday provided an incentive to management to find ways for increasing mine output and productivity. *Coal Age,* long the industry's most outspoken proponent of mine mechanization asked, "How to pay higher wages and yet reduce costs, and how to work shorter hours and yet produce the same tonnage?"[16] Industry data show that man-day productivity did, in fact, drop after the workday was shortened, both in 1932 and 1934.[17] Combined with the Lewis-negotiated wage increases during the same period, the shorter workday led to an increase in the unit cost of producing a ton of coal. Operators were thus pressured to introduce machinery. An unexpected increase in railroad freight rates further intensified these pressures.

Unlike the 1920s when operators were faced with union wages they thought were too high, the 1930s found the operators party to a contractual relation under threat of federal penalties; the Appalachian agreements were not to be broken as the Jacksonville agreement had been. And price competition did not express itself in the inhuman wage competition from which coal miners had suffered so badly during the 1920s.

In addition, the NRA code prices gave coal operators optimistic expectations concerning future earnings. Corporate borrowing for capital investment was facilitated during 1933 and 1934 by interest rates that had fallen to historically low levels.[18] The capital goods market responded by lowering prices and by making available a wide variety of new mining equipment. Several manufacturers were marketing equipment suitable for mining thin seams of coal and were developing auxiliary haulage equipment that complemented the loading machine.[19]

When the American Mining Congress held its annual convention in May 1934, it was attended by unusually large numbers of operators, who were anxious to examine the latest equipment on display. Ninety-three manufacturers sent salesmen to demonstrate the largest collection of mining equipment ever displayed for the industry. When they returned home, the operators placed orders for large numbers of new machines. The number of mobile loaders alone increased from 534 in use in 1934 to 657 in use a year later, then increased again to 980 in 1936 (appendix table B). The mechanization of coal loading had begun in earnest and would continue without interruption until hand loading became as obsolete as pick mining.

CHAPTER 11

Opportunities Lost

WRITING IN 1924 before mine mechanization had advanced, but when its potential for altering work relations was fully understood, Carter Goodrich believed that mechanical loading provided the miners' union with an opportunity to protect and even extend workers' control over their jobs.[1] The union, he proposed, could focus its efforts on improving the quality of working life by strengthening the control exercised by mine committees and local unions. And local union strength could be "greatly increased as the new methods break down the individualism of the scattered miners and throws them together into closer groups" working around the loading machine.

Goodrich had witnessed mechanical loaders at work and observed the reorganization of the labor process into small crews of miners working in close proximity and in cooperation with each other. These work groups, he believed, might become the foundation on which a new union could emerge, a union that would "exert a powerful influence over the quality of working life under the new technique." Such an opportunity would involve a new collective job control to replace the individual job control of the hand-loading era.

Goodrich understood that one of the fears of miners was that the independence traditionally associated with hand loading would be lost in the change to new technology and that this would be especially true if the payment system were changed. "Payment by the day, they feel, means a greater likelihood of the boss looking down the shirt collar," he wrote. Rather than a day-wage system, Goodrich suggested a modified tonnage system, which would involve payment based on "the tonnage of the whole group and divided equally among them." In this way, miners would be able to work as autonomous groups, providing their own internal discipline. He said, "Even if the new device is to take away the independence that went with the old-time isolation . . . it need not mean that the workers must be watched all day by a straw boss."

A democratic union, which drew its strength from work groups, pit committees, and local unions, could also give "the working miner . . . a real part in the government of coal." Supporting the goals of the Nationalization Research Committee, Goodrich argued that industry demand and prices could be stabilized with public ownership and control of the industry. A strong union built upon the foundation of workers' control at the mine site would represent the interests of coal miners in a nationalized industry, he believed.

What actually happened, of course, was quite the opposite. Rather than a new "collective freedom of workers' control" emerging from the technological revolution, the miners' union became dominated by one man whose rise to power necessitated breaking local control. By the early 1930s, John L. Lewis's control of the union had become so solidified that his policies and programs were virtually immune to challenge by the rank and file. His control of the union's biennial convention and the Scale Committee, where local unions voiced their concerns to the larger body, made it possible for him to block efforts of the membership to influence the impact of mechanization on job rights and workers' control.

The timing of the convention itself reduced rank-and-file influence on the union's bargaining goals. Originally, the union's convention had been held a short time before negotiations were to begin, so that bargaining demands could be formulated just prior to the time they were to be submitted to the operators. By the late 1930s, this timely connection had been broken, and the conventions were being held more than a year before negotiations. The Scale Committee used this time lag to justify ignoring local union demands. The committee said at one point, "We do not believe that this convention can adopt a scale of demands to present to the operators a year and two months from now, because no one knows what conditions may confront the mining industry . . . within that period of time."[2]

In addition to his control of the convention, Lewis had placed many of the district unions under trusteeship and appointed his own supporters to run these organizations. Formerly, the district officers had been elected by the rank and file and had been, therefore, more responsive to their demands and grievances. With this power to appoint district officers— officers who had the responsibility to enforce the contract and administer the grievance procedure—Lewis was in a position to implement his programs and policies for the industry. District officers or their appointees also served as delegates to the union's conventions, thus assuring Lewis further loyalty and support.

During the 1930s, union miners did not have the opportunity to express any opposition to the terms of their negotiated agreements, because Lewis ignored the traditional ratification process. In 1940, a local union from Fredericktown, Pennsylvania, summarized the problem in this manner:

> Whereas, we feel that we should have more say as to the kind of a contract that we have to work under; be it
>
> Resolved, That the International Convention go on record in favor of a referendum vote of the membership before the contract is signed.[3]

A part of Lewis's program involved a centralization of the bargaining structure in the industry, and his increased power within the union made that possible. In an earlier day, many of the terms and conditions of the labor agreements were negotiated at the local or subdistrict level, but under the new structure almost all the details of the agreement were negotiated by Lewis and applied to the whole industry. This, of course, was especially important in the mechanization movement during the 1930s. It had been in the more decentralized union of the 1920s that locals had been able to block the introduction of machinery by refusing to negotiate a wage scale for machine operators or by negotiating restrictive work rules.

The Appalachian agreements that Lewis negotiated reflected the success of his program to promote the stability of the industry through mechanization and to establish a businesslike union. Changes in the contract included (1) fixing day rates of wages for an increased number of job classes; (2) a fixed workday for all workers; (3) increased management rights, including the right to transfer workers from one job to another; (4) a loss of traditional job control by the tonnage miners (e.g., their loss of a claim to an individual workplace); (5) further limitations on the powers of the pit committee; and (6) the right of management to run the mines on multiple shifts. Most of these changes involved a loss of rights and privileges, especially of tonnage miners, without a corresponding increase in other advantages except monetary ones. Job rights were traded for incomes, or at least the promise of higher incomes.

A reading of the resolutions submitted by local unions to the union conventions in 1936, 1938, and 1940 shows clearly that many miners thought the price they had to pay for the Appalachian wage settlements was too high. They wanted their union to negotiate seniority rights in promotion, transfer, and layoff. They wanted the union to demand a tax on the output from machines, with the funds generated used to aid those laid off when the machines were installed. They wanted a payment system that assured them a share in the increased returns from the new technology. And they wanted the assurance that local union activists who spoke out for the protection of traditional job rights would not be discriminated against or blacklisted from employment. Most of these rank-and-file demands were ignored. By the 1930s, the union's bargaining demands were defined by Lewis, and his agenda was unchanged: to encourage mine mechanization and the rationalization of production.

It is true that the local, spontaneous strikes of coal miners in 1931 and 1932 were a manifestation of the militancy of the UMWA, which permitted it to reorganized and negotiate industrywide labor agreements, but this militancy did not express itself a few years later when the mine mechanization movement began in earnest in the Appalachian coalfields. By the time the machines were installed in the mines, miners had suffered economic hardships for nearly a decade. Tempered by these hard times, their militancy was now immobilized by a centralized union led by a man of considerable power. In some of the more depressed areas, mine workers' discontent was moderated by the promise of federal relief. A new union, a new labor contract, and hard times all worked to reduce the control miners had experienced since underground mining had first begun. The potential power that Carter Goodrich saw in the new technology, the opportunity to extend that control, was lost.

APPENDIX TABLES

NOTES

INDEX

APPENDIX

**Mechanization in Coal Production,
Selected Years 1900–1948**
(%)

| | Underground Coal | | All Coal | |
	Mechanically Undercut	Mechanically Loaded	Mechanically Cleaned	Strip Mined
1900	24.9			
1905	32.8			
1910	41.7		3.8	
1915	55.3		4.7	0.6
1920	60.7		3.3	1.5
1923	68.3	0.3	3.8	2.1
1924	71.5	0.7		2.8
1925	72.9	1.2		3.2
1926	73.8	1.9		3.0
1927	74.9	3.3	5.3	3.6
1928	76.9	4.5	5.7	4.0
1929	78.4	7.4	6.9	3.8
1930	81.0	10.5	8.3	4.3
1931	83.2	13.1	9.5	5.0
1932	84.1	12.3	9.8	6.3
1933	84.7	12.0	10.4	5.5
1934	84.1	12.2	11.1	5.8
1935	84.2	13.5	12.2	6.4
1936	84.8	16.3	13.9	6.4
1937		20.2	14.6	7.1
1938	87.5	26.7	18.2	8.7
1939	87.9	31.0	20.1	9.6
1940	88.4	35.4	22.2	9.4
1941	89.0	40.7	22.9	10.7
1942	89.7	45.2	24.4	11.5
1943	90.3	48.9	24.7	13.5
1944	90.5	52.9	25.6	16.3
1945	90.8	56.1	25.6	19.0
1946	90.8	58.4	26.0	21.1
1947	90.0	60.7	27.7	22.1
1948	90.7	64.3	30.2	23.3

Source: U.S. Bureau of Mines.
Note: Blank cells indicate zero.

TABLE B

Type of Loaders Used in Mechanically Loaded Coal, 1926–1948

	Mobile Loaders		Scraper Loaders		Pit-Car Loaders		Other Loaders	
	Percent of Output Mechanically Loaded	Number of Loaders	Percent of Output Mechanically Loaded	Number of Loaders	Percent of Output Mechanically Loaded	Number of Loaders	Percent of Output Mechanically Loaded	Number of Loaders
1926	73.9	205	14.7	133	4.9		6.5	
1928	54.8	397	7.2	130	19.1	1,040	18.9	
1929	43.4	488	4.1	126	39.6	2,521	12.9	
1930	42.7	545	3.5	150	40.7	2,876	13.1	
1931	40.8	583	3.1	146	40.3	3,428	15.8	
1932	41.4	548	3.2	128	35.1	3,112	20.3	
1933	47.2	523	2.6	93	30.2	2,453	20.0	657
1934	50.1	534	2.4	119	26.8	2,288	20.7	731
1935	52.3	657	2.4	78	23.5	2,098	21.8	849
1936	61.2	980	1.9	106	15.7	1,851	21.1	1,170
1938	68.0	1,405	1.2	117	6.6	1,392	24.2	1,872
1939	69.0	1,573	0.9	131	4.6	873	25.5	2,393
1940	68.3	1,720	0.8	116	2.7	697	28.2	2,919
1941	67.8	1,985	0.7	109	1.8	607	29.7	3,595
1942	68.8	2,301	0.6	93	1.4	481	29.2	4,103
1943	71.7	2,525	0.5	83	1.1	321	26.7	4,417
1944	74.0	2,737	0.5	87	0.7	241	24.8	4,567
1945	75.7	2,950	0.5	87	0.4	142	23.4	4,768
1946	76.2	3,200	0.4	75	0.3	93	23.1	4,991
1947	77.1	3,464	0.3	67	0.1	71	22.5	5,510
1948	78.6	3,980	0.3	56	0.1	37	21.0	5,757

Source: U.S. Bureau of Mines.
Note: Data for 1927 and 1937 were not available. Blank cells indicate unavailable data.

TABLE C

**Average Hourly Earnings for
Coal Miners, 1923–1948 ($)**

1923	0.82
1924	0.79
1925	0.77
1926	0.76
1927	0.73
1928	0.69
1929	0.66
1930	0.66
1931	0.63
1932	0.50
1933	0.49
1934	0.65
1935	0.72
1936	0.77
1937	0.83
1938	0.85
1939	0.86
1940	0.85
1941	0.96
1942	1.03
1943	1.10
1944	1.15
1945	1.20
1946	1.36
1947	1.58
1948	1.84

Source: U.S. Bureau of Census, *Historical Statistics of the U.S.*, pt. 1 (Washington, D.C.: Government Printing Office, 1975), p. 170.

TABLE D

Economic Indicators for Bituminous Coal Mining, 1923–1948

	Production (million tons)	Average Value per Ton[a] ($)	Employment	Number of Mines	Capacity Utilization[c] (%)
1923	565	2.68	704,793	9,331	63.8
1924	484	2.20	619,604	7,586	61.0
1925	520	2.04	588,493	7,144	69.5
1926	573	2.06	593,647	7,177	76.7
1927	518	1.99	593,918	7,011	68.2
1928	501	1.86	522,150	6,450	72.5
1929	535	1.78	502,993	6,057	78.8
1930	468	1.70	493,202	5,891	66.9
1931	382	1.54	450,213	5,642	57.1
1932	310	1.31	406,380	5,427	52.2
1933	334	1.34	418,703	5,555	59.7
1934	359	1.75	458,011	6,258	63.5
1935	372	1.77	462,403	6,315	63.9
1936	439	1.76	477,204	6,875	71.0
1937	446	1.94	491,864	6,584	69.0
1938	349	1.95	441,333	5,777	58.0
1939	395	1.84	421,788	5,820	63.6
1940	461	1.91	439,075	6,324	72.1
1941	514	2.19	456,981	6,822	77.2
1942	583	2.36	461,991	6,972	87.9
1943	590	2.69	416,007	6,620	94.2
1944	620	2.92	393,347	6,928	99.4
1945	578	3.06	383,100	7,033	93.2
1946	534	3.44	396,434[b]	7,333	93.2
1947	631	4.16	419,182[b]	8,700	83.6
1948	600	4.99	441,631[b]	9,079	72.4

Source: U.S. Bureau of Mines, *Minerals Yearbook,* Selected Years (Washington, D.C.: Government Printing Office); and Morton S. Baratz, *The Union and the Coal Industry* (New Haven: Yale Univesity Press, 1955), pp. 40–41.

a. Figures for the years 1923 to 1936, inclusive, and 1939, exclude selling expense.

b. Average number of men working daily.

c. Computed from figures on total production and estimated capacity production at 280 days per year.

NOTES

Preface

1. George Korson, *Coal Dust on the Fiddle* (Hatboro, Pa.: Folklore Associates, 1965), pp. 138–39.

2. See David Noble's excellent three-part article "Present Tense Technology," *democracy* (Summer, Fall, Winter 1983).

3. A major exception to this condition existed in a few states in an early period when convict labor was used. In Tennessee, for example, in the 1890s coal companies leased convicts from state prisons to replace miners and to break strikes. See Fran Ansley and Brenda Bell, eds., *Southern Exposure* 1 (1974): 144–59, for a discussion of working conditions for convict labor in Tennessee coal mines. For information on the deplorable conditions for convicts in Alabama coal mines, see Robert David Ward and Warren Williams Rogers, "Racial Inferiority, Convict Labor, and Modern Medicine: A Note on the Coalburg Affair," *Alabama History Quarterly* 44 (1982): 203–10.

CHAPTER 1. The Hand Loading of Coal

1. The first three sections of this chapter are based on Keith Dix, *Work Relations in the Coal Industry: The Hand-Loading Era, 1880–1930* (Morgantown: West Virginia University, 1977).

2. Where roof conditions permitted, the width of rooms was fixed to ensure miners a sufficient "fall" of coal for a full day's work. If the rooms were too large, the mining cycle, as described below, could not be completed in a normal day's work. *Mining Congress Journal* (Apr. 1926): 279.

3. Robert McCauley, "Geology, Technology and the Organization of Extraction in the Nineteenth Century South Wales Coal Industry" (unpublished manuscript, Harvard University).

4. D. E. Krebs, "Standard Panel System of Long Wall Mining, Worked Advancing," *Proceedings, West Virginia Coal Mining Institute* (1911): 135.

5. U.S. Geological Survey, *Mineral Resources of the United States, 1907* (Washington, D.C.: Government Printing Office, 1908), p. 52.

6. Interview, Dec. 19, 1979, at Morgantown, West Virginia. Mr. Raber is now deceased. This interview is published as a tribute to a kind and generous neighbor.

7. Interview, Mar. 15, 1982, at Eccles, West Virginia.

8. Interview, Oct. 27, 1976, at South Charleston, West Virginia.

9. Carter Goodrich, *The Miner's Freedom* (Boston: Marshall Jones, 1925), p. 37.

10. *Comparative Efficiency of Labor in the Bituminous Coal Industry Under Union and Non-Union Operation.* Evidence and testimony submitted to the U.S. Coal Commission by the Bituminous Operator's Special Committee, Sept. 10, 1923. West Virginia Collection, West Virginia University Library, p. 154. It is worth noting that in the shaft mines coming and going to the workplace was not as easy as in the drift mines. The mechanical means for entry and exit—the cage or man trip—was located on the surface under management's supervision, and miners who wanted to leave the mine early would have to wait until the coal had all been "caged." Over the years, as coal production came increasingly from shaft mines, it became more difficult for workers to leave the mine at will, and consequently their workday became more regimented and disciplined.

11. American Mining Congress, *1929 Yearbook on Coal Mine Mechanization* (Washington, D.C.), p. 7.

12. H. B. Lee, *Bloodletting in Appalachia* (Morgantown: West Virginia University, 1969), p. 188.

13. See Richard A. Simon, "The Development of Underdevelopment: The Coal Industry and Its Effect on the West Virginia Economy, 1880–1930" (Ph.D. diss., University of Pittsburgh, 1978), pp. 210–12.

14. These tactics constitute an important chapter in the history of this industry, but the story has been told numerous times through state and federal investigations, independent journalistic exposés, and eyewitness accounts. See, for example, U.S. Coal Commission, *Report, Part I: Principal Findings and Recommendations* (Washington, D.C.: Government Printing Office, 1925), pp. 153–82; Homer Morris, *Plight of the Bituminous Coal Miner* (Philadelphia: University of Pennsylvania Press, 1934), pp. 85–97; and *Report of the West Virginia Mining Investigation Commission, August 28, 1912* (Charleston, W.Va: and Senate Committee on Interstate Commerce, *Conditions in the Coal Fields of Pennsylvania, West Virginia, and Ohio,* 70th Cong., 1st sess. (Washington, D.C.: Government Printing Office, 1928).

15. Lee, *Bloodletting,* p. 12.

16. Mine workers' resistance to these abuses has been analyzed by Jon Amsden and Steve Brier in "Coal Miners on Strike: The Transformation of Strike Demands and the Formation of the National Union," *Journal of Interdisciplinary History* (Spring 1977): 583–616.

17. From several sources it has been possible to piece together a profile of this company, although there are many gaps in the record. The most important source has been the Justus Collins Papers in the West Virginia Collection, West Virginia University Library. Correspondence between Justus Collins and his brother Jairus, who managed the Collinses' coal mine for many years, and a few financial records for the company in 1932 were located in the Collins

Papers. Annual reports of the West Virginia Department of Mines have also been useful in preparing this section of the chapter.

18. West Virginia Department of Mines, *Annual Report, 1903* (Charleston, 1904), p. 270.

19. Justus Collins Papers.

20. Joseph T. Lambie, *From Mine to Market* (New York: New York University Press, 1954), p. 39.

21. See Justus Collins Papers.

22. Smokeless Fuel Company Contract, Nov. 26, 1924, West Virginia Collection, West Virginia University Library.

23. Morton Baratz, *The Union and The Coal Industry* (New Haven: Yale University Press, 1955), p. 19.

24. The company's financial statement shows that there was only an insignificant increase in the total rent payments from the company-owned houses. This would confirm the notion that no new employees were hired for the output expansion.

25. A decrease in the slack ratio would mean, other things remaining the same, a decrease in the weight of each car.

26. Dix, *Work Relations,* pp. 54–55.

27. Several interesting questions might be raised concerning the company's financial reports for 1932. They are not particularly relevant to the question of mine mechanization except that they affect the basic economic decisions of the firm. For example, why did the company accountant make it a practice to set aside a depletion allowance when the company leased its mining property and paid a ten-cent-per-ton royalty to the owner? And why did the company pay a $6,000 dividend to its stockholders during 1932, when operating losses were so large?

CHAPTER 2. Evolution of Underground Machinery

1. G. Hibberd, "A Century of Mechanical Coal-cutting," *Iron and Coal Trade Review* (Apr. 8, 1955): 783–91. Although cutting machines were first developed in Great Britain, they were slow to be adopted there. As late as 1930, only 31.1 percent of British coal was cut by machines. For an analysis of the mechanization movement in England, see H. H. Wilson and R. B. Dunn, "Mechanization in the Mines," *Convention Proceedings, National Association of Colliery Managers* 55 (1958): 13–28.

2. Hibberd, "Century of Mechanical Coal-cutting," p. 784.

3. *Black Diamond* (May 10, 1919): 480.

4. R. Shepherd and A. G. Withers, *Mechanized Cutting and Loading of Coal* (London: Odhams Press, 1960), pp. 16–17.

5. Hibberd, "Century of Mechanical Coal-cutting," p. 784.

6. Edward W. Parker, "Coal-Cutting Machinery," *Transactions of the American Institute of Mining Engineers* 29 (1899): 413–14.

7. Keith Dix, *Work Relations in the Coal Industry: The Hand-Loading Era, 1880–1930* (Morgantown: West Virginia University, 1977), p. 18.

8. In the late 1880s, Elmer A. Sperry, a man well known for his work with practical applications of electricity to industry, tried unsuccessfully to develop a commercially acceptable punch machine driven by an electric motor. See discussion below.

9. Parker, "Coal-Cutting Machinery," pp. 416–35.

10. Other examples can be found in various issues of *Coal Age*, for example Mar. 3, 1921, p. 395; May 5, 1921, p. 789; and Oct. 13, 1921, p. 589. See also *Coal Industry* (Dec. 1918): 457–78; American Mining Congress, *1928 Yearbook on Coal Mine Modernization* (Washington, D.C., 1928), pp. 168–33.

11. *Coal Industry* (Dec. 1918): 457.

12. *Coal Mine Management* (June 1924): 38. An excellent review of the status of mechanical loading in the early 1920s can be found in an article by L. A. Bean, *Coal Age* (Jan. 17, 1924): 66–71.

13. F. E. Cash and E. H. Johnson, *Mechanical Loading in Coal Mines* (Pittsburgh: Carnegie Institute of Technology, 1925).

14. *Coal Age* (Jan. 17, 1924): 71. See also the personal account of an engineer who used one of the original Stanley headers. He claimed, that "in entry driving, where it is desirable to quickly open up working places, it will probably be found possible to drive the necessary entries in about one-fourth of the time required by hand labor in the old way." *Colliery Engineer* (May 1891): 23.

15. E. M. Warner, "An Historical Review of American Continuous Miners," paper presented to the International Conference on Mining Machinery, Brisbane, Australia, July 4, 1979. See also *Mining Congress Journal* (June 1925): 296, for one coal operator's experience with the McKinley entry driver.

16. *Coal Age* (May 1, 1919): 786–87. See also the discussion below on the development work by the Jeffrey Company on this machine.

17. Ibid., p. 787.

18. *Mining Congress Journal* (June 1925): 301. It might have been that corporate policy toward development work on machinery was directly affected by labor costs, but inventive effort in the field had been going on for years before the tight labor markets in the World War I period.

19. Martin Hayduk (interviewed, March 8, 1978) worked with Edward O'Toole and remembers that two draftsmen were employed by the company to do nothing else but design and draw O'Toole's ideas. O'Toole was also provided with a well-equipped machine shop and several skilled machinists. U.S. Steel obviously wanted to encourage the inventor's efforts.

20. This discussion of the O'Toole mining system is based on the following

sources: C. E. Lawall, I. A. Given, and H. G. Kennedy, *Mining Methods in West Virginia* (Morgantown: West Virginia University, 1929), pp. 36–39; Cash and Johnson, *Mechanical Loading,* pp. 35–36; and *Coal Age* (May 28, 1925): 783–87.

21. In searching for the original Hamilton patent, I discovered that in 1903 the inventor also had patented a loading machine that incorporated a gathering device to pull the coal on to the conveyor. Drawings accompanying his patent application indicate that this gathering device was quite similar to the one Joseph Joy invented, perhaps coincidentally, in the same year. (See Patent 736,846, U.S. Patent Office, August 18, 1903. See also discussion of the Joy machine in the next chapter.)

22. *Mines and Minerals* (Nov. 1907): 185.

23. Ibid., p. 186.

24. Cash and Johnson, *Mechanical Loading,* p. 37.

25. *Coal Industry* (Dec. 1918): p. 465.

26. *Coal Age* (May 1, 1919): 788.

27. *Coal Age* (Feb. 5, 1925): 215.

28. Bert G. Norris, "Mechanical Mining of Coal, Early History and Development of Mining Machinery as Manufactured by the Jeffrey Manufacturing Company," (mimeo., no date).

29. George Dillig of Pittsburgh adapted the large steam shovel concept to underground mining, but his machine was severely limited by the height of the coal seam (see *Coal Age* (May 1, 1919): 788–89). In 1924, the Goodman Company introduced a small mechanical scoop, which could be operated by one man. This electro-hydraulic power shovel met with some success in the industry and continued to be used well into the 1930s in some coalfields. See American Mine Company, *1929 Yearbook on Coal Mine Mechanization,* p. 261.

30. *Mines and Minerals* (Sept. 1910): 66; and (Nov. 1910): 206–08. See also Cash and Johnson, *Mechanical Loading,* pp. 5–8.

31. Interview, May 26, 1978, at Clarksburg, West Virginia.

32. All of the mobile leaders also incorporated some form of conveyor to elevate and move the coal.

33. *Coal Age* (Dec. 3, 1925): 760.

34. *Coal Age* (Jan. 23, 1919): 176.

35. This section relies heavily on Bernard Drell, "The Role of the Goodman Manufacturing Company in the Mechanization of Coal Mining," (Ph.D. diss., University of Chicago, 1939).

36. "Half a Century Underground," *Electrical Mining* 7 (4). (The Goodman Company employees' magazine.)

37. This history is based on an article in *Black Diamond* (May 10, 1919): 480–81; and on Norris, "Mechanical Mining." See also *Business Week,* Mar. 19, 1949.

38. See for example an article by N. D. Levin, chief engineer of the Jeffrey Company, in *Coal Age* (Apr. 2, 1925).

39. Norris, "Mechanical Mining," p. 95.

40. Ibid., p. 97.

41. *Coal Age* (Dec. 30, 1920): 1321–22.

42. Ibid.

43. Ibid.

44. *Coal Age* (Apr. 2, 1925): 499. It is interesting to note that the trade journals opened their pages to manufacturers' representatives, who wrote articles that appeared to be scientific but were in reality promotions for specific products.

45. Norris, "Mechanical Mining," p. 101.

46. Ibid., p. 106.

47. Ibid., p. 107.

48. Ibid., p. 110.

49. The Joy loader, in contrast, was mounted on caterpillar tractor treads and thus was more mobile. With the development of rubber-tired shuttle cars in 1938, the use of Joy loaders and shuttle cars meant that tracks in the rooms were no longer needed. Jack Branter, a Jeffrey Company official, speculated in an interview (Mar. 9, 1979) that the company's longterm commercial relation with the captive steel mines probably explained why it was committed to track-mounted equipment for such a long period. The use of a mining machine that did not use steel track would deprive the steel industry of an important market.

50. American Mining Congress, *1938 Yearbook on Coal Mine Mechanization*, p. 135.

51. Interview, Oct. 12, 1979, at Mannington, West Virginia.

52. The difference of 700 between the number of mobile loaders in use in 1936 and those in use in 1940 is only an approximation of the number sold during this period.

Chapter 3. The Joy Loading Machine

1. I am indebted to Herman Van Houten for much of the information of Joseph Joy's early background and engineering career. Van Houten began working 1931 as Joy's private secretary and remained an employee and close friend of the inventor for many years. He was a vice president of Joy Manufacturing at the time I interviewed him on July 27, 1979, at Franklin, Pennsylvania. The story of Joy's early days is taken from the testimony given before a patent examiner in a hearing over a rival's claim to conception of the loading machine. See Archives Division, U.S. Patent Office, Washington, D.C.

(documents filed under U.S. Patent 1,206,064). See also the summary of the evidence in *Joy v. Morgan,* decided Jan. 7, 1924, *Federal Reporter* 295 F.931. Additional information has been obtained from a privately published document titled *My Work, 1914 . . . 1944,* by Joseph F. Joy (no date). Much of this chapter originally appeared in my article, "Joseph Joy and His Mobile Loading Machine," *West Virginia History* 41 (Spring 1980).

2. Draft copy of "Joy Manufacturing Company History," (mimeo, Jan. 1954).

3. U.S. Patent 772,152.

4. Thomas Hughes, "The Development Phases of Technology Change," *Technology and Culture* (July 1976): 425.

5. *Federal Reporter* 295 F.933.

6. Ibid.

7. *Federal Reporter* 295 F.943.

8. Ibid.

9. Ibid.

10. Bert G. Norris, "Mechanical Mining of Coal, Early History and Development of Mining Machinery as Manufactured by the Jeffrey Manufacturing Company" (mimeo., no date). Mr. Norris was employed by the Jeffrey Company from 1897 to 1950. It was during the early 1950s, after his retirement, that he wrote the personal account of the engineering history of the company. I am indebted to Jack Brantner, vice-president of Development for the Jeffrey Mining Machinery Division, for giving me access to the Norris manuscript.

11. *Federal Reporter* 295 F.231.

12. *Coal Age* (May 1920): 902.

13. Ibid.

14. U.S. patent 1,411,720.

15. Labor shortages were noted as early as 1915. *Mining Congress Journal* 2 (1916): 493.

16. See chapter 5.

17. Interview with Herman Van Houten July 27, 1979, at Franklin, Pennsylvania.

18. Ibid.

19. U.S. patent 1,306,064, pp. 1 and 4.

20. Letter from T. J. McNabe to Joy Manufacturing Co., Nov. 9, 1976, in the possession of Herman Van Houten. McNabe supervised the construction of the Joy loaders at Thayer and went with Joy to help them and to "get the 'bugs' out of them."

21. Robert Spence, *Land of the Guyandot, A History of Logan County* (Detroit: Harlo Press, 1976).

22. Not to be confused with the present-day Consolidation Coal Company.

23. Without a union, there was no organized resistance to the introduction of the loader. According to Spence, the miners may even have welcomed it at first, because they were told that those who operated the loaders would continue to be paid on a tonnage basis. This did not work out, however, and it later became common practice in both union and nonunion fields to pay machine operators a daily wage.

24. "Joy Manufacturing Company History."

25. For a discussion of UMWA policy relating to mechanization, see Stanley Miller, "The United Mine Workers: A Study on How Trade Union Policy Relates to Technological Change" (Ph.D. diss., University of Wisconsin, 1957). Also see chapter 6.

26. *Coal Age* (Oct. 22, 1925).

27. Ibid.

28. See discussion in chapter 6.

29. All quotations in this paragraph from *Coal Age* (Jan. 17, 1924): 74.

30. Interview with retired mine foreman Mike Murphy, Oct. 12, 1979, at Mannington, West Virginia.

31. Sales data were supplied by E. M. Warner, director of Engineering for the Joy Machinery Company. I have not been able to determine why the Pittsburgh Coal Company did not move ahead with mechanization in the early 1920s, since it apparently had been so committed to it at an earlier date. By 1927 this company along with others in western Pennsylvania, West Virginia, and Ohio had broken the union and were operating their mines on a nonunion basis.

32. "Joy Manufacturing Company History."

33. From the caption on the photo used in figure 20, in the possession of Herman Van Houten.

34. *Mining Congress Journal* (Dec. 1925): 628.

35. Ten of these models were donated to West Virginia University and are on display in White Hall, the College of Mineral and Energy Resources.

36. Based on Van Houten's impressions.

37. Letters quoted in Joy, *My Work, 1914* (no pagination).

CHAPTER 4. Transformation of the Miner's Job

1. The mechanized system of mining described herein continued in use long after the introduction of the continuous mining machine in 1948. It came to be known as the conventional mining system and as late as 1970 accounted for 46 percent of all coal mined underground. U.S. Bureau of Mines, *Minerals Yearbook, 1970* (Washington, D.C.: Government Printing Office), p. 342.

2. Keith Dix, *Work Relations in the Coal Industry: The Hand-loading Era, 1880–1930* (Morgantown: West Virginia University, 1977), p. 20.

3. Willard E. Hotchkiss, et al., *Mechanization, Employment, and Output Per Man it Bituminous-Coal Mining,* vol. 2 (Philadelphia: Work Projects Administration, 1939), p. 20. This document is the best single source on the development of early mine mechanization.

4. Ibid., p. 23.

5. Thomas A. Stroup, "Cause and Growth of Unionism Among Coal Miners," *Mining and Metallurgy* (Sept. 1923): 468.

6. U.S. Coal Commission, *Report, Part III: Bituminous Coal–Detailed Labor and Engineering Studies* (Washington, D.C.: Government Printing Office, 1925), pp. 1900–01.

7. *Coal Age* (Nov. 24, 1923): 834.

8. *Coal Age* (Dec. 4, 1924): 781–82.

9. *Coal Age* (Feb. 1931): 62.

10. *Coal Age* (Mar. 1930): 147.

11. *Proceedings, West Virginia Coal Mining Institute,* Wheeling, Nov. 27–28, 1931, Bulletin No. 17, p. 70.

12. U.S. Coal Commission, *Report,* p. 1993.

13. See F. E. Cash and E. H. Johnson, *Mechanical Loading in Coal Mines* (Pittsburgh: Carnegie Institute of Technology, 1925).

14. Ibid., p. 1.

15. See the discussion below on health and safety.

16. Cash and Johnson, *Mechanical Loading,* p. 26.

17. Interview, Mar. 15, 1982, at Eccles, West Virginia.

18. George Korson, *Coal Dust on the Fiddle* (Philadelphia: University of Pennsylvania Press, 1943), pp. 138–39. This song was recorded in 1940 in Welch, West Virginia.)

19. Ibid., p. 141.

20. Interview, Oct. 12, 1979, at Mannington, West Virginia.

21. Interview, May 26, 1978, at Clarksburg, West Virginia.

22. H. B. Humphrey, *Historical Summary of Coal-Mine Explosions in the United States, 1810–1958,* U.S. Bureau of Mines Bulletin 586 (Washington, D.C.: Government Printing Office, 1960), p. 165.

23. L. E. Young, "Reducing Accidents in Mechanized Loading," *1929 Yearbook on Coal Mine Mechanization* (Washington, D.C.: American Mining Congress, 1929), p. 64.

24. Ibid., p., 66.

25. A. V. Sproles, "Comparison on Accident Reduction in Hand and Machine Loading," *1929 Yearbook on Coal Mine Mechanization* (Washington, D.C.: American Mining Congress, 1929), p. 68.

26. Lyman Fearn, "Has Mechanized Mining Brought Safer Coal Mining?" *1933 Yearbook on Coal Mine Mechanization* (Washington, D.C.: American Mining Congress, 1933), p. 219.

27. D. Harrington, "Bringing Safety Home to the Mines," *1937 Yearbook on Coal Mine Mechanization* (Washington, D.C.: American Mining Congress, 1937), p. 318.

28. Otto Herres, "Mine Accidents and Their Effect on Production Costs," *1937 Yearbook on Coal Mine Mechanization* (Washington, D.C.: American Mining Congress, 1937), p. 312.

29. *Mining Congress Journal* (July 1927): 550.

30. Occasionally in the mining literature during this period the opposite view would be explicitly stated. The safety director of the Harlan County Coal Operators Association in 1934 made the following rather extraordinary statement regarding mine safety: "We often hear that coal mines are inherently unsafe and that there are countless hazards that are not found in any other industry; that accidents are bound to happen. Such statements are rash and unreliable. Most of the hazards in coal mining are man-made. Responsibility for accidents in mines must rest squarely on the shoulders of the operating officials." James F. Bryson, "Promoting Safety as a Sound Investment," *1934 Yearbook on Coal Mine Mechanization* (Washington, D.C.: American Mining Congress, 1934), p. 213.

31. *UMWA Journal* (Jan. 15, 1932): 6.

32. See, for example, the awards given in 1932, *UMWA Journal* (May 1, 1932): 14. See *Mining Congress Journal* (Dec. 1927): 922 for a description of the Holmes Safety Association. See also J. J. Sellers, "Safety Bonuses," *1937 Yearbook on Coal Mine Mechanization* (Washington, D.C.: American Mining Congress, 1937), p. 314; C. E. Young, "Safety Contests," *1938 Yearbook on Coal Mine Mechanization* (Washington, D.C.: American Mining Congress, 1938), pp. 319–25; F. S. Lenhart, "Promotion of Safety Education Through Meetings," *1934 Yearbook on Coal Mine Mechanization* (Washington, D.C.: American Mining Congress, 1934), pp. 239–40; and John Lyons, "Safety Training for Employees," *1938 Yearbook on Coal Mine Mechanization* (Washington, D.C.: American Mining Congress, 1938), pp. 300–03.

33. A. L. Hunt, "Successful Accident Prevention," *1933 Yearbook on Coal Mine Mechanization* (Washington, D.C.: American Mining Congress, 1933), p. 217.

34. U.S. Bureau of Mines, *Safety in the Mining Industry,* Information Circular 7485 (Washington, D.C.: Government Printing Office, 1949), p. 15.

35. Ibid.

36. U.S. Bureau of Mines, *Report of the Health and Safety Division, Fiscal Year 1949,* Information Circular 7562 (Washington, D.C.: Government Printing Office, 1950), p. 44.

37. U.S. Bureau of Labor Statistics, *Proceedings of the Seventeenth Annual*

Meeting of the International Association of Industrial Accident Boards and Commissions, Bulletin 536 (Washington, D.C.: 1931), p. 186.

38. Ibid., pp. 197–98.

39. *Mining Congress Journal* (July 1928): 485–86.

40. U.S. Bureau of Mines, *Falls of Roof: The No. 1 Killer in Bituminous Coal Mines*, Information Circular 7605 (Washington, D.C.: Government Printing Office, 1951), p. 2.

41. U.S. Bureau of Mines, *Roof Bolting in the United States*, Information Circular 7583 (Washington, D.C.: Government Printing Office, 1950), p. 3.

42. American Mining Congress, *1933 Yearbook on Coal Mine Mechanization*, (Washington, D.C.: American Mining Congress, 1933), p. 220.

43. Humphrey, *Historical Summary*, p. 41. The single most important cause of mine explosions was listed as "open lights and smoking," with electric arc being second and blasting and explosives third.

44. Hotchkiss et al., *Mechanization, Employment, and Output*, vol. I, pp. 23–24.

45. Senate Committee on Public Lands, *Investigation of Mine Explosion at Centralia, Illinois*, 80th Cong., 1st sess. (Washington, D.C.: Government Printing Office, 1947), p. 216.

46. *Mining Congress Journal* (Dec. 1925): 637.

47. J. J. Forbes, W. J. Fene, and H. B. Humphrey, *Coal-Mine Explosions and Metal-Mine Fires*, U.S. Bureau of Mines Information Circular 7572 (Washington, D.C.: Government Printing Office, 1950), p. 10.

48. Ibid., p. 11.

49. *Mining Congress Journal* (Dec. 1925); 633.

50. George S. Rice, *The Explosibility of Coal Dust*, U.S. Bureau of Mines Bulletin 20 (Washington, D.C.: Government Printing Office, 1911).

51. Quoted in Humphrey, *Historical Summary*, p. 166.

52. P. H. Burrell, "Rock Dusting," *1936 Yearbook on Coal Mine Mechanization* (Philadelphia: American Mining Congress, 1936), p. 330.

53. Irwing Hartman and H. P. Greenwald, *Uses of Wetting Agents for Allaying Coal Dust in Mines*, U.S. Bureau of Mines Information Circular 7131 (Washington, D.C.: Government Printing Office, 1940), p. 1.

54. Richard M. Gooding, ed., *Proceedings of the Symposium on Responsible Coal Mine Dust*, U.S. Bureau of Mines Information Circular 8458 (Washington, D.C.: Government Printing Office, 1969), p. 10.

CHAPTER 5. Miners' Responses to Technological Change

1. Sumner H. Slichter, *Union Policies and Industrial Management* (Washington, D.C.: Brookings, 1941), pp. 201–82.

2. Edward A. Wieck, *The American Miners' Association* (New York: Russell Sage, 1940), pp. 65–68.

3. Ibid., p. 89.

4. Stanley Miller, "The United Mine Workers: A Study on How Trade Union Policy Relates to Technological Change" (Ph.D. diss., Univ. of Wisconsin, 1957), p. 20.

5. Chris Evans, *History of the United Mine Workers of America from 1860 to 1890*, vol. 1 (Indianapolis: (no publisher given), 1918), p. 86.

6. Ibid., p. 90.

7. *Black Diamond* (May 10, 1919): 480.

8. These observations on the Ohio situation in the 1880s are based on the important research by Jon Amsden and Stephen Brier, "Coal Miners on Strike: The Transformation on Strike Demands and Formation of a National Union," *Journal of Interdisciplinary History* (Spring 1977): 599–616.

9. Quoted in ibid., p. 600.

10. Ohio Bureau of Labor Statistics, *Fourth Annual Report* (Columbus: Bureau of Labor Statistics, 1880), pp. 90–91.

11. Wage cuts were more or less accepted by miners in periods of depressed coal markets, but in 1884 "the reduction proposed by the . . . two strongest companies in the district, was made at a time when mining prices all over the state of Ohio remained unchanged." Evans, *History of the United Miner Workers*, pp. 112–13.

12. Ibid., p. 118.

13. Quoted in Amsden and Brier, "Coal Miners on Strike," p. 601.

14. Keith Dix, *Work Relations in the Coal Industry: The Hand-Loading Era, 1880–1930* (Morgantown: West Virginia University, 1977), p. 20.

15. Illinois Bureau of Labor Statistics, *Fourth Biennial Report* (Springfield: Bureau of Labor Statistics, 1886), p. 536.

16. Evans, *History of the United Mine Workers*, vol. 1, pp. 139–40.

17. While miners were accustomed to having tonnage rates cut when coal prices fell with swings in the business cycle and even with seasonal fluctuations in the demand for coal, the development of a national market for coal created a different situation, one in which there was a more or less continual downward pressure on coal prices.

18. Quoted in Evans, *History of the United Mine Workers*, p. 267.

19. Ibid., pp. 259–60.

20. Ibid.

21. The National Federation had, by 1889, changed its name to the National Progressive Union.

22. Evans, *History of the United Mine Workers*, vol. 2, p. 19.

23. J. E. George, "The Coal Miners' Strike of 1897," Quarterly Journal of Economics 12 (Oct. 1897–1898): 188.

24. Arthur Suffern, *Conciliation and Arbitration in the Coal Industry of America* (Boston: Houghton Mifflin, 1915), p. 44.

25. George, "Coal Miners' Strike," p. 186.

26. The irony of the notion that the eight-hour day was a victory for mine workers was recognized by the industry, if not by the union leadership. "Experiences with the craft has demonstrated that they want to earn all the money they can. . . . If a coal miner goes into the mine, has a good room and a chance to produce a large amount of coal, is it reasonable to expect him to let the opportunity to work several hours longer and earn more money pass by? . . . Organized labor throughout the country hailed the [eight-hour day] movement with vociferous expressions of delight. The indications are that the officials of the miners union will have to confront the difficulties of enforcing its provisions and not the operators" (*Coal and Coke* [Feb. 25, 1892]: 16).

27. Union leaders were expected to sanction strikes against operators who refused to comply with the wage-scale agreement, however. In 1889, for example, just three weeks after the interstate agreement was signed, a few Pennsylvania operators tried to alter established practices unilaterally, and the union was expected to bring them back in line by calling a strike. The trade journal *Coal and coke* (April 22, 1898: 12) reported on one such situation: "Miners employed at the Patton Coal Company, Patton, Pa., are on strike and seem to be bitter in their demands. Saturday next the company will begin machine mining at their Flannigan Run mine, and will try to put men to work loading coal after the machine by the day instead of the district price, 23 cents a ton. This the miners will try to prevent."

28. Arthur Suffern, *The Coal Miners Struggle for Industrial Status* (new York: Macmillan, 1926), p. 195.

29. *UMWA Journal* (July 31, 1902).

30. McAlister Coleman points out that Mitchell did not want to call a general strike because it would soon have depleted the union's treasury. As long as the soft-coal miners were working, they could be assessed a dollar a week to support the anthracite strikers. See *Men and Coal* (New York: Farrar and Rinehart, 1943), p. 70.

31. *UMWA Journal* (July 31, 1902). Emphasis added.

32. During a strike that began in 1919 in Illinois, operators claimed that the union had broken the contract by ceasing work. In this case, however, there was a fundamental difference of opinion over the expiration date of the contract and not a rejection of the inviolability principle.

33. *Coal and Coke* (April 8, 1898): 12.

34. Suffern, *Coal Miners Struggle*, pp. 227–31.

35. Ibid., pp. 240–57. Suffern studied nearly 7,000 grievances settled at various stages of the grievance procedure in Illinois in the years 1908 and 1910. He noted that many local strikes continued to occur even though the grievance

procedure was in operation, but there is no record of the number of such strikes. "In fact," he says, "there are no comprehensive and reliable data on the extent of merely local stoppages under the contract in any of the fields" (p. 246).

36. This summary of the role of the pit committee and the negotiated limitations on the power of the committee is based on Evelyn Preston, "The Pit Committee in the Illinois Coal Fields" (M.A. thesis, University of Wisconsin, 1923).

37. U.S. Commissioner of Labor, *Regulation and Restriction of Output*, H. Doc. 734, (Washington, D.C.: Government Printing Office, 1904), pp. 416–26.

38. Ibid., p. 442.

39. The controversy over the machine differential was a rather complicated one and persisted for several years. In Illinois, which adopted a statewide differential in 1889, the operators in low-coal seams argued that they needed a lower rate for loaders to justify the use of cutting machines. Failing to obtain a lower rate, operators in the Danville area removed their cutting machines and, for a while, returned to pick mining. Ibid., p. 422.

40. Quoted in Preston, *Pit Committee*, p. 43.

41. Ibid., pp. 44–46.

42. Ibid., p. 50.

43. Ibid., p. 44.

44. *Coal Trade Bulletin* (October 16, 1920): 296.

45. Preston, *Pit Committee*, p. 43.

CHAPTER 6. The Union and Mechanization

1. Richard P. Rothwell, ed., *The Mineral Industry, 1892* (New York: Scientific Publishing, 1893), p. 76, and U.S. Bureau of Mines, *Minerals Yearbook, 1942* (Washington, D.C.: Government Printing Office, 1943), p. 848.

2. U.S. Bureau of Mines, *Minerals Yearbook, 1942* (Washington, D.C.: Government Printing Office, 1942), p. 848.

3. The issue in question had its origin in the technology of undercutting machinery, which pulverized coal as it undercut the face. It was also related to the growing use, in the 1890s, of immigrant laborers who, in mining coal less skillfully than their counterparts, created a great deal of slack coal. Since the smaller sizes of coal had little or no market value in the early days of the industry, the operators installed screens to separate the coal by size. All coal less than, say, 1½ inches in diameter, was considered slack, or waste, and the miner was paid only for the coal that passed over the screen. The miners argued that payment for screened coal allowed for many abuses, as the screens were "known to vary all the way from ⅞ of an inch between the bars [of the screen]

to 2½ inches." Local agreements requiring payment on the basis of run-of-the-mine were negotiated in some fields, and laws in Ohio and Illinois requiring gross weight payment to miners were passed in the 1890s. But the practice continued until the operators agreed to discontinue it in 1916. For a detailed discussion of the economic pressures, the resistance of the miners, and the intervention of state government in this issue and how the issue related to technology, both in coal mining and coal utilization, see U.S. Commissioner of Labor, *Special Report on Regulation and Restriction of Output* (Washington, D.C.: Government Printing Office, 1914), pp. 394–430.

4. U.S. Bituminous Coal Commission, *Majority and Minority Reports* (Washington, D.C.: Government Printing Office, 1920), p. 19.

5. Ibid., p. 20.

6. The details of the penalty clause were not specified in the Washington Agreement. It was left to the various district and local negotiators to agree on wording of the contract on this point.

7. *Monthly Labor Review,* (Dec. 1917): 1182.

8. *UMWA Journal* (March 14, 1918): 26.

9. Sylvia Kopald, *Rebellion in Labor Unions* (New York: Boni and Livernash, 1924), pp. 50–123.

10. See discussion of attempts by the UMWA to discipline striking locals after 1947 in Keith Dix, *Work Stoppages and the Grievance Procedure in the Appalachian Coal Industry* (Morgantown: West Virginia University, Institute for Labor Studies, 1973), p. 54.

11. *Coal Age* (January 5, 1918); 25.

12. *Monthly Labor Review,* (December 1919): 61–63.

13. Before John White resigned as president of the union in October 1917, to take a job with the U.S. Fuel Administration, he appointed John L. Lewis as international statistician and manager of the *Journal.* Frank Hayes, White's successor, in turn appointed Lewis to act as vice-president of the union. When Hayes resigned in 1919, Lewis became president, a position he held until 1960. For the details of this transition of power in the UMWA, see Melvyn Dubofsky and Warren Van Tine, *John L. Lewis* (New York: Quadrangle, 1977), pp. 45–46.

14. Ibid., pp. 66–78.

15. U.S. Bituminous Coal Commission, *Reports,* pp. 14 and 118.

16. In addition, the operators wanted to eliminate the dues checkoff, to fix house rents, to instal time clocks at the mines, to make the union "legally responsible for the fulfillment of the contracts," and to have any contract they might sign expire in the spring.

17. U.S. Bituminous Coal Commission, *Reports,* pp. 14 and 118.

18. See chapter 2.

19. U.S. Bituminous Coal Commission, *Reports,* p. 105.

20. Ibid.

21. *Coal Trade Bulletin* (May 15, 1920): 140.

22. Ibid.

23. Ibid. (May 1, 1920): 116.

24. Ibid. (Sept. 18, 1920): 215.

25. Ibid. (Jan. 1, 1921): 75.

26. *Monthly Labor Review* (Nov. 1922): 4.

27. Union leaders believed that the operators' strategy was inspired by the nationwide open-shop drive of the 1920s—called the American plan—which was aimed at destroying collective bargaining. There seemed to be some basis for their belief, when the operators began demanding abolition of the union dues checkoff system, which had been in effect in the Central Competitive Field for many years. Ibid., p. 11.

28. Ibid., p. 14.

29. Ibid., p. 8.

30. U.S. Bureau of Labor Statistics, *Hours and Earnings in Bituminous Coal Mining, 1922, 1923 and 1926,* Bulletin 454 (Washington, D.C.: Government Printing Office, 1927), pp. 58–66.

31. Boris Emmet, *Labor Relations in the Fairmont, West Virginia, Bituminous Coal Field,* U.S. Bureau of Labor Statistics Bulletin 361 (Washington, D.C.: Government Printing Office, 1924), pp. 11–20.

32. Ibid., p. 15.

33. Ibid., p. 33.

34. Ibid., p. 35.

35. U.S. Bureau of Mines, *Mineral Resources of the United States, 1923,* pt. 2 (Washington, D.C.: Government Printing Office, 1926), p. 516.

36. Ibid., p. 22.

37. Ibid.

38. Ibid.

39. Dubofsky and Van Tine, *John L. Lewis,* p. 90; *UMWA Journal* (Jan. 1, 1924): 8–9.

40. Dubofsky and Van Tine, *John L. Lewis,* p. 91.

41. U.S. Coal Commission, *Report, Part II, Bituminous Coal—Detailed Labor and Engineering Studies* (Washington, D.C.: Government Printing Office, 1925), p. 1905.

42. Ibid., p. 1913.

43. Ibid., p. 1916.

44. U.S. Coal Commission, "Comparative Efficiency of Labor in the Bituminous Coal Industry under Union and Non-union Operation," submitted to the U.S. Coal Commission by the Bituminous Operators' Special Committee, Sept. 10, 1923, p. 182.

45. Bituminous Operators' Special Committee, *Briefs and Other Communication Submitted to the United States Coal Commission by the Bituminous*

Operators, 1923, vol. 4, pp. 59–60 (microfilm, West Virginia Collection, West Virginia University Library).

46. Quoted in United Miner Workers of America, *The United Mine Workers and the United States Coal Commission* (Indianapolis, Ind., n.d.), p. 28.

47. U.S. Coal Commission, *Report, Part I, Principal Findings and Recommendations* (Washington, D.C.: Government Printing Office), 1925), p. 272.

48. The text of the Jacksonville agreement can be found in U.S. Bureau of Labor Statistics Bulletin 419, *Trade Agreements, 1925* (Washington, D.C.: Government Printing Office, 1926), p. 99. An example of a subdistrict agreement for the Hocking Valley in Ohio can be located in the U.S. Bureau of Labor Statistics Bulletin 416, *Hours and Earnings in Anthracite and Bituminous Coal Mining* (Washington, D.C.: Government Printing Office, 1926), pp. 82–90.

49. *UMWA Journal* (Apr. 1, 1924): 11.

50. The U.S. Bureau of Labor Statistics reported that in the northern West Virginia agreement "all of the principal changes made, with one exception . . . are to the advantage of the operators." See Emmet, *Labor Relations in the Fairmont . . . Coal Field,* p. 46. One important change in work practice that benefited the hand loaders in Illinois involved the company agreement to accept loaded coal cars at the face so that miners did not have to push them from their rooms. "Agreement By and Between the Illinois Coal Operators Association . . . and the United Mine Workers of America, District Number 12," expiring March 31, 1927, ibid., p. 45.

51. See *Coal Age* (Apr. 10, 1924): 539; (Apr. 24, 1924): 609; and (May 1, 1924): 642.

52. Dubofsky and Van Tine believed that Lewis was locked into this position. He "could not confess his own weakness, request a wage revision, and suffer repudiation by his rank and file." *John L. Lewis,* p. 135.

53. Ibid.

54. Edmond M. Beame, "The Jacksonville Agreement: Quest for Stability in Coal," *Industrial and Labor Relations Review* (Jan. 1955); 198.

55. *Coal Age* (Aug. 7, 1924): 175.

56. Dubofsky and Van Tine, *John L. Lewis,* p. 134.

57. Beame, "Jacksonville Agreement," p. 199.

CHAPTER 7. Evolution of the UMWA's Mechanization Policy

1. See U.S. Coal Commission, "Comparative Efficiency of Labor in the Bituminous Coal Industry under Union and Non-union operation, submitted to the U.S. Coal Commission by the Bituminous Operators' Special Committee, Sept. 10, 1923.

2. For a good account of Mitchell's contribution to the development of the

UMWA and its policies, see J. M. Gowaskie, "John Mitchell: A Study in Leadership" (Ph.D. diss., Catholic University of America, 1968). A less scholarly treatment of the Mitchell years can be found in David J. McDonald and Edward A. Lynch, *Coal and Unionism* (Silver Spring, Md.: Cornelius Printing, 1939), pp. 48–76; and McAlister Coleman, *Men and Coal (New York: Farrar and Rinehart, 1943), pp.* 58–80. An explanation of the union's internal structure and the bargaining structure that evolved in the Central Competitive Field during Mitchell's tenure can be found in Frank J. Warne, *The Union Movement Among Coal-Mine Workers,* U.S. Department of Labor Bulletin 51 (Washington, D.C.: Government Printing Office, 1904), pp. 380–414.

3. A few contracts were signed in West Virginia, but generally the West Virginia operators were able to keep the state union free. See Arthur Suffern, *The Coal Miners Struggle for Industrial Status* (New York: Macmillan, 1926), pp. 63–107, 195.

4. Gowaskie, *John Mitchell,* p. 287.

5. See the discussion below on the role of the socialists in the UMWA.

6. Arthur C. Everling, "Tactics Over Strategy in the United Mine Workers of America" (Ph.D. diss., Pennsylvania State University, 1976), p. 18.

7. Philadelphia: American Book and Bible House, 1903.

8. Ibid., pp. 247 and 253.

9. Ibid., p. 248.

10. Ibid.

11. Ibid., p. 252.

12. Ibid., p. 249.

13. He believed in negotiating shorter hours, which would spread the available work around and thereby reduce layoffs.

14. See U.S. Commissioner of Labor, *Special Report on Regulation and Restriction of Output* (Washington, D.C.: Government Printing Office, 1914), pp. 383–481.

15. This section is based on Everling, "Tactics Over Strategy," and John H. M. Laslett, *Labor and the Left: A Study of Socialist and Radical Influence in the American Labor Movement, 1881–1924* (New York: Basic Books, 1970), chap. 6. The term *socialism* in this context does not necessarily imply party affiliation, although many miners did belong to the American Socialist Party during this period. The common thread that seems to tie together a wide range of left-wing political activists who thought of themselves as socialists was the support of a program of nationalization of industry.

16. Everling notes that Brophy was not part of the socialist movement and did not become a radical influence in the union until after 1921 ("Tactics Over Strategy, p. 24).

17. In 1915 Hayes dropped his association with the Socialists, and by the

time he became president of the union in 1917 he was hostile to them. Ibid., p. 21.

18. *UMWA Journal* (Apr. 12, 1894): 1.

19. *UMWA Journal* (Jan. 4, 1912).

20. Ibid.

21. *UMWA Journal* (Jan. 11, 1912): 6.

22. This discussion of Hayes is based on Everling, "Tactics Over Strategy," pp. 134–36; and John Brophy, *A Miner's Life* (Madison: University of Wisconsin Press, 1964), pp. 151–52.

23. UMWA, *Special Convention Proceedings, 1919* (Indianapolis: Bookwalter Ball Printing Co., 1919), vol. 1, pp. 374–92.

24. Ibid., p. 842.

25. Ibid., p. 869.

26. For a full discussion of Lewis's rise to power in the early 1920s and his behind-the-scene manipulation of the nationalization issue, see Everling, "Tactics Over Strategy," pp. 139–86.

27. Laslett, *Labor and the Left*, pp. 222–26.

28. Melvyn Dubofsky and Warren Van Tine, *John L. Lewis* (New York: Quadrangle, 1977), p. 73.

29. Everling, "Tactics Over Strategy," p. 164.

30. Quoted in Brophy, *Miner's Life*, pp. 160–61.

31. United Mine Workers of America, Nationalization Research Committee, *How to Run Coal* (Washington, D.C.: UMWA, 1922), pp. 10–12.

32. Quoted in Brophy, *Miner's Life*, p. 171. Brophy asserts that this statement accurately reflected Lewis's sentiments at the time.

33. Ibid., p. 175.

34. For an excellent summary of the events leading to Lewis's control of the UMWA, see Paul Clark's, *The Miners Fight for Democracy* (Ithaca: Cornell University Press, 1981), pp. 5–12.

35. UMWA, *Proceedings, 1927 Convention* (Indianapolis: Cornelius Printing Co., 1927), p. 215.

36. John L. Lewis, *The Miners' Fight for American Standards* (Indianapolis: Bell Publishing, 1925).

37. Dubofsky and Van Tine, *John L. Lewis*, p. 137.

38. Lewis, *Miners' Fight*, p. 15.

39. *Coal Trade Bulletin* (Feb. 16, 1925): 231.

40. Lewis, *Miners' Fight*, pp. 46–47.

41. Ibid., p. 108.

42. Ibid., p. 180.

43. The reader is referred to the following sources for accounts of the challenges to Lewis during the late 1920s, some of which revolved around the no-backward-step policy: Edward Dean Wickersham, "Opposition to the

International Officers of the United Mine Workers of America: 1919–1933"
(Ph.D. diss., Cornell University, 1951); Jack Richard Foster, "Union on Trial:
The United Mine Workers of America, District 11 of Indiana, 1930–1940
(Ph.D. diss., Ball State University, 1967): and Stanley Miller, "The United
Mine Workers: A Study on How Trade Union Policy Relates to Technological
Change" Ph.D. diss., University of Wisconsin, 1957).

44. Lewis, *Miners' Fight*, p. 98.

45. Morton S. Baratz, *The Union and the Coal Industry* (New Haven: Yale
University Press, 1955), p. 72.

46. *Coal Age* (Aug. 21, 1924): 261.

47. Ibid.

48. Ibid.

49. *Coal Trade Bulletin* (Aug. 1, 1924): 186.

50. See various issues of the then newly organized trade journal, *Coal Mine
Mechanization,* and especially Nov. 1924, and Feb. 1925. It is interesting to
note that incentive plans were reintroduced to the industry in the National
Bituminous Coal Wage Agreement of 1978, and continued in the 1981
Agreement.

51. UMWA, *Proceedings, 1927 Convention,* pp. 442–45.

52. Ibid., pp. 445–47.

53. Ibid., pp. 447–51.

54. Ibid., p. 452.

55. Ibid., p. 457.

56. One of the ways Lewis controlled debate on substantive issues and
determined union policy was by effective use of the committee system during
UMWA conventions. The hundreds of resolutions submitted by local unions
on a wide range of concerns were routinely disposed of by assigning them to
various standing committees made up of many Lewis appointees. Those related
to wages, hours, and working conditions were sent to the Scale Committee,
which in turn offered substitute resolutions to the convention delegate.
Through this process, local union resolutions expressing real issues facing the
working miner rarely got to the convention floor, the above-mentioned resolution from Belleville, Illinois, being an exception. Usually, the Scale Committee offered a single substitute motion for the hundreds of resolutions submitted
by local unions. Because of this weeding-out process, a review of local union
resolutions over the years reflects substantive workplace issues more accurately
than does debate on the convention floor. It is true that many resolutions sent
in by locals were simply copied from standard resolutions sent out by Lewis, but
others provide a rich source of information concerning changes in the labor
process and new management practices. These resolutions, which were printed
in the convention proceedings, also provided a means for locals to communi-
cate with each other in an increasingly centralized union.

CHAPTER 8. Union and Industry During the Great Depression

1. Edmond M. Beame, "The Jacksonville Agreement: Quest for Stability in Coal," *Industrial and Labor Relations Review* (Jan. 1955): 200.

2. Archives Service Center, University of Pittsburgh Library.

3. H. B. Lee, *Bloodletting in Appalachia* (Parsons, W. Va.: McClain Publishing, 1969), pp. 151–52. See also McAlister Coleman, *Men and Coal* (New York: Farrar and Rinehart, 1943), pp. 128–35.

4. See the Van A. Bittner Collection, West Virginia and Regional History Collection, West Virginia University Library. This collection contains an interesting financial and photographic record of the barracks built by union miners.

5. For details of the hardships suffered by miners and their families, see Senate Committee on Interstate Commerce, *Conditions in the Coal Fields of Pennsylvania West Virginia, and Ohio*, Vols. 1 and 2, 70th Cong., 1st sess. (Washington, D.C.: Government Printing Office, 1928).

6. Reprinted in *UMWA Journal* (Dec. 15, 1932).

7. *Coal Age* (Feb. 19, 1925); 296.

8. *Coal Trade Bulletin* (June 16, 1925): 87–88.

9. Ibid.

10. Ibid. (July 1, 1925): 103; and *Coal Age* (Feb. 26, 1925): 333.

11. Access to records of the major firms was unobtainable, so trade journals such as *Coal Age*, *Coal Trade Bulletin*, and *Black Diamond* were relied on for this information.

12. *Coal Age* (July 31, 1924): 160; and (May 1, 1924): 645.

13. For a review of the 1924 merger movement, see *Coal Age* (Mar. 19, 1925); and *Coal Trade Bulletin* (Dec. 1, 1924): 3.

14. *Coal Age* (Jan. 17, 1924): 76; and (Aug. 21, 1924): 262.

15. Ibid. (Feb. 7, 1924): 219.

16. Charles E. Beachley, *History of Consolidation Coal Company* (New York: Consolidation Coal Company, 1934), pp. 70 and 96.

17. West Virginia Department of Mines, *Annual Report* (Charleston, W. Va.), various years.

18. *Coal Age* (Mar. 19, 1925): 437.

19. Ibid. (Mar. 6, 1924): 361.

20. Willard E. Hotchkiss, et al., *Mechanization, Employment, and Output Per Man in Bituminous-Coal Mining*, vol. 2 (Philadelphia: Work Projects Administration, p. 377.

21. *Coal Age* (Jan. 17, 1924): 74 (emphasis added).

22. *Coal Trade Bulletin* (Aug. 1, 1924): 191.

23. *Coal Trade Bulletin* (Aug. 1, 1924): 186.

24. *Coal Age,* (July 31, 1924):: 159.

25. *Coal Trade Bulletin* (Nov. 17, 1924): 496.

26. *Coal Trade Journal* (Jan. 1, 1928): 53.

27. U.S. Bureau of Mines, *Mineral Resources of the United States, 1928*, vol. 2, (Washington, D.C.: Government Printing Office, 1930), p. 454.

28. *Monthly Labor Review* (May 1927): 133–35.

29. Ibid. (Nov. 1927): 139–40.

30. *Coal Age* (Feb. 1928): 115.

31. *Monthly Labor Review* (May 1928): 107.

32. *Coal Age* (June 1928): 387.

33. Ibid.

34. *Monthly Labor Review* (Aug. 1928): 110.

35. Edward D. Wickersham, "Opposition to the International Officers of the United Mine Workers of America: 1919–1933" (Ph.D. diss., Cornell University, 1951), pp. 192–93.

36. *UMWA Journal* (Sept. 15, 1928): 384.

37. Ibid.

38. The rate for machine operators in the Illinois agreement has an interesting origin and is worth noting. See *Coal Age* (Oct. 22, 1925): 564–65. In January 1921, UMWA local 5122 negotiated a contract with the Simplex Coal Company, in southern Indiana, at the time the company announced plans for opening an experimental mine using a locally manufactured loading machine. This local agreement, most likely the first formal union agreement dealing with the loading machine, specified that machine operators would be paid $1.50 an hour, or $12.00 a day, and helpers would be paid $7.50 a day. Some time later the nearby Ingle Coal Company decided to instal Joy loaders on a trial basis, and it, too, was able to negotiate a local agreement with the union. Here it was agreed that machine operators would receive the $12.00 a day that Simplex was paying, but the company agreed to increase the helpers rate to $8.14 a day. In the day-to-day operation of the Joy machine, the two men—the specified operator and the helper—shared the various tasks involved in using the loader, and they agreed to share the daily wages they were paid. Their combined income was $20.14, so that when the operator paid the helper $1.93 of his own wages, the two men each took home $10.07. Later, the miners asked the payroll office to split their pay for them, and thus the rate for working on the Joy loading machine became formalized. The rate appeared in other local agreements from time to time and then was accepted, as shown above, as the rate of pay for both loading machine and cutting machine operators in the Illinois statewide agreement. By 1928, however, the practice of sharing job responsibilities was discouraged, job classifications were more carefully defined, and wage differentials reestablished in the contract. In the Illinois mechanization agreement, the machine operator was paid $10.07, but helpers on the machines received $9.00 a day.

39. Wickersham, *Opposition to the International Officers,* p. 56.

40. U.S. Bureau of Mines, *Mineral Resources,* selected years (Washington, D.C.: Government Printing Office).

41. The popularity of the pit-car loader is reflected in the fact that the number in use in Illinois alone increased from less than 100 in 1927 to 2,162 in 1931. In that year, nearly half of the coal loaded by mechanical means in Illinois was loaded with pit-car loaders. Other states soon followed with orders for the conveyors, so that by 1931, the peak year, 3,428 were being used in Indiana, the far western states, and in some of the Pennsylvania fields. The pit-car loader was not, however, used to any great extent in the southern, nonunion coalfields. For example, in 1931 only 48 were reported in the mines of West Virginia. When the whole mechanization movement slowed under Depression conditions, pit-car loaders also were used less often; many were actually removed from the mines. When the coal operators began again to place orders for machinery after 1935, the pit-car loader was replaced by the fully mechanized mobile loading machines. By 1940 only 697 pit-car loaders were reported to still be in use in the nation's coal mines. See appendix, table B.

42. *Coal Age* (May 1929): 267.

CHAPTER 9. Government Intervention in the Industry

1. U.S. Bureau of Mines, *Mineral Resources,* selected years (Washington, D.C.: Government Printing Office).

2. Morton S. Baratz, *The Union and the Coal Industry* (New Haven: Yale University Press, 1955), p. 48.

3. Irving Bernstein, *Turbulent Years* (Boston: Houghton Mifflin, 1970), p. 16.

4. National Coal Association, *The Regional Sales Agency Plan* (Washington, D.C.: National Coal Association, 1931), p. 12.

5. *Coal Age* (Feb. 1933): 36.

6. Glenn L. Parker, *The Coal Industry, A Study in Social Control* (Washington, D.C.: American Council on Public Affairs, 1940), p. 164.

7. Ibid., pp. 165–66.

8. See ibid., p. 173, for an assessment of the role of sales agencies in stabilizing the coal industry. After reviewing several of the agencies established during the 1930s, he concluded that "there is little here of a stabilizing character."

9. Parker (ibid., p. 108) noted that the industry trade associations also played a role in the formulations of New Deal policies. "The National Recovery Administration idea was in part an outgrowth of the trade association

and trade practices movement." See also James P. Johnson, *The Politics of Soft Coal* (Urbana: University of Illinois Press, 1979), pp. 133–34.

10. Johnson, *Politics of Soft Coal,* pp. 112–13.

11. Ibid., pp. 123–24.

12. *Coal Age* (March 1932): 91.

13. Parker, *Coal Industry,* p. 105.

14. Ibid., p. 106.

15. Melvyn Dubofsky and Warren Van Tine, *John L. Lewis* (New York: Quadrangle, 1977), p. 185.

16. Ibid. pp. 185–86.

17. Parker, *Coal Industry,* p. 107.

18. *Coal Age* (Oct. 1933): 354.

19. Ibid., 325.

20. Quoted in Dubofsky and Van Tine, *John L. Lewis,* p. 191.

21. UMWA, *1934 Convention Proceedings* (Indianapolis, 1934), app. B, pp. 84–90.

22. Parker, *Coal Industry,* pp. 110–11.

23. Johnson, *Politics of Soft Coal,* p. 201.

24. *Coal Age* (Oct. 1934): 380.

25. Dubofsky and Van Tine, *John L. Lewis,* p. 192.

26. UMWA, *1934 Convention Proceedings,* p. 203.

27. *Coal Age* (Feb. 1934): 40.

28. Dubofsky and Van Tine, *John L. Lewis,* p. 192.

29. Quoted in Johnson, *Politics of Soft Coal,* p. 215.

30. For a review of the Guffey acts and an analysis of why they failed to stabilize the industry or promote its growth, see ibid., pp. 217–38.

CHAPTER 10. Miners' "Freedom" Under Increased Mechanization

1. See appendix, table D; and Waldo Fisher, *Economic Consequences of the Seven-hour Day and Wage Changes in the Bituminous Coal Industry* (Philadelphia: University of Pennsylvania Press, 1939), pp. 67–75. Fisher suggests but does not demonstrate that reductions in prices of loading machines at this time may also have led to increased purchases. See his footnote, p. 73.

2. Copies of the various Appalachian agreements were located in the UMWA *Convention Proceedings,* in *Coal Age;* and in the West Virginia Collection, West Virginia University Library.

3. Although Lewis controlled the union convention by various means noted above, local unions continued to submit resolutions to the conventions in the hope that some action would be taken on the problems of importance to their

membership. These resolutions reflected rank and file grievances and provide a rich source of material for understanding the changes taking place at the workplace during the 1930s.

4. UMWA, *1936 Convention Proceedings* (Washington, D.C.: 1936), vol. 3, p. 88.

5. UMWA, *1938 Convention Proceedings, Scale Resolutions* (Washington, D.C., 1938), p. 61.

6. UMWA, *1936 Proceedings*, vol. 3, p. 130.

7. See chapter 7 for a full discussion of this issue.

8. Fisher, *Economic Consequences*, p. 71.

9. U.S. Bureau of Mines. Coal output, employment, and number of days worked declined with the 1938 business recession but picked up again in 1939. Employment however, never again reached the 1937 level (see appendix, table D).

10. UMWA, *1936 Proceedings*, vol. 3, p. 52.

11. UMWA, *1938 Proceedings*, p. 35.

12. UMWA, *1940 Proceedings*, (Washington, D.C.: 1940), vol. 2, p. 53.

13. Convention delegates from across the coalfields complained that management regularly refused to rehire active union members. They charged that a new system requiring physical examinations for hiring and rehiring was used to discriminate against anyone the company, and therefore the company doctor, thought was undesirable.

14. UMWA, *1938 Proceedings*, p. 25.

15. Fisher, *Economic Consequences*, pp. 67–75.

16. *Coal Age* (Oct. 1933): 325.

17. Fisher, *Economic Consequences*, p. 70.

18. U.S. Census Bureau, *Historical Statistics* (Washington, D.C.: Government Printing Office), p. 1003.

19. Morton S. Baratz, *The Union and the Coal Industry* (New Haven: Yale University Press, 1955), p. 109.

CHAPTER 11. Opportunities Lost

1. Carter Goodrich, *The Miner's Freedom* (Boston: Marshall Jones, 1925). Quotations from Goodrich are found on pages 159–82.

2. UMWA, *1940 Convention Proceedings* (Washington, D.C., 1940), vol. 1, p. 455.

3. Ibid., vol. 2, p. 7.

INDEX

accidents: caused by electricity, 103–04; fatal, 97–98, 99, 100; lost-time, 99; most frequent causes of, 102–04; non-fatal, 98–99; responsibility for, 97, 102; roof-fall, 101–02
advertising, 52, 59
agreements. *See* labor agreements
Alabama, 11, 12
Allentown, Pa., 70
American Federation of Labor, 158
American Miners Association, 108–09
American Mining Congress: 1924 convention of, 34, 174–75; 1934 convention of, 210; 1935 convention of, 58; and safety issue, 94, 95; yearbook of, 94
American Socialist Party, 153–55, 156. *See also* nationalization movement
Amsterdam, Ohio, 205
anthracite strike of 1902, 119
Appalachian agreements (1933–1941): and impact of, on mechanization, 199, 210, 213; and labor agreements of 1920s, 200; Maximum Hours and Working Time provision of, 203–04, 205–06; and multiple shifts issue, 206; of 1933, 191–94, 210; of 1934, 196; of 1936, 197; and wage issue, 200–03; workers' reactions to, 192, 214; and work relations, 199–203
Appalachian Coals, Inc., 186, 188
Appalachian Joint Wage Conference, 205, 207

apprenticeship program, 5–6, 13
arc-wall cutting machine, 140

Baltimore, Md., 146
Belleville, Ill., 165, 180
Bernstein, Irving, *The Turbulent Years*, 185
Bethlehem Steel Company, 170
Bituminous Coal Commission, 130–38, 140
blacklisting, 15, 16, 207, 214
black lung disease, 93, 105
black miners, 11–12, 113–14
brakeman, 10, 85
Brazill, Ind., 48
Brewster, Thomas, 130
British miners, 156
Brophy, John: and Nationalization Research Committee, 158–59, 160; opposition of, to John L. Lewis, 161, 166–67; progressive ideals of, 142, 153
Bureau of Mines, 98–100
business unionism, 150–55

C&O Fuel Company, 91
Cannelton Coal Company, 53
Carbon Fuel, 90, 91
Carnegie Institute of Technology, 34, 82–83, 175
Carter v. Carter (1936), 197
Central Competitive Field (CCF), 68, 71; collective bargaining in, 117; and 1886 joint conference of, 115–16; and 1894 strike of, 117–18; and 1898

agreement, 125; and grievance proce-
dures in, 120; and Jacksonville agree-
ment, 146; and 1916 agreement,
127–28, 134–38; and 1927 strike of,
179. *See also* Illinois; Indiana; Ohio;
Pennsylvania
Centralia, Ill., 103
chain machines, 49, 75. *See also*
Gartsherrie chain machine
Charleroi Iron Works, 70
checkweighman, 14
Chicago, Ill., 114
Chicago, Wilmington, and Franklin
Coal Company, 72, 177
Chicago, Wilmington and Vermillion
Coal Company, 47
Claremont, N.H., 75
Clarkson loader, 84
Coal Age: and Appalachian agreement
(1933), 191; and Davis-Kelly bill, 188;
and issue of wages, 146–47, 177; and
Jacksonville agreement, 148; and Joy
loader, 68, 71; and management
techniques, 80, 81; and mine
mechanization, 174, 175, 210; and
movement to oust Lewis (1928), 180;
and NRA bituminous coal code, 194;
and 1934 UMWA convention, 196;
and penalty clause, 129–30; and scientific management, 165–66
coal code. *See* National Recovery Administration bituminous coal code
Coal Conservation Act, 197–98
coal dust, 104–06
Coal Dust on the Fiddle (George Korson),
85
"The Coal Loading Machine" (song), 85
coal loading machinery: advantages of,
82–83, 84, 94, 143; arrival of, in
mines, 34, 84–92; Carnegie Institute
of Technology study on, 82–83, 175;
and day-wage system, 165–67; defined, 135; development of, viii; disadvantages of, 85, 92, 143; effect of,
on production level, 82; and elimination of jobs, 107; exhibition of, at
American Mining Congress, 175;
hazards of, 84–85; Illinois workers'
acceptance of, 182–84; major manufacturers of, 46–60; purchase of, by

companies, 11, 87–88, 209–10;
operators of, 88, 91, 136, 140, 182;
opposition to, at 1934 UMWA convention, 195; and problems in change
from hand loading, 89; removal of,
from mines, 178; and reorganization
of work place, 88, 94; and right to install, 193; safety of, 83, 92–106;
technology of, in management practices, 79–80; use of, in 1920s, 32;
wage scale for operators of, 71, 176,
202; workers' reactions to, 53–54, 82,
84, 88, 91–92, 107, 134, 176. *See
also* Goodman Manufacturing Company; Hamilton Manufacturing
Company; Jeffrey Manufacturing
Company; Jones Coloder; Joy Manufacturing Company; machinery,
labor-saving; mobile loading
machines; Myers-Whaley loading
machines; pit car loader; scraper
loader
Coal Mine Management, 33
coal miners' pneumoconiosis. *See* black
lung disease
Coal Mining Institute of America, 33
Coal Operators Association, 120, 130
Coal Trade Bulletin, 177
Colburn Machine Tool Company, 74
collective bargaining, 14, 110, 117, 149
Collins, Jairus, 18
Collins, Justus, 18–19
Coloder Company, 32, 42
Columbus, Ohio, 42, 48
compensation, 99. *See also* unemployment
Consolidated Coal Company, 70
Consolidation Coal Company, 53, 168,
170, 174
contract, sanctity of, 119, 120, 124, 151
conveyors: chain, 51; installation of, 79;
and Joseph Joy's patent on, 61; and
long-wall mining system, 44; manufacture of, by Joy Manufacturing
Company, 75; safety of, 103; sectional, 45; self-loading, 34, 44. *See
also* haulage systems; Jeffrey Manufacturing Company; pit car loaders
convict labor, 221n3
Coombes, E. R., 76

cooperative mines, 171–73
"crowding of the mine," 204–05
Cumberland, Md., 108
cutting machines: and cutter-bar type, 29–30; development of, 28, 29; and Joseph Joy's patent on, 61; operators of, 8–9, 79; and workers' resistance to, 53–54. *See also* Sperry coal cutter

D. J. Kennedy Center, 71
Davis-Kelly bill (1932), 188
day-wage system: and Appalachian agreements, 200, 213; controversies surrounding, 163–67; establishment of, during 1920s, 182, 184; and Illinois agreement (1928), 184; and mechanization, 167; 1925 reduction of, 168; workers' objections to, 165, 166, 203
Debs, Eugene, 154
"Democratic management," 159
Depression. *See* Great Depression
digging and loading machines, 34, 38–44. *See also* Hamilton Manufacturing Company; Jones Coloder; Jeffrey Manufacturing Company; Myers-Whaley loading machines; Joy loading machine
dockage, 14, 120
Donaldson, John A., 65, 69, 70, 74
drift mining, 1, 2
drills. *See* tools, miners'

economic conditions, 13, 19, 96, 141–42, 178. *See also* market demand
Edenborn, William, 18
efficiency methods, 80
eight-hour-day: and Appalachian agreements, 192, 203; during hand loading period, 13; establishment of, 118; and Jacksonville agreement, 206; and miners' freedom, 118; in UMWA constitution, 116
Elkhorn, W. Va., 205
Engineering and Mining Journal, 112
Erwin, Wylie, 9–10, 84–86
Evans, Chris, 110, 115
Evansville, Ind., 70–71, 74
Ewart, William D., 48
explosions, 103–05
explosives, 78–79

Fairmont field (W. Va.), 11
Federal Coal Mine Inspections and Investigations Act (1941), 99
fire boss, 8, 9
foreman: discipline by, 16; duties of, 10, 14, 81–83; power of, in nonunion mines, 16; resistance of, to mechanization, 89–90; and safety, 91. *See also* section boss
Franklin, Pa., 74
Fredericktown, Pa., 213
free enterprise, 162–64
freight rate proposal, 145
Frick Company, 37

Gartsherrie chain machine, 28, 29, 31
Gary, Elbert H., 18
Gary, W. Va., 38
Gay, Harry S., 70
George's Creek field (Md.), 136
German, Adolph, 153
Gompers, Samuel, 158
Goodman, Herbert E., 47, 49
Goodman Manufacturing Company, 33, 47, 89; and competition with Jeffrey Manufacturing Company, 59; and electric-hydraulic power shovels, 47; and 460 mobile loader, 59; history of, 47–50; and power shovels, 225n29; and scrapers, 34, 46; and 660 mobile loader, 49; and 260 mobile loader, 49
Goodrich, Carter, *The Miner's Freedom*, 13, 211–14
government regulation: and Appalachian agreements, 191–94; during early 1930s, 187–89; and end of involvement in price-fixing, 198; of financial operations, 145; and mechanization, viii. *See also* U.S. Congress
Grant Town mine (W. Va.), 11–12
Great Depression, 21, 26, 126–27, 168–83. *See also* government regulation; nationalization movement; Pittsburgh plan
Greenbrier Coal Company, 27
Greenbrier mine: attempts to discourage unions at, 18; closure of coke-producing facility at, 17; cost of supplies at, 24; demand for coal at, 26; effects of Great Depression on, 26;

financial records at, 19, 20–22, 24,
26–27; haulage system at, 17; living
conditions of miners at, 15, 17,
25–27; management's control at, 24;
and mechanization, 26, 27; output at,
17, 26; recruitment of immigrants at,
18; size of workforce at, 17; as typical
of hand loading period, 16–17; wages
at, 26; workers' control at, 24
grievance procedures: and Appalachian
agreements, 192; development of,
119–21; on dockage, 120; for firing of
employees, 120; and grievance committee, 121, 123; and Illinois agreement (1928), 181; and labor
agreements of 1920s, 139–40
Guffey Act, 197

Hall, R. Dawson, 80
Hamilton, W. E., 39, 52–53, 61, 66
Hamilton Manufacturing Company, 33,
41; and loading machine, 55, 225n21;
and pit car loader, 34, 39–41, 42
hand loaders: duties of, 10–11; freedom
of, 211; and loss of jobs due to
mechanization, 82, 83, 87; wages for,
9, 182. See also hand loading
hand loading: advantages of, 85, 178;
compared to mechanical loading, 82,
83, 91; described, in southern W. Va.
mine, 9–11; disadvantages of, 81–82;
elimination of, vii, 77–79; and haulage systems, 7; and labor agreements,
138; and management policies, 19;
mechanization of methods of, 77; in
the 1930s, 1–27; supervision of, 13;
and workers' control of, ix, 5, 9; and
work relations, 77. See also Greenbrier
mine; long-wall mining system;
room-and-pillar mining system
Hanna Coal Company, 52
Harding, Warren G., 141, 145
Harlan County, Ky., 136
Harrington, Daniel, 100, 101
Harrison, J. W., 30
haulage systems: electric, 51, 79; hazards
of, 102–03; and mechanical loading,
83, 103; and use of locomotives, 2, 7,
17, 75, 79, 83; and use of mules, 2, 7,
17, 79, 81, 89. See also conveyors

Hayes, Frank, 153, 154, 156, 157,
235n13
Hibberd, G., 29, 30
hiring practices, 9, 149. See also right-
to-hire-and-fire policy
Hocking District labor agreement,
138–39
Hocking Valley (Ohio), 109–10, 112–
14, 176
Holden, W. Va., 44
housing, company-owned: abolition of,
under Appalachian agreements, 192;
dependency of miners on, 22; eviction
of union miners from, 147, 170; at
Greenbrier mine, 25–27; during hand
loading period, 17, 91; rent increase
on, 200–01, 202; study of, in 1920s,
81
Howat, Alexander, 153
How to Run Coal: Suggestions for a Plan
of Public Ownership, Public Control,
and Democratic Management in the Coal
Industry (Nationalization Research
Committee), 159
hydroelectric power. See substitute fuels

Illinois: black miners from, 114; coal
operators in, 115, 116; and 1897 strike
in, 118; grievance procedures in,
120–21; Jacksonville agreement period
in, 176–81; loading machines in, 165,
182–84; and 1919 strike in, 233n32;
pit committees in, 122; unions in,
108, 109, 117, 118, 180; and wage
issue in 1930s, 200; wildcat strikes in,
129. See also Central Competitive
Field
Illinois agreement (1928), 181–82,
184
Illinois Bureau of Labor, 114
immigrant labor, 18
incentive pay, 92, 182. See also tonnage
payment system
Indiana: coal operators in, 115; and 1897
strike in, 118; grievance procedures
in, 120; installation of loading
machines in, 166; and Jacksonville
agreement, 176–81; local unions in,
117, 118. See also Central Competitive
Field

industrial codes, 188–89
Ingersoll-Rand Company, 33
Ingersoll-Sargeant Company, 31
Ingle Coal Company, 71
injury rates (1930–1948), 98–99. *See
  also* accidents
International Association of Industrial
  Accident Boards and Commissions,
  100

Jacksonville, Fla., 146
Jacksonville agreement (1924), 138,
  145–48; abrogation of, 146–48, 178,
  180–81, 189, 196, 198; and day shift,
  206; effect of, on miners, 192; and
  eight-hour-day, 206; in Illinois and
  Indiana, 176–81; management's rights
  under, 206–07; renewal of (1927),
  179; and wage scale, 175, 176
Jeffrey, Joseph A., 29, 50
Jeffrey, R. K., 58
Jeffrey Manufacturing Company: and
  advertising, 52; and building of first
  Joy loader, 33, 65; Columbus plant of,
  139; and combination cutting and
  loading machine, 50; and competition
  with Joy Manufacturing Company,
  89; and design of Jones Coloder, 42;
  early history of, 29, 49, 50–59; as
  employer of Joseph Joy, 60, 64; and
  43A Shortwaloader, 34, 37, 42, 55,
  57; and 44A loader, 57, 58; and installation of cutter-bar-type undercutting machine, 110; and Jeffrey-Morgan
  34A and 34B entry drivers, 34, 35,
  36–37; and L400 mobile loader,
  58–59; and L600 mobile loader, 59;
  labor agreements at, 139; and lack of
  loading machine technology, 52–53;
  in 1930s, 47; and O'Toole mining and
  loading machine, 38; and pit car
  loader, 45; and purchase of patents to
  Hamilton loader, 41; and 33A coal
  loader, 53; and 34A entry driver, 35,
  64; and work on machines during
  World War I, 133
Johnson, Hugh, 190
Johnstown, Pa., 169
joint-scale movement (1898-1920s),
  118–19, 120, 121

Jones, James Elwood, 41–42, 61
Jones Coloder, 34, 42, 95
Jordan, U. G., 44, 88–92
Joseph A. Holmes Safety Association,
  97
Joy, Joseph Francis: birth of, 62; contributions of, to mechanization, 61,
  76; death of, 76; and design of
  chain-cutting machine, 75; and design of continuous drilling machine,
  75; and development of loading
  machine, 44, 55, 60, 62, 64, 65, 67;
  and dissociation from Joy Manufacturing Company, 75–76; early inventions of, 61, 62; employment history
  of, 60, 63, 64, 65, 67, 68–69, 75; financial difficulties of, 74–75; in Russia, 75; and organization of Joy
  Machine Company, 69; and organization of Joy Manufacturing Company, 70; and patent difficulties with
  Jeffrey Company, 66–67; and underground mining inventions, 73; as
  a young boy, 61–62; and work for
  U.S. Army, 75. *See also* Joy Manufacturing Company; Joy Machine
  Company
Joy Brothers, Incorporated, 75
Joy loading machine: advantages of, 44,
  50, 68, 89, 226 n49; early models of,
  64, 70–71, 89; effect of, on mining
  cycle, 69–70, 90; and 11BU loader,
  88–89, 177; and 5BU loader, 72–74,
  75, 88–89; and 4A and 4B loader, 71;
  and 4BU loader, 71–72, 74; and history of, 61–76; as mentioned in poem
  and song, 85, 86; in 1925, 34; patent
  awarded for, 61, 69; problems with,
  74, 175; and self-loading shuttle car,
  73–74; and 7BU loader, 86, 88–89;
  as used by Pittsburgh Coal Company,
  133; workers' reactions to, 72. *See also*
  Joy, Joseph Francis; Joy Manufacturing Company
Joy Machine Company, 69, 70–71, 74,
  75
Joy Manufacturing Company: and design
  of loading machine, 32, 60, 61; in
  1920s and 1930s, 46, 47; organization
  of, 70, 75; and purchase of Sullivan

Machinery Company, 76; workers' retaliation against representative of, 86–87. *See also* Joy loading machine

Kanawha field, 11, 54, 146
Knights of Labor, 109–10, 116, 117
Knoxville, Tenn., 44
Korson, George, *Coal Dust on the Fiddle,* 85

labor agreements, of 1920s: 138–41, 146, 149; between Hocking Valley and UMWA, 138; and Bituminous Coal Commission, 140; compared to Appalachian agreements, 200; and discipline issue, 140; and grievance issue, 139–40; during hand loading period, 138; in northern W. Va., 139–40, 146; term of, 138; wage issue in, 146. *See also* contract, sanctity of; Jacksonville agreement
Lang Coal Company, 71
Lauck, W. Jett, 187
Lawson, John, 153
Lechner, Francis M., 29, 49, 50, 61
Lechner Mining Machine Company, 50
Lechner-Slade chain-breast machine, 49
Lee, Howard B., 14, 169–70
Lever Act, 128, 131
Levin, N. D., 55, 57
Lewis, John L.: and Appalachian agreement, 194–95; and bid for presidency of AFL (1921), 158; business-oriented policies of, 155, 160–61; control of UMWA policies by, 161–62, 163, 168, 212–14, 240n56; economic recovery program of, 161–67; and government regulation, 187–88; and Guffey Act, 197; and Illinois agreement, 182; influence of John Mitchell on, 151, 153; and Jacksonville agreement, 146–47; and length of workday, 203, 204; and mechanization policy, 208–09; *The Miners' Fight for American Standards,* 161; and nationalization, 156–57, 158–59, 160–61; and NRA bituminous coal code, 190–91; and 1919 strike, 130; and 1922 strike, 137; and 1928 strike, 180; opposition to, 180–81; and state of industry during

Great Depression, 185; and UMWA membership drive, 189; and U.S. Coal Commission, 142, 145; and wage agreements of 1930s, 200, 203; and wage policies, 167, 208
Liberty Coal Company, 147
Link-Belt Company, 48, 49
loading machinery. *See* coal loading machinery
local unions. *See* unions
Logan County, W. Va., 70
long-wall mining system, 2, 4–5, 29, 30, 46, 48

McAuliffe, Eugene, 76
McDonald, Duncan, 153
McDowell County (W. Va.), 16
machinery, coal loading. *See* coal loading machinery
machinery, labor-saving: and Bituminous Coal Commission, 134; development of, 33, 80; impact of Illinois agreement on operators of, 181–82; use of, to improve production, 80; use of, at Greenbrier mine, 26; workers' acceptance of, 177; wages for operators of, 9, 132–33, 176, 228n23. *See also* coal loading machinery; mobile loading machines
McKinlay Mining and Loading Machine Company, 32
McKinlay entry driver, 34, 35–36
McNabe, T. J., 70
Main Island Creek Coal Company, 173
management: and control of workers, 14–16, 24, 91; cooperation of, with UMWA, 196–97; effect of, on union policies, 108; improvement of techniques of, 80–81; and loading machine technology, 79–80; policies of, during hand loading period, 19; problems of, during hand loading period, 19; responsibility of, for accidents, 94, 97, 102; rights of, under Appalachian agreements, 192–93, 206–07, 213; scientific, 79–84; studies of, in 1920s, 80–81, 82, 83; and U.S. Coal Commission, 143
Mann, Isaac, 18
Marietta Manufacturing Company, 36

Marion Shovel Company, 75
market demand, 3, 21, 126, 160
mass production system, 80
mechanical loaders. *See* coal loading machinery
Mechanization, 76
mechanization: adverse effects of, 115; and Appalachian agreements on, 192, 193, 198–99; Bituminous Coal Commission's recommendations on, 131–37; controversies surrounding, 135–36; and day-wage system, 167; early technology of, 78–79; economic factors contributing to, in 1930s, 199; effect of NIRA on, 190; effects of, on employment, 81, 115, 151; effects of, on wages, 111–12, 115, 163–64; efforts to block, in 1920s, 213; forces contributing to, viii, 198, 209–10; and grievance procedures, 120; hazards of, 90, 92–93, 100–01, 105; impact of, on hours of work, 204, 210; impact of, on miners, 86–87, 90, 199, 209, 212; and increase in output, 77; joint commission on, 207–09; John Lewis's views on, 161–64; John Mitchell's views on, 152; in 1920s, 173–76; problems of, in 1920s, 89; reluctance of nonunion states to accept, 182; report of U.S. Bureau of Labor Statistics on, 140–41; in Russia, 75; socialist views on, 153–55; and safety, 100–01; transition to, 182; unions' attitude toward, 110–14, 115, 126–27; and UMWA views on, 108, 124, 127, 128, 140–41, 143, 149, 181, 195; workers' resistance to, 40–41, 53–54, 77, 111, 168. *See also* coal loading machinery; technological change
Mechanized Mining Commission, 208
Mellon family, 65, 170–71
Mercer County (W. Va.), 18
merger movement, 173, 174–75
Milwaukee-Western Fuel Company, 173
mine committee. *See* pit committee
miners. *See* workers
The Miners' Fight for American Standards (John L. Lewis), 161
The Miner's Freedom (Carter Goodrich), 13

Mining and loading machines. *See* Jeffrey Manufacturing Company; McKinlay entry driver; O'Toole mining and loading machine
Mitch, William, 166
Mitchell, John, 119, 150–53, 154, 203
mobile loading machine: as designed by Joseph Joy, 55; development of, 28; as favored by the industry, 46; increase in use of, 210; and Jeffrey Manufacturing Company, 54. *See also* coal loading machinery
Monongahela Valley miner's strike (1859), 108
Monongah mine, 53
Morgan, E. C., 37, 53, 54, 61
Morgan-Gardner Electric Company, 47, 49
Morgan-Jeffrey entry driver, 54
Morrow, J.D.A., 171, 195–97, 207
motorman, 9, 10
mules. *See* haulage systems
multiple shifts, 213
Murphy, Mike, 59, 86–88
Myers-Whaley Company, 32, 33, 44
Myers-Whaley loading machines, 34, 43–44, 88, 177

National Bituminous Coal Commission, 197–98
National Civic Federation, 151
National Coal Association, 185–86, 188, 190, 194, 195–97
National Coal Board of Arbitration, 197
National Federation of Miners and Mine Laborers, 114–16
National Industrial Recovery Act (NIRA), 188–89, 190, 193–94, 197
nationalization movement, 154–55, 156–58, 159, 160–61, 167
Nationalization Research Committee, 154, 158–60, 212
National Miners Association, 109
National Policy Committee, 156, 180
National Recovery Administration (NRA) bituminous coal code, 190–94, 196–97
natural gas. *See* substitute fuels
New Deal, 145, 188, 190, 194, 199–203
Newdick, Norton, 42

New Orient mine (Ill.), 36, 177–78
New River Company, 55
"no-backward-step" wage policy, 137,
147–48, 162, 164, 176, 179
nonunion mines, 15–16, 125, 178–79,
182
Norfolk and Western Railroad, 17, 18
Norris, Bert, 53, 57, 64, 65, 65n10
Northern Illinois Mine Workers Union,
180
Northern West Virginia Coal Operators,
146, 148

Ohio: adoption of Pittsburgh plan in,
169; coal operators in, 115, 116; early
response to mechanization in, 110;
and 1897 strike in, 118; formation of
unions in, 108, 117, 118; as most
mechanized state, 113. *See also* Central Competitive Field
Ohio Bureau of Labor Statistics (1000),
111–12
Ohio Miners' Amalgamated Association, 110
oil. *See* substitute fuels
Oklahoma, 147–48
Old Ben Coal Corporation, 54, 76, 174
Old Ben Mining Company, 64
Oldroyd Machine Company, 33
*Organized Labor, Its Problems, Purposes
and Ideals and the Present and Future of
American Wage Earners,* 151
O'Toole, Colonel Edward, 37, 61, 224n19
O'Toole mining and loading machine,
34, 35, 38

Page, William N., 111
patents. *See* U.S. Patent Office; individual machines
Peabody Coal Company, 178–79
Peale, Rembrandt, 131
penalty clause, 128–30, 135, 136, 192,
209
Pennsylvania: adoption of Pittsburgh
plan in, 169; coal operators in, 115,
116; and 1897 strike in, 118; grievance
procedures in, 120; labor agreements
of 1924 in, 146; local unions in, 117,
118; and 1933 strike in, 191; wage
scale for loading machine operators

in, 202. *See also* Central Competitive
Field
Pennsylvania Coal and Coke Corporation, 97
Philadelphia Exhibition (1876), 29
piece-rate system, 14
Pike County Coal Company, 71
pillar removal system, 3–4, 83, 95
Pinkerton Detective Agency, 112, 113
pit car loader, 34, 55, 57, 183–84,
243n41
pit committee: and Appalachian
agreements, 213; attempts to limit actions of, 123–24; duties of, 121–22;
and local unions, 121–25; and
mechanization, 175; and Pittsburgh
plan, 169; structure of, 139
Pittsburgh, Pa., 109
Pittsburgh Coal Company, 69, 94–95;
during hand loading period, 13; and
employment of Joseph Joy by, 64, 67,
68–69; expansion of, in 1920s, 173,
174; and Jeffrey Company, 52; and Joy
loading machines, 65, 67–68, 72,
133; Morrow as president of, 196; and
Somers no. 2 mine, 54, 59, 65, 67;
union-busting plan at, 168–69, 170–
71. *See also* Pittsburgh plan
Pittsburgh plan, 168–69, 171–72, 175
Plumb, Glenn, 157
Pocahontas, Va., 64, 201
Pocahontas field, 17, 18, 21, 42, 54
Pocahontas Fuel Company, 41–42, 52,
95
Point Pleasant, W. Va., 36
Presidential Coal Commission (1923),
34, 162
Preston County, W. Va., 87
price of coal: competition for, under
mechanization, 198; decrease in, per
ton, 185; during handloading period,
19; and safety precautions, 93–94; and
size of coal, 20; and tonnage rate system, 232n17; under NRA bituminous
coal code, 193–94
price fixing, 186–87, 196–98
production: for coal, 21, 24, 126, 185,
186–87; daily quotas set for, 81; at
Greenbrier mine, 26; and impact of
hours of work on, 204; increase of,

with mechanization, 78–79, 80, 82, 84; and merger movement of 1924, 173; variable costs of, 19, 22; workers' control of, 24, 81–82

Progressive Mine Workers, 181. *See also* American Socialist Party; Brophy, John; nationalization movement

pulmonary disease, 105, 107. *See also* black lung disease

punching machine, 29, 30, 31. *See also* Sperry coal punching machine

Pursglove, Joseph, 148

Raber, Howard, 7–9
Rae, John, 117
rail strike of 1877, 109
Ratchford, M. D., 150
Red Ash, Va., 202
Reed, George W., 178
C. Reiss Coal Company, 173
Reorganized United Mine Workers of America (1930–1931), 180–81
reward system. *See* tonnage payment system
right-to-hire-and-fire policy, 181, 192–93, 206–07
Robinson, H. W., 131
Rochester and Pittsburgh Coal and Iron Company, 171
Rockefeller, John D., Jr., 170–71
roof bolting, 102
room-and-pillar mining system: advantages of, 5; disadvantages of, 4; at Greenbrier mine, 17; in W. Va., 7, 9–11; process of tasks involved, 2–3, 4, 5, 14; and use of pit car loaders with, 55
Roosevelt, Franklin Delano, 190–91, 194, 197, 198
Russelton, Pa., 205

safety: advocacy of, 95–96; impact of mechanization on, 92–93, 94–96, 97, 104; improvement of, during 1940s, 99–100; laws enacted on, during handloading period, 14; management's responsibility for, 94; and 1938 UMWA mechanization study, 208; operators' responsibility for, 230n30; pit committee's role in, 122; record of,

from 1930–1948, 97–98; resolution of problems of, 93; in UMWA constitution, 116; workers' responsibility for, 94, 96–98

sales agencies, 185–86, 188, 193–94
Saskatchewan, Canada, 70
scabs, 11, 12, 147, 170
Scale Committee. *See* UMWA, Scale Committee of
Schwab, Charles M., 170–71
scientific management, 79–84
scraper loader, 34, 46. *See also* Goodman Manufacturing Company, and scrapers
Searles, Ellis, 160
Seatonville, Ill., 47
section boss, 8, 10, 88, 89, 92. *See also* foreman
Sessions, Francis C., 50
Sherman Antitrust Act, 186
shift work, 91, 206
Shortwaloader. *See* Jeffrey Manufacturing Company
shuttle cars, 75
Siney, John, 109
Slade, Frank N., 48, 49
Smither, W. Va., 53
Smokeless Fuel Company, 19
socialists. *See* American Socialist Party
Somers no. 2 mine. *See* Pittsburgh Coal Company
Somerset County, Pa., 62
Spence, Robert, 70
Sperry, Elmer A., 47, 48, 49, 224n8
Sperry coal cutter, 48
Sperry coal punching machine, 47, 48
Sperry Electrical Mining Machine Company, 47–48
spies, company-hired, 15
spragger. *See* brakeman
stores, company-owned: abolition of under Appalachian agreement, 192; dependency of miners on, 22, 25–27, 91; during hand loading period, 17; at Greenbrier mine, 22, 25–27; price increases at, 201; profits of, 15
Straitsville Central Mining Company, 111–12
strikes: attempts to discourage, 121; during hand loading period, 16; of 1894,

117–18; of 1897, 118; local, 108, 120–21, 189; of 1919, 130–31; of 1922, 137–38, 141, 145; of 1924, 169, 170; of 1927, 179; of 1928, 180; of 1931, 214; of 1932, 214; of 1933, 191; in violation of UMWA orders, 124–25. See also wildcat strikes
strip mining, 99
Stroup, Thomas A., 80
substitute fuels, 126, 142, 155
Sullivan Machinery Company, 30–31, 33, 75, 76
supervision of work force, 13, 14, 81, 83. See also foreman; section boss
Sweet, Albert L., 47, 48
Switchback, W. Va., 201–02

Taylor, Frederick W., 80
technological change: disadvantages of, 101–02, 151–52; during 1920s, 89–91, 160; and grievance procedures, 120; health and safety problems linked to, 92, 93, 104, 107; impact of, x, 89–91, 142; union resistance to, 70–71; and UMWA policies, 107–08; workers' response to, viii, 53–54, 68–69, 107–25, 175, 178, 209
technology, defined, vii
Thayer Engineering Company, 70
Thompson, Sanford E., 80
time clocks, 206
tonnage payment system: acceptance of, by industry, 79; advantages of, 165, 166; as established by Appalachian agreement, 200, 202–03; for hand loaders, 14, 182; and impact of hours of work on, 204–06; reduction of, in 1925, 168; as related to coal prices, 232n17; as suggested by Carter Goodrich, 211; and UMWA mechanization, 208
tools, miners', 5–7
The Turbulent Years (Irving Bernstein), 185
Tuscarawas Valley (Ohio), 110

undercutting machinery: introduction of, 6; invention of, 50; and Jeffrey Manufacturing Company, 51, 52; in nineteenth century, 28, 30; and pit

committee's rules governing use of, 122; prevalence of, in 1920s, 78; workers' objections to, 110–11, 132
unemployment, 84, 115, 185
unions: abrogation of contracts of, 11; and competition with nonunion mines, 147–48; and control of workplace, 152; efforts to discourage organization of, 7, 15–16, 18; goals of, during hand loading period, 14; and issue of wage scales in, 124; local, 108, 109–10, 114, 122; Midwest struggles of, 176–81; and protection of workers' rights, 124; resistance of, to new technology, 70–71; response of, to mechanization, viii, 107, 110–14, 126–27, 143–45; right of, to organize, 189–90; and struggle to form, 124
union-busting, 113, 169–72. See also Pittsburgh plan
Union Pacific Coal Company, 44, 76
United Mine Workers of America (UMWA): and cooperative mines, 172–73; and 1890 convention, 116–17; formation of, 110, 116–19, 125; and National Coal Association, 195–97; Nationalization Research Committee of, 154; National Policy Committee of, 156; and 1909 convention, 156–57; and 1919 convention, 156–58; and 1921 convention, 158–59; and 1924 convention, 147, 160–61; and 1927 convention, 165–67; and 1930 convention, 201; and 1934 convention, 195–96; and 1936 convention, 204–05, 214; and 1938 convention, 207–08, 214; and 1940 convention, 208, 214; and nonunion mines, 125; policies of, and management, 108, 109; rank-and-file rebellion against, 180–81; recognition of, by operators, 189–90; and relationship with local unions, 108, 109–10, 122–23, 124, 128; reorganization of, 189–90; and sanctity of the contract, 119, 124; Scale Committee of, 167, 195, 201, 205, 212; socialist influence in, 153–55; United Mine Workers and the United States Coal Commission, 144;

view of, on mechanization, 68, 108, 119, 124, 127, 128, 134, 140–41, 144, 207–09; view of, on safety, 96; view of U.S. Coal Commission by, 142; and wage agreement of 1941, 208–09

UMWA *Journal:* and Jacksonville agreement, 146; and nationalization issue, 160; prohibition of political discussion in, 151; and reduction in wages, 118; socialist views in, 154–55; and U.S. Coal Commission, 144

U.S. Bureau of Labor Statistics, 140–41

U.S. Bureau of Mines: experiments with coal dust of, 104–05; and miners' safety, 93–94, 100–01; pre-World War I, 93–94; and study of roof-bolting, 102; on transition to mechanization, 100–01, 182–83; and use of explosives, 78–79, 103–04

U.S. Coal and Coke Company, 52

U.S. Coal Commission, 13, 42, 80, 82, 141–45, 149

U.S. Commissioner of Labor, 122–23

U.S. Congress: and Coal Conservation Act, 198; and Guffey Act, 197; investigation of coal industry by, 137; and nationalization movement, 157; and U.S. Coal Commission, 141; and Watson bill (1928), 188

U.S. Department of the Interior, 141–42, 198

U.S. Department of Labor, 137

U.S. Fuel Administration, 128–29, 156

U.S. Industrial Commission, 150

U.S. Justice Department, 186–87

U.S. Patent Office, 61, 62, 64, 65–66

United States Steel Company, 37

U.S. Supreme Court, 186–87, 197

Van Houten, Herman, 75, 226n1

Veasly, William H., 11–12

ventilating systems, 51

wages: and Appalachian agreements, 191–92, 196, 202–03, 214; concessions of 1928 of, 181; as dependent on work done, 6, 23; during hand loading period, 15, 16, 22, 26; grievance procedures concerning, 120; impact of mechanization on, 92, 111–12, 115,

162–64, 198, 210; increase of, in 1902, 119; and Jacksonville agreement (1924), 146, 147; and Lewis's economic recovery program, 163–64; for machine operators, 132–33, 140, 242n38; and nationalization, 156; and 1917 wage scale, 168, 176, 178; and 1924 labor agreements, 146; and 1934 UMWA convention, 195; and 1940 UMWA convention, 208; and NRA bituminous coal code, 190–91; in nonunion mines, 136; reductions of, in 1928, 179–80; and strike of 1894, 118; in UMWA constitution, 116; and union efforts concerning, 108–09, 124, 136; and Watson bill, 187–88. *See also* day-wage system; dockage; "no-backward-step" wage policy

Walker, John, 153

Warner, E. M., 36

Washington agreement, 127–30

Watson, James E., 188

Watson, Little, and Company mine, 48

Watson bill (1928–1929), 164, 188

Westinghouse, 47

West Virginia: coal operators in, 115; and 1897 strike in, 118; hand loading in, 7–9, 11–12, 15, 16, 19; as member of Appalachian Coals, Inc., 186; mine work experience in, 84–86; 1923 labor agreement in, 139–40; 1924 labor agreements in, 146; and 1924 strike in, 169–70; room-and-pillar method used in, 7–8, 9–11; UMWA organization drive in, 189

West Virginia Coal and Coke Company, 173

West Virginia Coal Mining Institute, 81

West Virginia Department of Mines, 11, 90

Wheeling, W. Va., 7

Whitcomb Company, 31

White, John P., 131, 133, 134, 151, 155, 235n13

wildcat strikes, 128, 129, 136

Wilson, Woodrow, 130–31

Winding Gulf Collieries, 18

workday: and Appalachian agreements, 196, 203–06, 213; and loss of miners' freedom, 206; and NRA bituminous coal code, 190–91; reduction in, 209–10. *See also* eight-hour-day; work schedule

workers: intimidation of, by owners, 14, 15; relationship of, with owners, ix, 125; responsibility of, for safety, 94, 100; rights movement of, 155–56; rights of, 124; role of, in Appalachian agreements, 194–95; reaction of, to mechanization, viii, 33, 53–54, 84, 100, 107. *See also* workers' control; workers' freedom

workers' compensation laws, 105

workers' control: attempts to limit, 121, 150, 199; during hand loading period, 18; and labor agreements of 1920s, 138–41; and local union bargaining power, 110; loss of, x, 169, 184, 192, 203, 213, 214; of management, 19; and mechanization, 127, 184, 212; of production, 13, 24, 33, 79, 81–82, 88; role of union in preserving, 124

workers' freedom, 199, 204, 206

working conditions, 11–13, 115, 119

work schedule, 9, 22, 84–85

workweek, 192, 196, 203

World War I, 126–28

Yearbook on Mechanization (American Mining Congress), 94

Young, L. E., 13

Zern, E. N., 33, 40–41